1

The Fanon Reader

Frantz Fanon

Edited and introduced by
Azzedine Haddour

Pluto Press

LONDON

This anthology first published 2006 by Pluto Press
345 Archway Road, London N6 5AA

www.plutobooks.com

British Library Cataloguing in Publication Data
A catalogue record for this book is available from the British Library

ISBN   0 7453 1565 8 hardback
ISBN   0 7453 1560 7 paperback

10   9   8   7   6   5   4   3   2   1

Designed and produced for Pluto Press by
Chase Publishing Services Ltd, Fortescue, Sidmouth, EX10 9QG
Typeset from disk by Stanford DTP Services, Northampton
Printed and bound in the European Union by
Antony Rowe Ltd, Chippenham and Eastbourne, England

Contents

Acknowledgements

My first thanks are due to Laura Peters, Katherine MacDonald and Anne Beech for reading the 'Foreword', providing useful suggestions to improve it. I should also like to thank Debjani Roy and Robert Webb, and Sophie Richmond, the copy-editor, for their work on this book.

The editor and publisher gratefully acknowledge the permission to reproduce the copyright material in this anthology:

'The Negro and Laguage', 'The Woman of Colour and the White Man', 'The Man of Colour and the White Woman', 'The Fact of Blackness' and 'The Negro and Psychopathology', in *Black Skin, White Masks*, trans. Charles Lam Markmann, Pluto Press, 1986. Copyright © Éditions de Seuil, 1952.

'West Indians and Africans' and 'Racism and Culture' in *Toward the African Revolution*, trans. Haakon Chevalier, Monthly Review Press, 1967. Copyright © François Maspero, 1964.

'Algeria Unveiled', in *Studies in a Dying Colonialism*, Monthly Review Press, 1965. Copyright © François Maspero, 1959.

'On National Culture', in *The Wretched of the Earth*, MacGibbon & Kee, 1965. Copyright © François Maspero, 1961.

For the sake of clarity, some minor changes have been made to the original translations.

Foreword:
Postcolonial Fanonism

Frantz Fanon was born in Fort-de-France, Martinique, in 1925. In the period between 1939 and 1943 he received his secondary education at a local private *lycée* where he was taught by Aimé Césaire, the author of *Cahiers d'un retour au pays natal* and *Discours sur le colonialisme* and the founder of negritude. Nurtured on the values of French culture, Fanon, a member of the black elite, believed in the fiction of assimilation. During the Second World War he volunteered to serve under the tricolour and defend mother France from the threat of fascism. Major Salan awarded him the *Croix de guerre* for bravery. However, to his dismay, Fanon learnt that his French comrades serving with him, the freedom-fighters, were prejudiced. He returned home at the end of the war a changed person, marked by his encounter with racism. In 1947 he went to study psychiatry at the University of Lyon. In 1951, he successfully completed and defended his thesis. Fanon became more aware of his blackness in a white culture, acutely conscious of his subject position as a psychoanalyst of culture and as the object of its racism. In France, he was treated as a Negro. His encounter with racism embittered him throughout his life. *Black Skin, White Masks* is an autobiographical account of this encounter: it articulates his disillusionment with a culture in which he was brought up; a culture that he perceived as his own, but in which he was discriminated against. In 1953, a year before the Algerian War ignited, Fanon was appointed as Head of the Psychiatric Ward at the Blida-Joinville Hospital in Algeria. In 1956, he resigned his post and became an active militant in the course of the Algerian War of liberation and in the cause of African freedom. His commitment to his ideas led him to espouse the revolutionary causes of Algeria and Africa. He became, according to Sartre, the spokesperson and the main theoretician of the Algerian Revolution.

In 'The Impossible Life of Frantz Fanon', Albert Memmi sketches for us four different stages in Fanon's biography. 'In his short life', he writes, 'Frantz Fanon experienced at least three serious failures.'[1] The first consists in his disavowal of his West Indian identity and in his identification with the colonizer's cultural models, which are French and white. The second failure was the outcome of his disillusionment with these models; his encounter with racism in mainland France ultimately led him to renounce his Frenchness. Subsequently, he discovered Algeria and espoused its political causes. In fact, he became the intellectual and spokesperson of the Algerian Revolution, but Algeria was not the last stage. Memmi argues that although Fanon never abandoned Algeria, he relinquished the Algerian nationalistic point of view and moved to embrace Africa. Implicitly, Memmi suggests that the internal conflicts within the Front de Libération Nationale (FLN) caused Fanon to abandon the narrowness of its political concerns in order to champion a universalistic conception of politics. On this universal politics he founded a new brand of humanism.

Memmi's four stages could be reformulated thus: Fanon's West Indian background and his identification with France, the two earlier stages, inform *Black Skin, White Masks*; the two later stages, his identification with Algeria and Africa, *The Wretched of the Earth*. Memmi's reading of Fanon's biography reproduces the bifid structure which certain critics impose on the work of Fanon: earlier versus late Fanon; his psychoanalysis in *Black Skin, White Masks* versus revolutionary praxis in *The Wretched of the Earth*.

According to Memmi, the two first stages, that is his ambivalent relationship with Martinique and France, continued until quite late in his life. Prior to his encounter with racism in mainland France, Fanon believed in the fiction of assimilation. *Black Skin, White Masks* captures this ambivalent relationship with the land of his birth (Martinique) and that of his adoptive culture (France). Memmi maintains that:

The identification of the former Black slave with the White nation which enslaved and then apparently adopted him, inevitably contains a subtle poison: the success of the operation – if one can speak of success – demands that the Black man renounce himself as Black. It must be admitted that for a long time the Black himself consented to the White man's monstrous demand. This is understandable: it is not up to the powerful to become more like the weak; assimilation takes place from the dominated to the dominant; from the dominated culture to the dominating culture, hardly ever in the inverse sense. [...] Now as one of the results of this unnatural effort, the war waged by the White against the Black also brings about a war of the Black against himself, a war that is perhaps even more destructive, for it is unremittingly carried on from within.[2]

In the above, Memmi summarizes pithily the problematic at the core of *Black Skin, White Masks*: the neurosis from which the Black suffers; the 'war' which the Black wages against him/herself. Memmi draws a portrait of Fanon that reflects the psychological complex of Jean Veneuse, who felt abandoned both by his mother country and his adoptive country France. After his encounter with racism, Memmi argues, Fanon proclaimed 'the end of the "White Illusion"'. He had to 'take off his White mask, which he believed he had to wear in order to get ahead in the world'.[3] However, what is puzzling for Memmi is that Fanon's disillusionment did not 'mark a new era of self-affirmation'; it did not galvanize him to fight to deliver his people, and ultimately himself, from the fetters of colonialism and from its racial prejudice. Memmi asserts that:

When a dominated man has understood the impossibility of assimilation to the dominator, he generally returns to himself, to his people, to his past, sometimes, as I have indicated, with excessive vigor, transfiguring this people and this past to the point of creating counter-myths. When Fanon finally discovered the fraud of assimilating West Indians into French citizens, he broke with France and the French with all the passion of which his fiery temperament was capable.[4]

Memmi describes Fanon's identification with Algeria as a substitution for 'an unattainable identification with Martinique'.[5] Unlike Césaire, Fanon never returned to self. He never turned to negritude to resolve his dilemma, but rather turned against it. Memmi attributes this rejection to Sartre's sway over him.[6] I agree with Memmi that Sartre imparted a negative view of negritude to Fanon. However, Memmi seems to ignore the Hegelian influence that Alexandre Kojève exerted on Fanon. This influence is central to Fanon's views on violence and to his humanist project. Echoing Kojève, he maintains in 'The Negro and Hegel' that freedom could not be obtained without risking life:

I demand that notice be taken of my negating activity insofar as I pursue something other than life; insofar as I do battle for the creation of a human world – that is, of a world of reciprocal recognitions.[7]

To return to the issue of negritude, Memmi misinterprets the ambivalent ways in which Fanon deploys the notion of negativity. It is true, as Memmi suggests, that Fanon employs this notion to chide Sartre for reducing negritude to a negative term in a dialectical schema, the workings of which should overcome capitalism and abolish its classist and paradoxically racist economy. But, as intimated in the above quotation, the 'negating activity' does have a positive signification. Fanon's definition of this activity is akin to Kojève's: it is bound up with the notion of Desire directed toward other Desires, which is to say the Desire of the Slave for recognition. It is important to note that while, for Kojève, it is work that restores the humanity (and ultimately the subjecthood) of the Slave, Fanon does not hold this idealized view of work. Since it was exploitative and dehumanizing in the colonial context, Fanon renounces work (literally resigns his post) and undertakes to fight instead for the dignity of the oppressed. Determined not to capitulate to racism, to what he calls 'the inessentiality of servitude', Fanon is now 'willing to accept the convulsions of death'.[8] Clearly, 'The Negro and Hegel' announces the incendiary language of *The Wretched of the Earth*. The Second World War was a landmark: just as the West Indians experienced what Fanon describes as their 'first metaphysical experience' (that is the realization that they were black and not white, their coming-into-consciousness which politically went hand in hand with their celebration of negritude), Martinique was made into a French Department. According to Memmi, Fanon felt betrayed by Martinique after its departmentalization. It could not provide him with 'the psychological and material resources to succeed in his combat against the oppressor'.[9] Because of its 'failure' to liberate itself from the fetters of French colonialism, Martinique proved itself 'incapable of furnishing him with the psychological and historical remedy to his tragic situation'.[10] He had to channel his revolt against colonial France and Algeria was therefore 'uniquely suited to Fanon's neurosis'.[11]

Like Martinique, Algeria was one of the departments of France. Like Fanon, the Algerian elite were steeped in French culture. Unlike the advocates of negritude, this elite revolted against France once it discovered the sham of assimilation. 'Fundamentally, [negritude]', Bulham writes, 'presented neither a total departure from the white world it denounced nor a program of transformative action, objectively transforming oppressive conditions.'[12] For the revolutionary Fanon, Algeria became 'the embellished substitute of his lost home'.[13] Three factors would nevertheless conspire against Fanon's integration into 'his country of adoption': the facticity of colour, language and religion.[14] Memmi concludes that:

one cannot shed his identity so easily. A Black man does not get rid of his negritude by calling it a mirage: nor can anyone exchange his cultural, historical and social singularity for another, by a simple act of will not even in the service of a revolutionary ethic.[15]

It is Memmi's view that the universalist schema put forward by Fanon in the concluding section of *The Wretched of the Earth* drowns the singularities of 'all those accursed differences'. As we will see, Memmi misinterprets Fanon's universalism. He fails to comprehend that Fanon rejects the mythic rhetoric of negritude because it obfuscates the cultural, national and ethnic differences that traverse the notion of blackness.

Memmi uses the concept of negritude in a confusing way, conflating Fanon's blackness (his colour) with the movement of negritude, which was set up by Césaire, Senghor and Damas. Through the work of this conflation, Memmi proceeds to disparage Fanon's critique of negritude, which he passes as a rejection of self. Memmi reads *Black Skin, White Masks* from the perspective of a Fanon exasperated by the facticity of his negritude. He describes Fanon's work as an autobiographical account, composed of lyrical prose which 'break[s] up into short poems of bitterness or rage'.[16] Memmi laments '[Fanon's] totally negative and very questionable conception of Negritude'.[17] For Memmi, negritude is not just the recognition of belonging to an oppressed group, but an 'affirmation of self; it is protest, reconstruction of a culture, at least of its potential. Positive adherence to a group, and the decision to contribute to a collective future.' Memmi rebukes Fanon for his 'disdainful abandonment of Blackness [...] in the name of universalism and the universal man [that] rests on a misconception'.[18] Memmi holds an essentialist conception of identity, which reproduces the very abstraction he criticizes in Fanon. In fact, Fanon's new humanism is at variance with this essentialist conception of identity; it predicated upon an ethics which, in order to attain a universal plane, must acknowledge differences and must be anchored in history.

As I have shown elsewhere, in the concluding pages of *Black Skin, White Masks* and *The Wretched of the Earth*, Fanon formulates two protean models of cultural belonging: two incompatible views on cultural assimilation, underwritten by two nationalistic discourses that are mutually exclusive.[19] In *Black Skin, White Masks*, he subscribes to the colonial doctrine of assimilation, attempting to reconcile his personal destiny with that of the French nation. He is still 'interested in the future of France, in French values, in the French nation'. Rejecting negritude – what he calls 'Negro nationality' – he asks: 'What have I to do with a black empire?'[20] In no way does he jeopardize '[this] future in the name of a mythic past'.[21] Instead, he seeks to be an actively involved participant in the future of the nation. It is the failure to fulfil this aspiration that motivates him to relinquish Frenchness and embrace the nationalist cause of the FLN. Colonial practice in Algeria will ultimately lead him to the realization that assimilation and colonialism are contradictory terms. I will have occasion to elaborate on the exclusion of the colonized from the political life of the nation, a factor that goes some way to explaining why Fanon forsakes the culture in which he has been brought up. In his letter of resignation, he denounces assimilation as a sham: 'the lawlessness, the inequality, the multi-daily murder of man [which] were raised to the status of legislative principles'.[22] He concludes that decolonization is the only way out of the absolute dehumanization in which the colonized lived. The colonial doctrine of assimilation succeeded only in denying the colonized an historical agency. In *The Wretched of the Earth*, Fanon represents a nationalistic view which empowers the colonized to be the same as other peoples in history. He subscribes to a worldview which articulates, in the phraseology of Denis Hollier, 'the pure openness of historical synchronicity'. Simply put: 'That history [...] is never strictly of one's own. That history means risking one's past in the other's language [...] a history that is no longer exclusively its own.'[23] It is in this sense that we must interpret the oft-cited statement that '[n]ational consciousness, which is not nationalism, is the only thing that will give us an international dimension'.[24] Consciousness of self is a prerequisite for the enunciating subject and, crucially, for establishing discursive relations with others. Transposing an existential phenomenology onto the plane of international politics, Fanon holds that communication is impossible without the realization of the self and of the existence of others. National consciousness must not be an inward-looking process, which shuts the ex-colonized nations within some kind of political solipsism after their decolonization. On the contrary, national consciousness is a precondition for opening up dialogue with other independent peoples. Nation-building, he insists:

[must be] accompanied by the discovery and encouragement of universalizing values. Far from keeping aloof from other nations, therefore, it is national liberation which leads the nation to play its part on the stage of history. It is at the heart of national consciousness that international consciousness lives and grows.[25]

Fanon's view agrees with Hollier's characterization of post-Enlightenment history as 'the register – or the concert – of what could, allegorically, be called the united nations'.[26] According to such a conception of history and international relations, nations can share the same history without losing their differences.

Fanon's warning against the nefarious effects of reactionary and bigoted nationalisms anticipates what Homi Bhabha calls 'the ethnonationalist "switchbacks" of our times, the charnel houses of ethnic cleansing: Bosnia, Rwanda, Kosovo, Gujarat, Sudan'.[27] The new humanism, inaugurated by Fanon in *The Wretched of the Earth*, projects '[a] vision of the global future, *post* colonialism and after decolonization', predicated upon 'an ethical and political *project* [...] that must go beyond "narrow-minded nationalism" or bourgeois nationalist formalism'.[28]

*   *   *

In the early 1960s, after his death, Fanon became the symbol of anti-colonial struggle in the Third World. At the same time, in the United States, black political activists involved in the civil rights movement embraced his views. The initial infatuation with Fanon gave rise to a militant trend in Fanonian scholarship. This trend was, however, short-lived and had abated by the end of the 1960s and early 1970s. At the time, Fanon became important in the field of social sciences, namely in departments of politics, sociology and psychology, and, as a result, a number of biographical works came into fruition. It is worth noticing that much of this interest in Fanon was taking place outside mainland France and his adoptive country, Algeria.

Indeed, Christiane Achour laments the fact that Fanon was relegated to oblivion in France and Algeria; she thanks Alice Cherki for saving him from the dereliction of forgetfulness with the publication of her book *Frantz Fanon, Portrait*.[29] After a long period of neglect, Achour remarks, a number of colloquia in the 1980s renewed interest in the work of Fanon. It is indeed ironic that this revival appeared at a moment when Algeria was in the grip of civil unrest and the socialist project envisaged by Fanon and undertaken by the FLN, his comrades-in-arms, was politically bankrupt. Certainly, the irony is not at Fanon's expense, the caution he issued against the pitfalls of nationalism shows he had the foresight to anticipate this bankruptcy. Fanon insists that nationalism leads to a blind alley if it does not develop into a pedagogy nurturing social and political consciousness, and giving rise to a new humanism.

As Achour suggests, Fanon is a relatively minor figure in France and Algeria. However, Achour glosses over the fact that this marginal character came from the outside to occupy a central role in the Anglo-American critical circles. It was predominantly in English, Cultural Studies and Postcolonial Studies programmes that he emerged as a global figure in the 1980s. The main question here is: how did Fanon come to be considered as the chief exponent of postcolonial theorizing? To provide a quick answer: the appropriation of Fanon as leading figure in this field of critical inquiry must be sought at the level of cultural politics.

Kobena Mercer offers some clues to this complex question. In 'Busy in the Ruins of a Wretched Phantasia', he writes:

As a result of epochal shifts over the past ten to fifteen years, from post-Fordism to post-Communism, there probably isn't anyone whose identity has not been touched by the bewildering uncertainties of living in a world with no stable center. [...] These changed circumstances profoundly alter the way in which Fanon's writings speak to our contemporary crises. Whereas earlier generations prioritized the Marxist themes of Fanon's later work, above all *The Wretched of the Earth*, published in 1961 at the height of the optimism of the post-war social movements, the fading fortunes of the independent left during the 1980s provided the backdrop to renewed interest in *Black Skin, White Masks*, Fanon's first and his most explicitly psychoanalytical text.[30]

This renewed interest in Fanon in the 1980s owed much to the 1986 Pluto edition, prefaced by Homi Bhabha, who, with his Cultural Studies approach and his psychoanalytical interpretation, opened up new readings. These new readings brought the issues of language, sexuality and race to the fore. According to Stuart Hall, *Black Skin, White Masks*, which explores the interrelationship between psychoanalysis and politics, the issues of colonialism, gender, race and sexuality, 'provides the privileged ground of Fanon's "return" and of the contestation over him'.[31] The perceived 'symptomatic break between Fanon's early and late work' is, in Hall's view, dubious in its attempt to privilege Fanon's political commitment over his psychoanalytical theory.[32] Hall takes a converse position: he seems to privilege the latter. Indeed, he proclaims that the revolutionary politics of Fanon, his 'incendiary Third Worldism', has become dated, if not obsolete.

Thus Hall defends Bhabha's 'strategic reading' of Fanon against the criticism mounted by the materialists. In particular, Hall points out that Bhabha departs at a certain point from Fanon. In fact, according to Hall, Bhabha's reading has less to do with Fanon than with his own agenda to promote postcolonial studies in the 1980s. The location of Bhabha's interpretation of Fanon must not be overlooked. Nonetheless, his 'Foreword: Framing Fanon' to the new translation of *The Wretched of the Earth*[33] represents a remarkable departure from his readings of Fanon which are dismissed by critics for not taking into account the most obvious historical and political contexts from which the work of Fanon emerged.

In his 'Foreword: Framing Fanon', Bhabha raises a number of crucial questions regarding the relevance of Fanon today:[34] Has Fanon become obsolete? Has the new humanism which he inaugurates in the concluding section of *The Wretched of the Earth* turned out to be nothing but a vain plea? What grounds for optimism does he allow us, if any? What is to be salvaged from his ethics and politics in this age of globalization? Bhabha raises two crucial points: the first concerns the ethical dimension of Fanon's brand of nationalism and appraises whether his views on decolonization are still relevant to our postcolonial/global world; the second focuses on the issue of violence. To engage effectively with Bhabha's 'Foreword', I will discuss these two points in reverse order.

To read the theme of violence out of context, without accounting for the wider historical specificities of Fanon's text and the context of its ethical preoccupations, is to commit violence against Fanon. Let us first address his view of violence. In *The Wretched of the Earth*, he calls for the abolition of colonialism and for the expulsion of the colonizer. Decolonization, he argues, is nothing but the 'complete calling in question of the colonial situation';[35] it is a 'violent phenomenon', a 'programme of complete disorder' from which emerges a 'historical process' leading to decolonization; it is 'the meeting of two forces, opposed to each other by their very nature'[36] and involved in a 'murderous struggle'. This violence has marked the history of the colonized people. Colonialism is not an ideology, in the sense that it has never sought to hide or dress up its violence: its agents openly speak a brutal language.[37] 'Colonialism is not a thinking machine,' argues Fanon, 'nor a body endowed with reasoning faculties.' It is maintained by naked violence: 'violence in its natural state, and it will only yield when confronted with greater violence.'[38] Put in other words: 'The native's challenge to the colonial world is not a rational confrontation of points of view. It is not a treatise on the universal.'[39]

Nevertheless, the theme of violence does not constitute the centrality of Fanon's project; a project which, as it emerges in the concluding section of *The Wretched of the Earth*, discourses on universal humanism. Violence, for Fanon, is just a moment, a negative instance in the process of decolonization, which must pass through two phases: the breaking-up of the colonial state and the emergence of the postcolonial nation. This is how Fanon describes the ultimate purpose of decolonization:

> ... it influences individuals and modifies them fundamentally. It transforms spectators crushed with their inessentiality into privileged actors, with the grandiose glare of history's floodlight upon them. It brings a natural rhythm into existence, introduced by new men, and with it a new language and a new humanity. Decolonization is the veritable creation of new men. [...] the 'thing' which has been colonized becomes man during the same process by which it frees itself.[40]

The theme of violence cannot be comprehended without 'exploring the processes by which decolonization turns into the project of nation building', a stage prior to 'constructing a world-system based on the ideals of global equity'.[41] Bhabha describes this stage as a moment of 'fundamental importance in the colonized's pyscho-affective equilibrium'. Bhabha borrows from Fanon the term 'psycho-affective' to demarcate the space within which 'the citizen and individual develop and grow'.[42] Taking his cue from Fanon, he inscribes violence in this space, the site where political citizenship is enacted and re-enacted.

Bhabha is right to remark that the exclusion of the colonized from the public sphere led them to adopt 'the reactive vocabulary of violence and retributive justice'.[43] This violence arises from the simple fact that colonialism created a diremption between the ideals of French Republicanism and the practices of political citizenship. To grasp Fanon's 'approach to the phenomenology of decolonization', his views on colonial violence, it is important to underscore 'the internal dissonance [...] between the free standing of citizen and the segregated status of the subject – the double political destiny of the same'.[44] Bhabha is vague in his discussion of the political economy of assimilation or what he calls 'the double political destiny of the same'. As I have argued elsewhere,[45] the *senatus-consulte* of 1863 and 1865 worked to expropriate the colonized and deny them subject status.

The *senatus-consulte* of 1863 had two devastating consequences on colonized Algeria. First, it displaced the social structures of traditional life and precipitated the collapse of its political economy. Second, and most importantly, it facilitated the expropriation of Algeria's most fertile land. Let me here open a parenthesis to note that, because of this historical factor, Fanon assigns to the expropriated peasantry a revolutionary role in the Algerian War. The *senatus-consulte* of July 1865 stipulated that the Arabs and Berbers were subjects; it allowed them to apply for French citizenship, provided they relinquish their 'personal status', namely their Muslim identity. In reality, the offer of citizenship amounted to nothing: the Muslims would not renounce their cultural identity; moreover, the colonial administration would thwart the assimilationist laws always proposed but never promulgated. The *senatus-consulte* of 1865 produced a fracture at the core of French citizenship: it subjected the colonized to French laws but denied the rights of political citizenship. This fracture also manifested itself in the form of a disjunction between the public and private spheres, between personal life and the life of the nation, between past and present. Excluded from the benefits that political citizenship bequeathed to citizens, the colonized were confined to the private sphere of domestic life or religion to enact and re-enact their sense of identity and cultural belonging. This exclusion from the public, that is, from the political life of the nation, forced the colonized to fall back on 'archaic' cultural practices inherited from a congealed past. The religious formalism that gave rise, both in colonial times and subsequently, to fundamentalism, or what Bhabha calls 'ethno-nationalist religious conflicts', was nothing but the consequences of this colonial policy, which denied the colonized subject status and political participation. The ideology of assimilation put in place a regime of apartheid, characterized by its Manichaean violence, compartmentalizing and segregating the nation into a French Algeria, which enjoyed the rights of political citizenship, and a native Algeria, to which these rights were denied.

To be sure, the rhetoric of assimilation went against the grain of France's Republicanism. It rendered citizenship an 'unstable, unsustainable psycho-affective site in the conflict between political and legal assimilation, and the respect for, and recognition of, Muslim ethical and cultural affiliations'.[46] Bhabha highlights the pernicious effects of the laws instituted by the *senatus-consulte*, which divested the colonized Muslims of their identity. But he is oblivious to the material consequences that these laws had in dispossessing them of their land: the root cause of violence.

Fanon has been dismissed as an 'apostle of violence': a preacher of hate. He has been compared to Hitler, Sorel and Pareto. Hannah Arendt has denounced him for 'glorify[ing] violence for violence's sake' and for expressing 'a much deeper hatred of bourgeois society than the conventional Left'.[47] Sartre, on the other hand, thinks that Fanon's *The Wretched of the Earth* represents 'the moment of the boomerang, the third stage of violence': a returning violence that comes back to assail its perpetrators.[48] The violence inflicted upon the colonized was, in Sartre's view, systemic: it could be seen in the expropriation of the colonized, the pulverization of their social structures. This was achieved by brutal force. The result of the violence was the objective condition of the colonized, that is their immiseration, their unemployment, their chronic malnutrition, famine, disease. Sartre argues that, in order to overcome this condition, violence must be confronted with violence. Echoing Fanon, Sartre is adamant that the violence involving colonizer and colonized in the context of Algeria's decolonization was the sum total of colonial oppression. Sartre puts the blame squarely on the colonizer: the violence of the colonized was nothing but the interiorization of a single violence, that of the colonizer. Sartre distinguishes between the gratuitous violence of the latter and that of the colonized '[which] is no less than man reconstructing himself'.[49] Unlike Arendt, for whom Fanon's incendiary language announces 'the end of politics', and, unlike Sartre, who 'fanned' it and for whom violence represented 'the fiery, first breath of human freedom',[50] Bhabha proposes a different reading. The following passage well illustrates the distance Bhabha takes from Arendt and Sartre:

Fanon, the phantom of terror, might be only the most intimate, if intimidating, poet of the vicissitudes of violence. But poetic justice can be questionable even when it is exercised on behalf of the wretched of the earth. And if, as I have argued, the lesson of Fanon lies in his fine adjustment of the balance between the politician and the psychiatrist, his skill in altering the 'scale' between the social dimension and the psycho-affective relation, then we have to admit that he is in danger of losing his balance when, for instance, he writes: 'Violence can thus be understood to be the perfect mediation. The colonized man liberates himself in and through violence. The praxis enlightens the militant because it shows him the means and the end.' Knowing what we now know about the double destiny of violence, we must ask: Is violence ever a *perfect* mediation? Is it not simply rhetorical bravura to assert that *any* form of secular, material mediation can provide a transparency of political action (or ethical judgment) that reveals 'the means *and* the end'? Is the clear mirror of violence not something of a mirage in which the dispossessed see their reflections but from which they cannot slake their thirst?[51]

Bhabha's re-reading of Fanon still reproduces Henry Louis Gates's 'Critical Fanonism': he characterizes him as a contradictory and 'polemical' figure, 'dialectically rich', hypostatizing the complexities of our global culture.[52] In Bhabha's critical account, the work of Fanon provides valuable insights into the segregated economy of our globalized world. Nevertheless, Bhabha's treatment of the issue of violence is one-sided and rather superficial in that it does not account for the historical context of Fanon's political intervention in colonial Algeria. Implicitly and explicitly, Bhabha intimates that violence mars Fanon's ethics of decolonization. Bhabha concludes his discussion of the question of violence with rhetorical questions. It is easy to sit on the fence and depict Fanon as 'the intimate, if intimidating, poet of the vicissitudes of violence' and 'the phantom of terror', projecting for the colonized the phantasmata of violence. Bhabha presents Fanon as deluded because he confuses the means with the ends of colonial violence. It is important to stress that, for Fanon, violence is not a mediating agency between the means and the end, as Bhabha intimates. Rather, it is a feature of the Manichaean economy which structures the colonial space. Bhabha introduces Fanon as performing a difficult balancing act, one in which he risks losing his bearings and precipitating the colonized into blind violence. In his analysis, Bhabha crucially does not distinguish between the different levels within which violence operates in Fanon's discourse. In particular, it is necessary to recognize that Fanon's account of the politics that generated colonial violence should be situated at the level of description. Having acknowledged this: the systemic violence of colonialism cannot be attributed to him. At the prescriptive level, he endorses violence, only as a last resort, to combat a system that could not be overhauled without being dismantled. Bhabha's conflation of these two levels results in his overlooking the larger picture in Fanon's description of the violence of colonialism. Bhabha misses the significance of Fanon's discerning analyses of colonial violence. In today's world, where violence and terror have gone global, what conclusions might we draw from Fanon's *The Wretched of the Earth*? Should we keep on blaming Fanon for the colonial violence, which he internalized and struggled against, and overlook the fact that the very Manichaeism that previously governed the economy of colonial societies is now generating violence and terror on a global scale?

To be fair, Bhabha astutely remarks that globalization has reproduced the Manichaeism of colonial politics.

[T]he economic 'solutions' to inequality and poverty subscribed to by the IMF and the World Bank, for instance, have 'the feel of the colonial ruler', according to Joseph Stiglitz, once senior vice president and chief economist of the World Bank. 'They help to create a dual economy in which there are pockets of wealth ... But a dual economy is not a developed economy.' It is the reproduction of dual, unequal economies as effects of globalization that render poor societies more vulnerable to the 'culture of conditionality', through which what is purportedly the granting of loans turns, at times, into the peremptory enforcement of policy.[53]

This dual economy, argues Bhabha, has created divided worlds, which are mutually exclusive: the haves and the have-nots. Bhabha conjures the spirit of Fanon's *The Wretched of the Earth* in his pronouncements against the pernicious effects of this economy on the Third World.

I acquiesce with Bhabha's perspicacious view that *The Wretched of the Earth* transcends its specificities 'because of the peculiarly grounded, historical stance it takes towards the future'.[54] He reinscribes Fanon's Manichaean language within 'the anticolonial spatial tradition'.[55] Clearly, Bhabha has reconsidered his previous position with regard to the conceptual opposition that marks Fanon's thinking. 'This critical language of duality', Bhabha remarks, 'is part of the *spatial* imagination that seems to come so naturally to geopolitical thinking of a progressive, postcolonial cast of mind: margin and metropole, centre and periphery, the global and the local, the nation and the world.'[56] Nonetheless, Bhabha's understanding of this geopolitics is not consistent with his deconstructive take on Fanon: his pronouncements that put the dialectical operation at work in *The Wretched of the Earth* out of commission. In addition, one might ask: what is so progressive about this language of duality that stems from colonial practice, a language that he has thus far dismissed? Arguably, Fanon's language is progressive in as much as it anticipates the Manichaean economy which governs globalization; an economy which has reproduced in our postcolonial world the compartmentalized societies of the colonial era.

Let me now turn to the first point raised by Bhabha and examine the significance of Fanon's ethics. According to Bhabha, this ethics:

introduces a *temporal* dimension into the discourse of decolonization. It suggests that the *future* of the colonized world – 'The Third World must start over a new history of Man ...' – is imaginable, or acheivable, only in the process of resisting the peremptory and polarizing choices that the superpowers impose on their 'client' states. Decolonization can truly be achieved only with the destruction of the Manichaeanism of the cold war; and it is this belief that enables the insights of *The Wretched of the Earth* to be effective beyond its publication in 1961 (and the death of its author in that year), and to provide us with salient and suggestive perspectives on the state of the decompartmentalized world after the dismemberment of the Berlin Wall in 1989.[57]

The dismantling of the Berlin Wall has been hailed by some critics as a movement towards the completion of the project of globalization, the advent of open society, the triumph of freedom in the world and the liberalization of the market. Paradoxically, this movement has reinstated the Manichaeism that determined the politics of the old colonial regimes. Fanon's ethics of decolonization calls for a different kind of globalization, for a new world order in which segregated economies must be abolished. Fanon envisages the emergence of a new humanism, freed from the weight of the colonial past and from the ideological conflict of the Cold War.

In *The Wretched of the Earth*, Fanon wages war at two fronts: against colonialism in Algeria and in the Third World, and against capitalism in the post-independence period. His struggle to unshackle Algeria from the chains of colonial domination is concomitant with his commitment to liberate the Third World from Europe's hegemony. After decolonization, he maintains, the Third World could find itself subjected to an insidious neocolonialism. In his view, genuine decolonization cannot be attained without implementing a policy that ensures its ideological independence or non-alignment; for in the period of post-independence, he fears that the Third World will be drawn into 'the framework of cut-throat competition between capitalism and socialism'.[58] The end of direct colonial rule (which hitherto depended on territorial occupation of former Third World countries) does not necessarily mean the end of colonialism. In the postcolonial period, decolonization necessitates a cultural and political revolution which must guarantee economic independence from the West.

The prospect of seeing the Third World mortgage its future to capitalism fills Fanon with fear and trepidation. He warns that the Third World might become a 'factor' in the ideological conflict of the

Cold War. The aid from the developed countries often comes with strings attached; it is employed as a tool of ideological control and manipulation. In Fanon's view, however, it must not be perceived as a charitable gesture, endowing its sponsors with some moral authority. Aid is nothing but 'reparation'. He draws a parallel between the situation of the Third World after the anti-colonial wars and that of Western Europe after the Second World War. He perceptively notes that, just as Nazi Germany was made to compensate Western European countries, the latter should pay for the damage they inflicted on the Third World. He underscores that the poverty of the latter is the outcome of a long history of 'domination, of exploitation and pillage'.[59] As he eloquently puts it, 'Europe is literally the creation of the Third World. The wealth which smothers her is that which was stolen from the under-developed people.' In prophetic language which conjures up the abject poverty of today's Africa, he writes:

The mass of the people struggle against the same poverty, flounder about making the same gestures and with their shrunken bellies outline what has been called the geography of hunger. It is an under-developed world, a world inhuman in its poverty; but it is a world without doctors, without engineers and without administrators. Confronting this world the European opulence is literally scandalous, for it has been founded on slavery, it has been nourished with the blood of slaves and it comes from the soil and subsoil of that underdeveloped world.[60]

What is even more reprehensible is the fact that this 'geography of hunger' still persists in the twenty-first century. This troubling fact confirms Fanon's astute remark that 'the primary Manichaeism which governed colonial society is preserved intact during the period of decolonization'.[61] This geography is characterized by the Manichaeism of the colonial world as a divided world, made up of separate zones, inhabited by different species and with its segregated economies. The plight of the Third World is indeed a scar on Europe's conscience. The relief programmes, intended to alleviate the chronic famines which plagued and still plague Africa, Europe's handouts, must not conceal the brutal history of colonial exploitation. Of course, Europe could eradicate this 'geography of hunger' if it were to give up its programmes of weapons of mass destruction. Fanon is adamant that:

Those literally astronomical sums of money which are invested in military research, those engineers who are transformed into technicians of nuclear war, could in the space of fifteen years raise the standards of living of under-developed countries by sixty per cent. So we see that the true interests of under-developed countries do not lie in the protraction nor in the accentuation of this cold war.[62]

Let us note in passing that Fanon's views here run counter to the portrayal of them by critics who have denounced him for preaching violence. One could not underscore enough the significance of the humanist dimension of his critique; for he conceives of this humanism within a 'socialist regime, a regime which is completely orientated towards the people as a whole and based on the principle that man is the most precious of all possessions'.[63]

Fanon warns against nationalism that is subtended by a bourgeois ideology, substituting colonial antagonism with class conflict: displacing the colonizer only to replace the latter with the *évolués*, the middle-class elite that is steeped in French colonial culture. This elite does not represent, for Fanon, the revolutionary force that will call a halt to colonialism. On the contrary, it epitomizes an emergent neocolonialism that will perpetuate the misery of the exploited masses. This perhaps goes some way towards addressing Memmi's question of why Fanon relinquishes the politics of negritude.

Fanon's call to liberate the Third World through development has fallen on deaf ears. Governments in the Third World did not heed Fanon's warning against the pitfalls of nationalist consciousness. Self-styled revolutionary movements in the Third World and in Africa failed to achieve a genuine decolonization. Nationalism was not harnessed by a pedagogy fostering a social and political emancipation. This failure has fatally undermined Fanon's project to 'put Africa in motion, to cooperate in its organization, in its regrouping, behind revolutionary principles, to participate in the ordered movement of a continent'.[64] What Africa's postcolonial history shows – and this is no fault of Fanon's – is the reverse of his efforts to protect Africa from 'passing through the middle-class chauvinistic national phase with its procession of wars and death-tolls'.[65] In postcolonial Africa, myriad dictatorships have been installed and propped up by the West. To echo Bulhan, home-grown dictators sponsored by Europe have instituted the ultimate form of oppression: 'auto-colonialism'. Sad to say, 'these African tyrants of today, many of them products of colonial servitude, rule with lethal arms sent as "aid" by more "developed countries" in a manner reminiscent of the way firearms and gunpowder were [used in] … Africa during the slave trade.'[66]

I concur with Bhabha that *The Wretched of the Earth* raises important political questions with respect to the project of decolonization, questions that have become acute since the end of the Cold War. I also agree with Bhabha that Fanon's work 'provides a genealogy for globalization that reaches back to the complex problems of decolonization'.[67] Bhabha incisively points out that:

Fanon's proleptic proposal that the postcolonial narrative of independent nation building could enter its international phase only after the end of the Cold War telescopes that long history of neglect into our times, whence it reveals the poignant proximity of the incomplete project of decolonization to the dispossessed subjects of globalization.[68]

What Bhabha divulges here is the failure of postcolonial studies to deal effectively with the problems that globalization poses for emergent postcolonial nations. Two practical conclusions could be drawn from Bhabha: (1) that globalization has instituted an insidious neocolonialism; (2) that the most powerful members of the international community have failed in their responsibility to help the wretched of the earth, to lift them from the doldrums, from the depths of colonial and postcolonial misery.

By way of conclusion, let us recall Kebena Mercer's contentious view that the 'decentring' of the subject and the epochal shifts in the 1980s and 1990s (both spurred by the economy of globalization) renewed interest in Fanon's early work *Black Skin, White Masks* and rendered obsolete *The Wretched of the Earth*. This view chimes with Hall's and subscribes to Bhabha's post-structuralist reading of *Black Skin, White Masks*. In 'Framing Fanon', the thrust of Bhabha's argument goes against the grain of this thinking. His critique of *The Wretched of the Earth* throws into relief difficult questions. For instance, how are we to resolve the question of postcolonial domination, and what strategies are we to adopt against the progress of an insidious neocolonialism? It must be said that Bhabha does not provide effective answers to these pertinent questions. What emerges from his critique is the depressing thought that while postcolonial theorizing has thrived thanks to the work of Fanon and at times in spite of it, neocolonialism has been consolidating its rules of domination and expanding its spheres of influence, and that globalization is sapping the foundations of deconstructive postcolonialism, rendering its rhetoric almost obsolete – the rhetoric of difference that is leading to political apathy and indifference. It has stolen the ground from critics like Hall, Mercer and Bhabha, who attempted to read Fanon deconstructively, leaving them with nothing to offer but Fanon, expurgated of the rhetoric of violence – the very same violence against which Fanon struggles and which rules over our postcolonial world. In an age where oppression lurks behind globalization, reading Fanon is urgent. It is important to revisit *The Wretched of the Earth* and to re-read it as we enter into a new age of globalized terror and violence.

Section One:

Culture and Racism

1
The Negro and Language

I ascribe a basic importance to the phenomenon of language. That is why I find it necessary to begin with this subject, which should provide us with one of the elements in the coloured man's comprehension of the dimension of *the other*. For it is implicit that to speak is to exist absolutely for the other.

The black man has two dimensions. One with his fellows, the other with the white man. A Negro behaves differently with a white man and with another Negro. That this self-division is a direct result of colonialist subjugation is beyond question…. No one would dream of doubting that its major artery is fed from the heart of those various theories that have tried to prove that the Negro is a stage in the slow evolution of monkey into man. Here is objective evidence that expresses reality.

But when one has taken cognizance of this situation, when one has understood it, one considers the job completed. How can one then be deaf to that voice rolling down the stages of history: 'What matters is not to know the world but to change it.'

This matters appallingly in our lifetime.

To speak means to be in a position to use a certain syntax, to grasp the morphology of this or that language, but it means above all to assume a culture, to support the weight of a civilization. Since the situation is not one-way only, the statement of it should reflect the fact. Here the reader is asked to concede certain points that, however unacceptable they may seem in the beginning, will find the measure of their validity in the facts.

The problem that we confront in this chapter is this: the Negro of the Antilles will be proportionately whiter – that is, he will come closer to being a real human being – in direct ratio to his mastery of the French language. I am not unaware that this is one of man's attitudes face to face with Being. A man who has a language consequently possesses the world expressed and implied by that language. What we are getting at becomes plain: mastery of language affords remarkable power. Paul Valéry knew this, for he called language 'the god gone astray in the flesh'.[1]

4 Culture and Racism

In a work now in preparation I propose to investigate this phenomenon.[2] For the moment I want to show why the Negro of the Antilles, whoever he is, has always to face the problem of language. Furthermore, I will broaden the field of this description and through the Negro of the Antilles include every colonized man.

Every colonized people – in other words, every people in whose soul an inferiority complex has been created by the death and burial of its local cultural originality – finds itself face to face with the language of the civilizing nation; that is, with the culture of the mother country. The colonized is elevated above his jungle status in proportion to his adoption of the mother country's cultural standards. He becomes whiter as he renounces his blackness, his jungle. In the French colonial army, and particularly in the Senegalese regiments, the black officers serve first of all as interpreters. They are used to convey the master's orders to their fellows, and they too enjoy a certain position of honour.

There is the city, there is the country. There is the capital, there is the province. Apparently the problem in the mother country is the same. Let us take a Lyonnais in Paris: he boasts of the quiet of his city, the intoxicating beauty of the quays of the Rhône, the splendour of the plane trees and all those other things that fascinate people who have nothing to do. If you meet him again when he has returned from Paris, and especially if you do not know the capital, he will never run out of its praises: Paris-city-of-light, the Seine, the little garden restaurants, know Paris and die....

The process repeats itself with the man of Martinique. First of all on his island: Basse-Pointe, Marigot, Gros-Morne and, opposite, the imposing Fort-de-France. Then, and this is the important point, beyond his island. The Negro who knows the mother country is a demigod. In this connection I offer a fact that must have struck my compatriots. Many of them, after stays of varying length in metropolitan France, go home to be deified. The most eloquent form of ambivalence is adopted toward them by the native, the-one-who-never-crawled-out-of-his-hole, the *bitaco*. The black man who has lived in France for a length of time returns radically changed. To express it in genetic terms, his phenotype undergoes a definitive, an absolute mutation.[3] Even before he had gone away, one could tell from the almost aerial manner of his carriage that new forces had been set in motion. When he met a friend or an acquaintance, his greeting was no longer the wide sweep of the arm: with great reserve our 'new man' bowed slightly. The habitually raucous voice hinted at a gentle inner stirring as of rustling breezes. For the Negro knows that over there in France there is a stereotype of him that will fasten on to him at the pier in Le Havre or Marseille: 'Ah come fom Mahtinique, it's the fuhst time Ah've eveh come to Fance.' He knows that what the poets call the *divine gurgling* (listen to Creole) is only a halfway house between pidgin-nigger and French. The middle class in the Antilles never speak Creole except to their servants. In school the children of Martinique are taught to scorn the dialect. One avoids *Creolisms*. Some families completely forbid the use of Creole and mothers ridicule their children for speaking it.

> My mother wanting a son to keep in mind
> if you do not know your history lesson
> you will not go to mass on Sunday in
> your Sunday clothes
> that child will be a disgrace to the family
> that child will be our curse
> shut up I told you you must speak French
> the French of France
> the Frenchman's French
> French French[4]

Yes, I must take great pains with my speech, because I shall be more or less judged by it. With great contempt they will say of me, 'He doesn't even know how to speak French.'

In any group of young men in the Antilles, the one who expresses himself well, who has mastered the language, is inordinately feared; keep an eye on that one, he is almost white. In France one says, 'He talks like a book.' In Martinique, 'He talks like a white man.'

The Negro arriving in France will react against the myth of the *R*-eating man from Martinique. He will become aware of it, and he will really go to war against it. He will practise not only rolling his *R* but embroidering it. Furtively observing the slightest reactions of others, listening to his own speech, suspicious of his own tongue – a wretchedly lazy organ – he will lock himself into his room and read aloud for hours – desperately determined to learn *diction*.

Recently an acquaintance told me a story. A Martinique Negro landed at Le Havre and went into a bar. With the utmost self-confidence he called, 'Waite*rrr*! Bing me a beeya.' Here is a genuine intoxication. Resolved not to fit the myth of the nigger-who-eats-his-Rs, he had acquired a fine supply of them but allocated it badly.

There is a psychological phenomenon that consists in the belief that the world will open to the extent to which frontiers are broken down. Imprisoned on his island, lost in an atmosphere that offers not the slightest outlet, the Negro breathes in this appeal of Europe like pure air. For, it must be admitted, Aimé Césaire was generous – in his *Cahier d'un retour au pays natal*. This town of Fort-de-France is truly flat, stranded. Lying there naked to the sun, that 'flat, sprawling city, stumbling over its own common sense, winded by its load of endlessly repeated crosses, pettish at its destiny, voiceless, thwarted in every direction, incapable of feeding on the juices of its soil, blocked, cut off, confined, divorced from fauna and flora'.[5]

Césaire's description of it is anything but poetic. It is understandable, then, when at the news that he is getting into France (quite like someone who, in the colloquial phrase, is 'getting a start in life') the black man is jubilant and makes up his mind to change. There is no thematic pattern, however; his structure changes independently of any reflective process. In the United States there is a centre directed by Pearce and Williamson; it is called Peckham. These authors have shown that in married couples a biochemical alteration takes place in the partners and, it seems, they have discovered the presence of certain hormones in the husband of a pregnant woman. It would be equally interesting – and there are plenty of subjects for the study – to investigate the modifications of body fluids that occur in Negroes when they arrive in France. Or simply to study through tests the psychic changes both before they leave home and after they have spent a month in France.

What are by common consent called the human sciences have their own drama. Should one postulate a type for human reality and describe its psychic modalities only through deviations from it, or should one not rather strive unremittingly for a concrete and ever new understanding of man?

When one reads that after the age of twenty-nine a man can no longer love and that he must wait until he is forty-nine before his capacity for affect revives, one feels the ground give way beneath one. The only possibility of regaining one's balance is to face the whole problem, for all these discoveries, all these inquiries lead only in one direction: to make man admit that he is nothing, absolutely nothing – and that he must put an end to the narcissism on which he relies in order to imagine that he is different from the other 'animals'.

This amounts to nothing more nor less than *man's surrender*.

Having reflected on that, I grasp my narcissism with both hands and I turn my back on the degradation of those who would make man a mere mechanism. If there can be no discussion on a philosophical level – that is, the plane of the basic needs of human reality – I am willing to work on the psychoanalytical level – in other words, the level of the 'failures', in the sense in which one speaks of engine failures.

The black man who arrives in France changes because to him the country represents the Tabernacle; he changes not only because it is from France that he received his knowledge of Montesquieu, Rousseau and Voltaire, but also because France gave him his physicians, his department heads, his innumerable little functionaries – from the sergeant-major 'fifteen years in the service' to the policeman who was born in Panissières. There is a kind of magic vault of distance, and the man who is leaving next week for France creates round himself a magic circle in which the words *Paris, Marseille, Sorbonne, Pigalle* become the keys to the vault. He leaves for the pier and the amputation of his being diminishes as the silhouette of his ship grows clearer. In the eyes of those who have come to see him off he can read the evidence of his own mutation, his power. 'Good-bye bandanna, good-bye straw hat. …'

Now that we have got him to the dock, let him sail; we shall see him again. For the moment, let us go to welcome one of those who are coming home. The 'newcomer' reveals himself at once; he answers only in French and often he no longer understands Creole. There is a relevant illustration in folklore. After several months of living in France, a country boy returns to his family. Noticing a farm implement, he asks his father, an old don't-pull-that-kind-of-thing-on-me peasant, 'Tell me, what does one call that apparatus?' His father replies by dropping the tool on the boy's feet and the amnesia vanishes. Remarkable therapy.

There is the newcomer, then. He no longer understands the dialect, he talks about the Opéra, which he may never have seen except from a distance, but above all he adopts a critical attitude toward his compatriots. Confronted with the most trivial occurrence, he becomes an oracle. He is the one who knows. He betrays himself in his speech. At the Savannah, where the young men of Fort-de-France spend their leisure, the spectacle is revealing: everyone immediately waits for the newcomer to speak. As soon as the school day ends, they all go to the Savannah. This Savannah seems to have its own poetry. Imagine a square about 600 feet long and 125 feet wide, its sides bounded by worm-eaten tamarind trees, one end marked by the huge war memorial (the nation's gratitude to its children), the other by the Central Hotel; a miserable tract of uneven cobbles, pebbles that roll away under one's feet; and, amid all this, three or four hundred young fellows walking up and down, greeting one another, grouping – no, they never form groups, they go on walking.

'How's it going?'
'OK. How's it with you?'
'OK.'

And that goes on for fifty years. Yes, this city is deplorably played out. So is its life.

They meet and talk. And if the newcomer soon gets the floor, it is because they were *waiting for him*. First of all to observe his manner: the slightest departure is seized on, picked apart and, in less than forty-eight hours, it has been retailed all over Fort-de-France. There is no forgiveness when one who claims a superiority falls below the standard. Let him say, for instance, 'It was not my good fortune, when in France, to observe mounted policemen', and he is done for. Only one choice remains to him: throw off his 'Parisianism' or die of ridicule. For there is also no forgetting: when he marries, his wife will be aware that she is marrying a joke, and his children will have a legend to face and to live down.

What is the origin of this personality change? What is the source of this new way of being? Every dialect is a way of thinking, Damourette and Pichon said. And the fact that the newly returned Negro adopts a language different from that of the group into which he was born is evidence of a dislocation, a separation. Professor D. Westermann, in *The African Today* (p. 331), says that the Negroes' inferiority complex is particularly intensified among the most educated, who must struggle with it unceasingly. Their way of doing so, he adds, is frequently naïve:

The wearing of European clothes, whether rags or the most up-to-date style; using European furniture and European forms of social intercourse; adorning the Native language with European expressions; using bombastic phrases in speaking or writing a European language; all these contribute to a feeling of equality with the European and his achievements.

On the basis of other studies and my own personal observations, I want to try to show why the Negro adopts such a position, peculiar to him, with respect to European languages. Let me point out once more that the conclusions I have reached pertain to the French Antilles; at the same time, I am not unaware that the same behaviour patterns obtain in every race that has been subjected to colonization.

I have known – and unfortunately I still know – people born in Dahomey or the Congo who pretend to be natives of the Antilles; I have known, and I still know, Antilles Negroes who are annoyed when they are suspected of being Senegalese. This is because the Antilles Negro is more 'civilized' than the African, that is, he is closer to the white man; and this difference prevails not only in back streets and on boulevards but also in public service and the army. Any Antilles Negro who performed his military service in a Senegalese infantry regiment is familiar with this disturbing climate: on one side he has the Europeans, whether born in his own country or in France, and on the other he has the Senegalese. I remember a day when, in the midst of combat, we had to wipe out a machine-gun nest. The Senegalese were ordered to attack three times and each time they were forced back. Then one of them wanted to know why the toubabs[6] did not go into action. At such times, one no longer knows whether one *is toubab* or 'native'. And yet many Antilles Negroes see nothing to upset them in such European identification; on the contrary, they find it altogether normal. That would be all we need, to be taken for niggers! The Europeans despise the Senegalese and the Antilles Negro rules the black roost as its unchallenged master. Admittedly as an extreme example, I offer a detail that is at least amusing. I was talking recently with someone from Martinique who told me with considerable resentment that some Guadeloupe Negroes were trying to 'pass' as Martinicans. But, he added, the lie was rapidly discovered, because they are more savage than we are; which, again, means they are farther away from the white man. It is said that the Negro loves to jabber; in my own case, when I think of the word *jabber* I see a gay group of children calling and shouting for the sake of calling and shouting – children in the midst of play, to the degree to which play can be considered an initiation into life. The Negro loves to jabber and, from this theory, it is not a long road that leads to a new proposition: the Negro is just a child. The psychoanalysts have a fine start here and the term *orality* is soon heard.

But we have to go farther. The problem of language is too basic to allow us to hope to state it all here. Piaget's remarkable studies have taught us to distinguish the various stages in the mastery of language, and Gelb and Goldstein have shown us that the function of language is also broken into periods and steps. What interests us here is the black man confronted by the French language. We are trying to understand why the Antilles Negro is so fond of speaking French.

Jean-Paul Sartre, in *Orphée noir*, which prefaces the *Anthology de la nouvelle poésie nègre et malgache*, tells us that the black poet will turn against the French language; but that does not apply in the Antilles. Here I share the opinion of Michel Leiris, who, discussing Creole, wrote not so long ago:

Even now, despite the fact that it is a language that everyone knows more or less, though only the illiterate use it to the exclusion of French, Creole seems already predestined to become a relic eventually, once public education (however slow its progress, impeded by the insufficiency of school facilities everywhere, the paucity of reading matter available to the public and the fact that the physical scale of living is often too low) has become common enough among the disinherited classes of the population.

And, the author adds:

In the case of the poets that I am discussing here, there is no question of their deliberately becoming 'Antilleans' – on the Provençal picturesque model – by employing a dead language which, furthermore, is utterly devoid of all external radiance regardless of its intrinsic qualities; it is rather a matter of their asserting, in opposition to white men filled with the worst racial prejudices, whose arrogance is more and more plainly demonstrated to be unfounded, the integrity of their personalities.[7]

If there is, for instance, a Gilbert Gratiant who writes in dialect, it must be admitted that he is a rarity. Let us point out, furthermore, that the poetic merit of such creation is quite dubious. There are, in contrast, real works of art translated from the Peul and Wolof dialects of Senegal, and I have found great interest in following the linguistic studies of Sheik Anta Diop.

Nothing of the sort in the Antilles. The language spoken officially is French; teachers keep a close watch over the children to make sure they do not use Creole. Let us not mention the ostensible reasons. It would seem, then, that the problem is this: in the Antilles, as in Brittany, there is a dialect and there is the French language. But this is false, for the Bretons do not consider themselves inferior to the French people. The Bretons have not been civilized by the white man.

By refusing to multiply our elements, we take the risk of not setting a limit to our field; for it is essential to convey to the black man that an attitude of rupture has never saved anyone. While it is true that I have to throw off an attacker who is strangling me, because I literally cannot breathe, the fact remains solely on the physiological foundation. To the mechanical problem of respiration it would be unsound to graft a psychological element, the impossibility of expansion.

What is there to say? Purely and simply this: when a bachelor of philosophy from the Antilles refuses to apply for certification as a teacher on the ground of his colour, I say that philosophy has never saved anyone. When someone else strives and strains to prove to me that black men are as intelligent as white men, I say that intelligence has never saved anyone; and that is true, for, if philosophy and intelligence are invoked to proclaim the equality of men, they have also been employed to justify the extermination of men.

Before going any farther I find it necessary to say certain things. I am speaking here, on the one hand, of alienated (duped) blacks and, on the other, of no less alienated (duping and duped) whites. If one hears a Sartre or a Cardinal Verdier declare that the outrage of the colour problem has survived far too long, one can conclude only that their position is normal. Anyone can amass references and quotations to prove that 'colour prejudice' is indeed an imbecility and an iniquity that must be eliminated.

Sartre begins *Orphée noir* thus: 'What then did you expect when you unbound the gag that had muted those black mouths? That they would chant your praises? Did you think that when those heads that our fathers had forcibly bowed down to the ground were raised again, you would find adoration in their eyes?'[8] I do not know; but I say that he who looks into my eyes for anything but a perpetual question will have to lose his sight; neither recognition nor hate. And if I cry out, it will not be a black cry. No, from the point of view adopted here, there is no black problem. Or at any rate, if there is one, it concerns the whites only accidentally. It is a story that takes place in darkness and the sun that is carried within me must shine into the smallest crannies.

Dr H.L. Gordon, attending physician at the Mathari mental hospital in Nairobi, declared in an article in *The East African Medical Journal* (1943): 'A highly technical skilled examination of a series of 100 brains of normal Natives has found naked eye and microscopic facts indicative of inherent new brain inferiority.... Quantitatively,' he added, 'the inferiority amounts to 14.8 percent.'[9]

It has been said that the Negro is the link between monkey and man – meaning, of course, white man. And only on page 108 of his book does Sir Alan Burns come to the conclusion that 'we are unable to accept as scientifically proved the theory that the black man is inherently inferior to the white, or that he comes from a different stock'. Let me add that it would be easy to prove the absurdity of statements such as this:

It is laid down in the Bible that the separation of the white and black races will be continued in heaven as on earth and those blacks who are admitted into the Kingdom of Heaven will find themselves separately lodged in certain of those many mansions of Our Father that are mentioned in the New Testament.

Or this: 'We are the chosen people – look at the colour of our skins. The others are black or yellow: that is because of their sins.'

Ah, yes, as you can see, by calling on humanity, on the belief in dignity, on love, on charity, it would be easy to prove, or to win the admission, that the black is the equal of the white. But my purpose is quite different: what I want to do is help the black man to free himself of the arsenal of complexes that has been developed by the colonial environment. M. Achille, who teaches at the Lycée du Parc in Lyon, once during a lecture told of a personal experience. It is a universally known experience. It is a rare Negro living in France who cannot duplicate it. Being a Catholic, Achille took part in a student pilgrimage. A priest, observing the black face in his flock, said to him, 'You go 'way big Savannah what for and come 'long us?' Very politely Achille gave him a truthful answer and it was not the young fugitive from the Savannah who came off the worse. Everyone laughed at the exchange and the pilgrimage proceeded. But if we stop right here, we shall see that the fact that the priest spoke pidgin-nigger leads to certain observations:

1. 'Oh, I know the blacks. They must be spoken to kindly; talk to them about their country; it's all in knowing how to talk to them. For instance....' I am not at all exaggerating: a white man addressing a Negro behaves exactly like an adult with a child and starts smirking, whispering, patronizing, cozening. It is not one white man I have watched, but hundreds; and I have not limited my investigation to any one class but, if I may claim an essentially objective position, I have made a point of observing such behaviour in physicians, policemen, employers. I shall be told, by those who overlook my purpose, that I should have directed my attention elsewhere, that there are white men who do not fit my description.

To these objections I reply that the subject of our study is the dupes and those who dupe them, the alienated, and that if there are white men who behave naturally when they meet Negroes, they certainly do not fall within the scope of our examination. If my patient's liver is functioning as it should, I am not going to take it for granted that his kidneys are sound. Having found the liver normal, I leave it to its normality, which is normal, and turn my attention to the kidneys: as it happens, the kidneys are diseased. Which means simply that, side by side with normal people who behave naturally in accordance with a human psychology, there are others who behave pathologically in accordance with an inhuman psychology. And it happens that the existence of men of this sort has determined a certain number of realities to the elimination of which I should like to contribute here.

Talking to Negroes in this way gets down to their level, it puts them at ease, it is an effort to make them understand us, it reassures them....

The physicians of the public health services know this very well. Twenty European patients, one after another, come in: 'Please sit down.... Why do you wish to consult me? ... What are your symptoms? ...' Then comes a Negro or an Arab: 'Sit there, boy.... What's bothering you? ... Where does it hurt, huh? ...' When, that is, they do not say: 'You not feel good, no?'

2. To speak pidgin to a Negro makes him angry, because he himself is a pidgin-nigger-talker. But, I will be told, there is no wish, no intention to anger him. I grant this; but it is just this absence of wish, this lack of interest, this indifference, this automatic manner of classifying him, imprisoning him, primitivizing him, decivilizing him, that makes him angry.

If a man who speaks pidgin to a man of colour or an Arab does not see anything wrong or evil in such behaviour, it is because he has never stopped to think. I myself have been aware, in talking to certain patients, of the exact instant at which I began to slip....

Examining this seventy-three-year-old farm woman, whose mind was never strong and who is now far gone in dementia, I am suddenly aware of the collapse of the *antennae* with which I touch and through which I am touched. The fact that I adopt a language suitable to dementia, to feeble-mindedness; the fact that I 'talk down' to this poor woman of seventy-three; the fact that I condescend to her in my quest for a diagnosis, are the stigmata of a dereliction in my relations with other people.

What an idealist, people will say. Not at all: it is just that the others are scum. I make it a point always to talk to the so-called *bicots*[10] in normal French and I have always been understood. They answer me as well as their varying means permit; but I will not allow myself to resort to paternalistic 'understanding'.

'G'morning, pal. Where's it hurt? Huh? Lemme see – belly ache? Heart pain?'

With that indefinable tone that the hacks in the free clinics have mastered so well.

One feels perfectly justified when the patient answers in the same fashion. 'You see? I wasn't kidding you. That's just the way they are.'

When the opposite occurs, one must retract one's pseudopodia and behave like a man. The whole structure crumbles. A black man who says to you: 'I am in no sense your boy, Monsieur....' Something new under the sun.

But one must go lower. You are in a bar, in Rouen or Strasbourg and you have the misfortune to be spotted by an old drunk. He sits down at your table right off. 'You – Africa? Dakar, Rufisque, whorehouse, dames, café, mangoes, bananas....' You stand up and leave, and your farewell is a torrent of abuse: 'You didn't play big shot like that in your jungle, you dirty nigger!'

Mannoni has described what he calls the Prospero complex. We shall come back to these discoveries, which will make it possible for us to understand the psychology of colonialism. But we can already state that to talk pidgin-nigger is to express this thought: 'You'd better keep your place.'

I meet a Russian or a German who speaks French badly. With gestures I try to give him the information that he requests, but at the same time I can hardly forget that he has a language of his own, a country, and that perhaps he is a lawyer or an engineer there. In any case, he is foreign to my group and his standards must be different.

When it comes to the case of the Negro, nothing of the kind. He has no culture, no civilization, no 'long historical past'.

This may be the reason for the strivings of contemporary Negroes: to prove the existence of a black civilization to the white world at all costs.

Willy-nilly, the Negro has to wear the livery that the white man has sewed for him. Look at children's picture magazines: out of every Negro mouth comes the ritual 'Yassuh, boss.' It is even more remarkable in motion pictures. Most of the American films for which French dialogue is dubbed in offer the type-Negro: 'Sho' good!'

In one of these recent films, *Requins d'acier*, one character was a Negro crewman in a submarine who talked in the most classic dialect imaginable. What is more, he was all *nigger*, walking backward, shaking at the slightest sign of irritation on the part of a petty officer; ultimately he was killed in the course of the voyage. Yet I am convinced that the original dialogue did not resort to the same means of expression. And, even if it did, I can see no reason why, in a democratic France that includes sixty million citizens of colour, dubbing must repeat every stupidity that crosses the ocean. It is because the Negro has to be shown in a certain way; and from the Negro in *Sans pitié* – 'Me work hard, me never lie, me never steal' – to the servant girl of *Duel in the Sun* one meets the same stereotype.

Yes, the black man is supposed to be a good nigger; once this has been laid down, the rest follows of itself. To make him talk pidgin is to fasten him to the effigy of him, to snare him, to imprison him, the eternal victim of an essence, of an *appearance* for which he is not responsible. And naturally, just as a Jew who spends money without thinking about it is suspect, a black man who quotes Montesquieu had better be watched. Please understand me: watched in the sense that he is starting something. Certainly I do not contend that the black student is suspect to his fellows or to his teachers. But outside university circles there is an army of fools: what is important is not to educate them, but to teach the Negro not to be the slave of their archetypes.

That these imbeciles are the product of a psychological-economic system I will grant. But that does not get us much farther along.

When a Negro talks of Marx, the first reaction is always the same: 'We have brought you up to our level and now you turn against your benefactors. Ingrates! Obviously nothing can be expected of you.' And then too there is that bludgeon argument of the plantation-owner in Africa: our enemy is the teacher.

What I am asserting is that the European has a fixed concept of the Negro and there is nothing more exasperating than to be asked: 'How long have you been in France? You speak French so well.'

It can be argued that people say this because many Negroes speak pidgin. But that would be too easy. You are on a train and you ask another passenger: 'I beg your pardon, sir, would you mind telling me where the dining car is?'

'Sure, fella. You go out door, see, go corridor, you go straight, go one car, go two car, go three car, you there.'

No, speaking pidgin-nigger closes off the black man; it perpetuates a state of conflict in which the white man injects the black with extremely dangerous foreign bodies. Nothing is more astonishing than to hear a black man express himself properly, for then in truth he is putting on the white world. I have had occasion to talk with students of foreign origin. They speak French badly: little Crusoe, alias Prospero, is at ease then. He explains, informs, interprets, helps them with their studies. But with a Negro he is completely baffled; the Negro has made himself just as knowledgeable. With him this game cannot be played, he is a complete replica of the white man. So there is nothing to do but to give in.[11]

After all that has just been said, it will be understood that the first impulse of the black man is to say *no* to those who attempt to build a definition of him. It is understandable that the first action of the black man is a *reaction,* and, since the Negro is appraised in terms of the extent of his assimilation, it is also understandable why the newcomer expresses himself only in French. It is because he wants to emphasize the rupture that has now occurred. He is incarnating a new type of man that he imposes on his associates and his family. And so his old mother can no longer understand him when he talks to her about his *duds*, the family's *crummy joint*, the *dump* ... all of it, of course, tricked out with the appropriate accent.

In every country of the world there are climbers, 'the ones who forget who they are' and, in contrast to them, 'the ones who remember where they came from'. The Antilles Negro who goes home from France expresses himself in dialect if he wants to make it plain that nothing has changed. One can feel this at the dock where his family and his friends are waiting for him. Waiting for him not only because he is physically arriving, but in the sense of waiting for the chance to strike back. They need a minute or two in order to make their diagnosis. If the voyager tells his acquaintances, 'I am so happy to be back with you. Good Lord, it is hot in this country, I shall certainly not be able to endure it very long,' they know: a European has got off the ship.

In a more limited group, when students from the Antilles meet in Paris, they have the choice of two possibilities:

- either to stand with the white world (that is to say, the real world) and, since they will speak French, to be able to confront certain problems and incline to a certain degree of universality in their conclusions;

- or to reject Europe, 'Yo',[12] and cling together in their dialect, making themselves quite comfortable in what we shall call the *Umwelt* of Martinique; by this I mean – and this applies particularly to my brothers of the Antilles – that when one of us tries, in Paris or any other university city, to study a problem seriously, he is accused of self-aggrandizement and the surest way of cutting him down is to remind him of the Antilles by exploding into dialect. This must be recognized as one of the reasons why so many friendships collapse after a few months of life in Europe.

My theme being the disalienation of the black man, I want to make him feel that whenever there is a lack of understanding between him and his fellows in the presence of the white man there is a lack of judgement.

A Senegalese learns Creole in order to pass as an Antilles native: I call this alienation.

The Antilles Negroes who know him never weary of making jokes about him: I call this a lack of judgement.

It becomes evident that we were not mistaken in believing that a study of the language of the Antilles Negro would be able to show us some characteristics of his world. As I said at the start, there is a retaining-wall relation between language and group.

To speak a language is to take on a world, a culture. The Antilles Negro who wants to be white will be the whiter as he gains greater mastery of the cultural tool that language is. Rather more than a year ago in Lyon, I remember, in a lecture I had drawn a parallel between Negro and European poetry, and a French acquaintance told me enthusiastically, 'At bottom you are a white man.' The fact that I had been able to investigate so interesting a problem through the white man's language gave me honorary citizenship.

Historically, it must be understood that the Negro wants to speak French because it is the key that can open doors that were still barred to him fifty years ago. In the Antilles Negro who comes within this study we find a quest for subtleties, for refinements of language – so many further means of proving to himself that he has measured up to the culture.[13] It has been said that the orators of the Antilles have a gift of eloquence that would leave any European breathless. I am reminded of a relevant story: in the election campaign of 1945, Aimé Césaire, who was seeking a deputy's seat, addressed a large audience in the boys' school in Fort-de-France. In the middle of his speech a woman fainted. The next day, an acquaintance told me about this and commented: '*Français a té tellement chaud que la femme là tombé malcadi.*'[14] The power of language!

Some other facts are worth a certain amount of attention: for example, Charles-André Julien introducing Aimé Césaire as 'a Negro poet with a university degree', or again, quite simply, the expression, 'a great black poet'.

These ready-made phrases, which seem in a commonsense way to fill a need – for Aimé Césaire is really black and a poet – have a hidden subtlety, a permanent rub. I know nothing of Jean Paulhan except that he writes very interesting books; I have no idea how old Roger Caillois is, since the only evidence I have of his existence are the books of his that streak across my horizon. And let no one accuse me of affective allergies; what I am trying to say is that there is no reason why André Breton should say of Césaire, 'Here is a black man who handles the French language as no white man today can.'[15]

And, even though Breton may be stating a fact, I do not see why there should be any paradox, anything to underline, for in truth M. Aimé Césaire is a native of Martinique and a university graduate.

Again we find this in Michel Leiris:

If in the writers of the Antilles there does exist a desire to break away from the literary forms associated with formal education, such a desire, oriented toward a purer future, could not take on an aspect of folklore. Seeking above all, in literature, to formulate the message that is properly theirs and, in the case of some of them at least, to be the spokesmen of an authentic race whose potentials have never been acknowledged, they scorn such devices. Their intellectual growth took place almost exclusively within the framework of the French language and it would be artifice for them to resort to a mode of speech that they virtually never use now except *as* something learned.[16]

But we should be honoured, the blacks will reproach me, that a white man like Breton writes such things.

Let us go on....

2
Racism and Culture[1]

The unilaterally decreed normative value of certain cultures deserves our careful attention. One of the paradoxes immediately encountered is the rebound of egocentric, sociocentric definitions.

There is first affirmed the existence of human groups having no culture; then of a hierarchy of cultures; and finally, the concept of cultural relativity.

We have here the whole range from overall negation to singular and specific recognition. It is precisely this fragmented and bloody history that we must sketch on the level of cultural anthropology.

There are, we may say, certain constellations of institutions, established by particular men, in the framework of precise geographical areas, which at a given moment have undergone a direct and sudden assault of different cultural patterns. The technical, generally advanced development of the social group that has thus appeared enables it to set up an organized domination. The enterprise of deculturation turns out to be the negative of a more gigantic work of economic, and even biological, enslavement.

The doctrine of cultural hierarchy is thus but one aspect of a systematized hierarchization implacably pursued.

The modern theory of the absence of cortical integration of colonial peoples is the anatomic-physiological counterpart of this doctrine. The apparition of racism is not fundamentally determining. Racism is not the whole but the most visible, the most day-to-day and, not to mince matters, the crudest element of a given structure.

To study the relations of racism and culture is to raise the question of their reciprocal action. If culture is the combination of motor and mental behaviour patterns arising from the encounter of man with nature and with his fellow man, it can be said that racism is indeed a cultural element. There are thus cultures with racism and cultures without racism.

This precise cultural element, however, has not become encysted. Racism has not managed to harden. It has had to renew itself, to adapt itself, to change its appearance. It has had to undergo the fate of the cultural whole that informed it.

The vulgar, primitive, over-simple racism purported to find in biology – the Scriptures having proved insufficient – the material basis of the doctrine. It would be tedious to recall the efforts then undertaken: the comparative form of the skulls, the quantity and the configuration of the folds of the brain, the characteristics of the cell layers of the cortex, the dimensions of the vertebrae, the microscopic appearance of the epidermis, etc....

Intellectual and emotional primitivism appeared as a banal consequence, a recognition of existence.

Such affirmations, crude and massive, give way to a more refined argument. Here and there, however, an occasional relapse is to be noted. Thus the 'emotional instability of the Negro', the 'subcritical integration of the Arab', 'the quasi-generic culpability of the Jew' are data that one comes upon among a few contemporary writers. The monograph by J. Carothers, for example, sponsored by the World Health Organization, invokes 'scientific arguments' in support of a physiological lobotomy of the African Negro.

These old-fashioned positions tend in any case to disappear. This racism that aspires to be rational, individual, genotypically and phenotypically determined, becomes transformed into cultural racism. The object of racism is no longer the individual man but a certain form of existing. At the extreme, such terms as 'message' and 'cultural style' are resorted to. 'Occidental values' oddly blend with the already famous appeal to the fight of the 'cross against the crescent'.

The morphological equation, to be sure, has not totally disappeared, but events of the past thirty years have shaken the most solidly anchored convictions, upset the chequerboard, restructured a great number of relationships.

The memory of Nazism, the common wretchedness of different men, the common enslavement of extensive social groups, the apparition of 'European colonies', in other words the institution of a colonial system in the very heart of Europe, the growing awareness of workers in the colonizing and racist countries, the evolution of techniques, all this has deeply modified the problem and the manner of approaching it.

We must look for the consequences of this racism on the cultural level.

Racism, as we have seen, is only one element of a vaster whole: that of the systematized oppression of a people. How does an oppressing people behave? Here we rediscover constants.

We witness the destruction of cultural values, of ways of life. Language, dress, techniques, are devalorized. How can one account for this constant? Psychologists, who tend to explain everything by movements of the psyche, claim to discover this behaviour on the level of contacts between individuals: the criticism of an original hat, of a way of speaking, of walking....

Such attempts deliberately leave out of account the special character of the colonial situation. In reality the nations that undertake a colonial war have no concern for the confrontation of cultures. War is a gigantic business and every approach must be governed by this datum. The enslavement, in the strictest sense, of the native population is the prime necessity.

For this its systems of reference have to be broken. Expropriation, spoliation, raids, objective murder, are matched by the sacking of cultural patterns, or at least condition such sacking. The social panorama is destructured; values are flaunted, crushed, emptied.

The lines of force, having crumbled, no longer give direction. In their stead a new system of values is imposed, not proposed but affirmed, by the heavy weight of cannons and sabres.

The setting up of the colonial system does not of itself bring about the death of the native culture. Historic observation reveals, on the contrary, that the aim sought is rather a continued agony than a total disappearance of the pre-existing culture. This culture, once living and open to the future, becomes closed, fixed in the colonial status, caught in the yoke of oppression. Both present and mummified, it testifies against its members. It defines them in fact without appeal. The cultural mummification leads to a mummification of individual thinking. The apathy so universally noted among colonial peoples is but the logical consequence of this operation. The reproach of inertia constantly directed at 'the native' is utterly dishonest. As though it were possible for a man to evolve otherwise than within the framework of a culture that recognizes him and that he decides to assume.

Thus we witness the setting up of archaic, inert institutions, functioning under the oppressor's supervision and patterned like a caricature of formerly fertile institutions....

These bodies appear to embody respect for the tradition, the cultural specificities, the personality of the subjugated people. This pseudo-respect in fact is tantamount to the most utter contempt, to the most elaborate sadism. The characteristic of a culture is to be open, permeated by spontaneous, generous, fertile lines of force.

The appointment of 'reliable men' to execute certain gestures is a deception that deceives no one. Thus the Kabyle *djemaas* named by the French authority are not recognized by the natives. They are matched by another *djemaa* democratically elected. And naturally the second as a rule dictates to the first what his conduct should be.

The constantly affirmed concern with 'respecting the culture of the native populations' accordingly does not signify taking into consideration the values borne by the culture, incarnated by men. Rather, this behaviour betrays a determination to objectify, to confine, to imprison, to harden. Phrases such as 'I know them', 'that's the way they are', show this maximum objectification successfully achieved. I can think of gestures and thoughts that define these men.

Exoticism is one of the forms of this simplification. It allows no cultural confrontation. There is on the one hand a culture in which qualities of dynamism, of growth, of depth can be recognized. As against this, we find characteristics, curiosities, things, never a structure.

Thus in an initial phase the occupant establishes his domination, massively affirms his superiority. The social group, militarily and economically subjugated, is dehumanized in accordance with a polydimensional method.

Exploitation, tortures, raids, racism, collective liquidations, rational oppression take turns at different levels in order literally to make of the native an object in the hands of the occupying nation.

This object man, without means of existing, without a *raison d'être*, is broken in the very depth of his substance. The desire to live, to continue, becomes more and more indecisive, more and more phantom-like. It is at this stage that the well-known guilt complex appears. In his first novels, Wright gives a very detailed description of it.

Progressively, however, the evolution of techniques of production, the industrialization, limited though it is, of the subjugated countries, the increasingly necessary existence of collaborators, impose a new attitude upon the occupant. The complexity of the means of production, the evolution of economic relations inevitably involving the evolution of ideologies, unbalance the system. Vulgar racism in its biological form corresponds to the period of crude exploitation of man's arms and legs. The perfecting of the means of production inevitably brings about the camouflage of the techniques by which man is exploited, hence of the forms of racism.

It is therefore not as a result of the evolution of people's minds that racism loses its virulence. No inner revolution can explain this necessity for racism to seek more subtle forms, to evolve. On all sides men become free, putting an end to the lethargy to which oppression and racism had condemned them.

In the very heart of the 'civilized nations' the workers finally discover that the exploitation of man, at the root of a system, assumes different faces. At this stage racism no longer dares appear without disguise. It is unsure of itself. In an ever greater number of circumstances the racist takes to cover. He who claimed to 'sense', to 'see through' those others, finds himself to be a target, looked at, judged. The racist's purpose has become a purpose haunted by bad conscience. He can find salvation only in a passion-driven commitment such as is found in certain psychoses. And having defined the symptomatology of such passion-charged deliria is not the least of Professor Baruk's merits.

Racism is never a super-added element discovered by chance in the course of the investigation of the cultural data of a group. The social constellation, the cultural whole, are deeply modified by the existence of racism.

It is a common saying nowadays that racism is a plague of humanity. But we must not content ourselves with such a phrase. We must tirelessly look for the repercussions of racism at all levels of sociability. The importance of the racist problem in contemporary American literature is significant. The Negro in motion pictures, the Negro and folklore, the Jew and children's stories, the Jew in the café, are inexhaustible themes.

Racism, to come back to America, haunts and vitiates American culture. And this dialectical gangrene is exacerbated by the coming to awareness and the determination of millions of Negroes and Jews to fight this racism by which they are victimized.

This passion-charged, irrational, groundless phase, when one examines it, reveals a frightful visage. The movements of groups, the liberation, in certain parts of the world, of men previously kept down, make for a more and more precarious equilibrium. Rather unexpectedly, the racist group points accusingly to a manifestation of racism among the oppressed. The 'intellectual primitivism' of the period of exploitation gives way to the 'medieval, in fact prehistoric fanaticism' of the period of the liberation.

For a time it looked as though racism had disappeared. This soul-soothing, unreal impression was simply the consequence of the evolution of forms of exploitation. Psychologists spoke of a prejudice having become unconscious. The truth is that the rigour of the system made the daily affirmation of a superiority superfluous. The need to appeal to various degrees of approval and support, to the native's cooperation, modified relations in a less crude, more subtle, more 'cultivated' direction. It was not rare, in fact, to see a 'democratic and humane' ideology at this stage. The commercial undertaking of enslavement, of cultural destruction, progressively gave way to a verbal mystification.

The interesting thing about this evolution is that racism was taken as a topic of meditation, sometimes even as a publicity technique.

Thus the blues – 'the black slave lament' – was offered up for the admiration of the oppressors. This modicum of stylized oppression is the exploiter's and the racist's rightful due. Without oppression and without racism you have no blues. The end of racism would sound the knell of great Negro music....

As the all-too-famous Toynbee might say, the blues are the slave's response to the challenge of oppression.

Still today, for many men, even coloured, Armstrong's music has a real meaning only in this perspective.

Racism bloats and disfigures the face of the culture that practises it. Literature, the plastic arts, songs for shopgirls, proverbs, habits, patterns, whether they set out to attack it or to vulgarize it, restore racism. This means that a social group, a country, a civilization, cannot be unconsciously racist.

We say once again that racism is not an accidental discovery. It is not a hidden, dissimulated element. No superhuman efforts are needed to bring it out.

Racism stares one in the face for it so happens that it belongs in a characteristic whole: that of the shameless exploitation of one group of men by another which has reached a higher stage of technical development. This is why military and economic oppression generally precedes, makes possible and legitimizes racism.

The habit of considering racism as a mental quirk, as a psychological flaw, must be abandoned.

But the men who are a prey to racism, the enslaved, exploited, weakened social group – how do they behave? What are their defence mechanisms?

What attitudes do we discover here?

In an initial phase we have seen the occupying power legitimizing its domination by scientific arguments, the 'inferior race' being denied on the basis of race. Because no other solution is left it, the racialized social group tries to imitate the oppressor and thereby to deracialize itself. The 'inferior race' denies itself as a different race. It shares with the 'superior race' the convictions, doctrines and other attitudes concerning it.

Having witnessed the liquidation of its systems of reference, the collapse of its cultural patterns, the native can only recognize with the occupant that 'God is not on his side'. The oppressor, through the inclusive and frightening character of his authority, manages to impose on the native new ways of seeing and, in particular, a pejorative judgement with respect to his original forms of existing.

This event, which is commonly designated as alienation, is naturally very important. It is found in the official texts under the name of assimilation.

Now this alienation is never wholly successful. Whether or not it is because the oppressor quantitatively and qualitatively limits the evolution, unforeseen, disparate phenomena manifest themselves.

The inferiorized group had admitted, since the force of reasoning was implacable, that its misfortunes resulted directly from its racial and cultural characteristics.

Guilt and inferiority are the usual consequences of this dialectic. The oppressed then tries to escape these, on the one hand by proclaiming his total and unconditional adoption of the new cultural models and, on the other, by pronouncing an irreversible condemnation of his own cultural style.[2]

Yet the necessity that the oppressor encounters at a given point to dissimulate the forms of exploitation does not lead to the disappearance of this exploitation. The more elaborate, less crude economic relations require a daily coating, but the alienation at this level remains frightful.

Having judged, condemned, abandoned his cultural forms, his language, his food habits, his sexual behaviour, his way of sitting down, of resting, of laughing, of enjoying himself, the oppressed *flings himself* upon the imposed culture with the desperation of a drowning man.

Developing his technical knowledge in contact with more and more perfected machines, entering into the dynamic circuit of industrial production, meeting men from remote regions in the framework of the concentration of capital, that is to say, on the job, discovering the assembly line, the team, production 'time', in other words yield per hour, the oppressed is shocked to find that he continues to be the object of racism and contempt.

It is at this level that racism is treated as a question of persons. 'There are a few hopeless racists, but you must admit that on the whole the population likes....'

With time all this will disappear.

This is the country where there is the least amount of race prejudice....

At the United Nations there is a commission to fight race prejudice.

Films on race prejudice, poems on race prejudice, messages on race prejudice....

Spectacular and futile condemnations of race prejudice. In reality, a colonial country is a racist country. If in England, in Belgium or in France, despite the democratic principles affirmed by these respective nations, there are still racists, it is these racists who, in their opposition to the country as a whole, are logically consistent.

It is not possible to enslave men without logically making them inferior through and through. And racism is only the emotional, affective, sometimes intellectual explanation of this inferiorization.

The racist in a culture with racism is therefore normal. He has achieved a perfect harmony of economic relations and ideology. The idea that one forms of man, to be sure, is never totally dependent on economic relations, in other words – and this must not be forgotten – on relations existing historically and geographically among men and groups. An ever greater number of members belonging to racist societies are taking a position. They are dedicating themselves to a world in which racism would be impossible. But everyone is not up to this kind of objectivity, this abstraction, this solemn commitment. One cannot with impunity require of a man that he be against 'the prejudices of his group'.

And, we repeat, every colonialist group is racist.

'Acculturized' and deculturized at one and the same time, the oppressed continues to come up against racism. He finds this sequel illogical, what he has left behind him inexplicable, without motive, incorrect. His knowledge, the appropriation of precise and complicated techniques, sometimes his intellectual superiority as compared to a great number of racists, lead him to qualify the racist world as passion-charged. He perceives that the racist atmosphere impregnates all the elements of the social life. The sense of an overwhelming injustice is correspondingly very strong. Forgetting racism as a consequence, one concentrates on racism as cause. Campaigns of deintoxication are launched. Appeal is made to the sense of humanity, to love, to respect for the supreme values....

Race prejudice in fact obeys a flawless logic. A country that lives, draws its substance from the exploitation of other peoples, makes those peoples inferior. Race prejudice applied to those peoples is normal.

Racism is therefore not a constant of the human spirit.

It is, as we have seen, a disposition fitting into a well-defined system. And anti-Jewish prejudice is no different from anti-Negro prejudice. A society has race prejudice or it has not. There are no degrees of prejudice. One cannot say that a given country is racist but that lynchings or extermination camps are not to be found there. The truth is that all that and still other things exist on the horizon. These virtualities, these latencies circulate, carried by the life-stream of psycho-affective, economic relations....

Discovering the futility of his alienation, his progressive deprivation, the inferiorized individual, after this phase of deculturation, of extraneousness, comes back to his original positions.

This culture, abandoned, sloughed off, rejected, despised, becomes for the inferiorized an object of passionate attachment. There is a very marked kind of overvaluation that is psychologically closely linked to the craving for forgiveness.

But behind this simplifying analysis there is indeed the intuition experienced by the inferiorized of having discovered a spontaneous truth. This is a psychological datum that is part of the texture of History and of Truth.

Because the inferiorized rediscovers a style that had once been devalorized, what he does is in fact to cultivate culture. Such a caricature of cultural existence would indicate, if it were necessary, that culture must be lived and cannot be fragmented. It cannot be had piecemeal.

Yet the oppressed goes into ecstasies over each rediscovery. The wonder is permanent. Having formerly emigrated from his culture, the native today explores it with ardour. It is a continual honeymoon. Formerly inferiorized, he is now in a state of grace.

Not with impunity, however, does one undergo domination. The culture of the enslaved people is sclerosed, dying. No life any longer circulates in it. Or, more precisely, the only existing life is dissimulated. The population that normally assumes here and there a few fragments of life, which continues to attach dynamic meanings to institutions, is an anonymous population. In a colonial system these are the traditionalists.

The former emigré, by the sudden ambiguity of his behaviour, causes consternation. To the anonymity of the traditionalist he opposes a vehement and aggressive exhibitionism.

The states of grace and aggressiveness are the two constants found at this stage. Aggressiveness being the passion-charged mechanism making it possible to escape the sting of paradox.

Because the former emigré is in possession of precise techniques, because his level of action is in the framework of relations that are already complex, these rediscoveries assume an irrational aspect. There is an hiatus, a discrepancy between intellectual development, technical appropriation, highly differentiated modes of thinking and of logic on the one hand and a 'simple, pure' emotional basis on the other....

Rediscovering tradition, living it as a defence mechanism, as a symbol of purity, of salvation, the decultured individual leaves the impression that the mediation takes vengeance by substantializing itself. This falling back on archaic positions having no relation to technical development is paradoxical. The institutions thus valorized no longer correspond to the elaborate methods of action already mastered.

The culture put into capsules, which has vegetated since the foreign domination, is revalorized. It is not reconceived, grasped anew, dynamized from within. It is shouted. And this headlong, unstructured, verbal revalorization conceals paradoxical attitudes.

It is at this point that the incorrigible character of the inferiorized is brought out for mention. Arab doctors sleep on the ground, spit all over the place, etc....

Negro intellectuals consult a sorcerer before making a decision, etc....

'Collaborating' intellectuals try to justify their new attitude. The customs, traditions, beliefs, formerly denied and passed over in silence are violently valorized and affirmed.

Tradition is no longer scoffed at by the group. The group no longer runs away from itself. The sense of the past is rediscovered, the worship of ancestors resumed....

The past, becoming henceforth a constellation of values, becomes identified with the Truth.

This rediscovery, this absolute valorization almost in defiance of reality, objectively indefensible, assumes an incomparable and subjective importance. On emerging from these passionate espousals, the native will have decided, 'with full knowledge of what is involved', to fight all forms of exploitation and of alienation of man. At this same time, the occupant, on the other hand, multiplies appeals to assimilation, then to integration, to community.

The native's hand-to-hand struggle with his culture is too solemn, too abrupt an operation to tolerate the slightest slip-up. No neologism can mask the new certainty: the plunge into the chasm of the past is the condition and the source of freedom.

The logical end of this will to struggle is the total liberation of the national territory. In order to achieve this liberation, the inferiorized man brings all his resources into play, all his acquisitions, the old and new, his own and those of the occupant.

The struggle is at once total, absolute. But then race prejudice is hardly found to appear.

At the time of imposing his domination, in order to justify slavery, the oppressor had invoked scientific argument. There is nothing of the kind here.

A people that undertakes a struggle for liberation rarely legitimizes race prejudice. Even in the course of acute periods of insurrectional armed struggle one never witnesses the recourse to biological justifications.

The struggle of the inferiorized is situated on a markedly more human level. The perspectives are radically new. The opposition is the henceforth classical one of the struggles of conquest and of liberation.

In the course of struggle the dominating nation tries to revive racist arguments but the elaboration of racism proves more and more ineffective. There is talk of fanaticism, of primitive attitudes in the face of death, but once again the now crumbling mechanism no longer responds. Those who were once unbudgeable, the constitutional cowards, the timid, the eternally inferiorized, stiffen and emerge bristling.

The occupant is bewildered.

The end of race prejudice begins with a sudden incomprehension.

The occupant's spasmed and rigid culture, now liberated, opens at last to the culture of people who have really become brothers. The two cultures can affront each other, enrich each other.

In conclusion, universality resides in this decision to recognize and accept the reciprocal relativism of different cultures, once the colonial status is irreversibly excluded.

Section Two:

Race, Gender and Sexuality

3
The Woman of Colour
and the White Man

Man is motion toward the world and toward his like. A movement of aggression, which leads to enslavement or to conquest; a movement of love, a gift of self, the ultimate stage of what by common accord is called ethical orientation. Every consciousness seems to have the capacity to demonstrate these two components, simultaneously or alternatively. The person I love will strengthen me by endorsing my assumption of my manhood, while the need to earn the admiration or the love of others will erect a value-making superstructure on my whole vision of the world.

In reaching an understanding of phenomena of this sort, the analyst and the phenomenologist are given a difficult task. And, if a Sartre has appeared to formulate a description of love as frustration, his *Being and Nothingness* amounting only to an analysis of dishonesty and inauthenticity, the fact remains that true, authentic love – wishing for others what one postulates for oneself, when that postulation unites the permanent values of human reality – entails the mobilization of psychic drives basically freed of unconscious conflicts.

Left far, far behind, the last *sequelae* of a titanic struggle carried on against *the other* have been dissipated. Today I believe in the possibility of love; that is why I endeavour to trace its imperfections, its perversions.

In this chapter devoted to the relations between the woman of colour and the European, it is our problem to ascertain to what extent authentic love will remain unattainable before one has purged oneself of that feeling of inferiority or that Adlerian exaltation, that overcompensation, which seem to be the indices of the black *Weltanschauung*.

For after all we have a right to be perturbed when we read, in *Je suis Martiniquaise*: 'I should have liked to be married, but to a white man. But a woman of colour is never altogether respectable in a white man's eyes. Even when he loves her. I knew that.'[1] This passage, which serves in a way as the conclusion of a vast delusion, prods one's brain. One day a woman named Mayotte Capécia, obeying a motivation whose elements are difficult to detect, sat down to write 202 pages – her life – in which the most ridiculous ideas proliferated at random. The enthusiastic reception that greeted this book in certain circles forces us to analyse it. For me, all circumlocution is impossible: *Je suis Martiniquaise* is cut-rate merchandise, a sermon in praise of corruption.

Mayotte loves a white man to whom she submits in everything. He is her lord. She asks nothing, demands nothing, except a bit of whiteness in her life. When she tries to determine in her own mind whether the man is handsome or ugly, she writes, 'All I know is that he had blue eyes, blond hair and a light skin, and that I loved him.' It is not difficult to see that a rearrangement of these elements in their proper hierarchy would produce something of this order: 'I loved him because he had blue eyes, blond hair and a light skin.' We who come from the Antilles know one thing only too well: blue eyes, the people say, frighten the Negro.

When I observed in my introduction that, historically, inferiority has been felt economically, I was hardly mistaken.

There were evenings, unhappily, when he had to leave me alone in order to fulfil his social obligations. He would go to Didier, the fashionable part of Fort-de-France inhabited by the 'Martinique whiteys', who are perhaps not too pure racially but who are often very rich (it is understood that one is white above a certain financial level), and the 'France whiteys', most of them government people and military officers.

Among André's colleagues, who like him had been marooned in the Antilles by the war, some had managed to have their wives join them. I understood that André could not always hold himself aloof from them. I also accepted the fact that I was barred from this society because I was a woman of colour; but I could not help being jealous. It was no good his explaining to me that his private life was something that belonged to him alone and that his social and military life was something else, which was not within his control; I nagged so much that one day he took me to Didier. We spent the evening in one of those little villas that I had admired since my childhood, with two officers and their wives. The women kept watching me with a condescension that I found unbearable. I felt that I was wearing too much makeup, that I was not properly dressed, that I was not doing André credit, perhaps simply because of the colour of my skin – in short, I spent so miserable an evening that I decided I would never again ask André to take me with him.[2]

It was Didier, the preserve of the richest people in Martinique, that magnetized all the girl's wishes. And she makes the point herself: one is white above a certain financial level. The houses in this section had long dazzled the lady. I have the feeling, however, that Mayotte Capécia is laying it on: she tells us that she did not go to Fort-de-France until she was grown, at about the age of eighteen; and yet the mansions of Didier had beguiled her childhood. There is an inconsistency here that becomes understandable when one grasps the background. It is in fact customary in Martinique to dream of a form of salvation that consists of magically turning white. A house in Didier, acceptance into that high society (Didier is on a hill that dominates the city) and there you have Hegel's subjective certainty made flesh. And in another way it is quite easy to see the place that the dialectic of being and having[3] would occupy in a description of this behaviour. Such, however, is not the case with Mayotte. She is looked at with distaste. Things begin their usual course.... It is because she is a woman of colour that she is not accepted in this society. Her resentment feeds on her own artificiality. We shall see why love is beyond the reach of the Mayotte Capécias of all nations. For the beloved should not allow me to turn my infantile fantasies into reality: on the contrary, he should help me to go beyond them. The childhood of Mayotte Capécia shows us a certain number of characteristics that illustrate the line of orientation she follows as an adult. And each time there is a movement or a contact, it will have a direct relation to her goal. It would seem indeed that for her white and black represent the two poles of a world, two poles in perpetual conflict: a genuinely Manichaean concept of the world; the word has been spoken, it must be remembered – white or black, that is the question.

I am white: that is to say that I possess beauty and virtue, which have never been black. I am the colour of the daylight....

I am black: I am the incarnation of a complete fusion with the world, an intuitive understanding of the earth, an abandonment of my ego in the heart of the cosmos, and no white man, no matter how intelligent he may be, can ever understand Louis Armstrong and the music of the Congo. If I am black, it is not the result of a curse, but it is because, having offered my skin, I have been able to absorb all the cosmic *effluvia*. I am truly a ray of sunlight under the earth....

And there one lies body to body with one's blackness or one's whiteness, in full narcissistic cry, each sealed into his own peculiarity

– with, it is true, now and then a flash or so, but these are threatened at their source.

From the first this is how the problem appears to Mayotte – at the fifth year of her age and the third page of her book: 'She took her inkwell out of the desk and emptied it over his head.' This was her own way of turning whites into blacks. But she quite soon recognized the futility of such attempts; and then there were Loulouze and her mother, who told her that life was difficult for a woman of colour. So, since she could no longer try to blacken, to negrify the world, she was going to try, in her own body and in her own mind, to bleach it. To start, she would become a laundress: 'I charged high prices, higher than elsewhere, but I worked better, and since people in Fort-de-France like their linens clean, they came to me. In the end, they were proud to have their laundry done by Mayotte.'[4]

I am sorry that Mayotte Capécia has told us nothing about her dreams. That would have made it easier to reach her unconscious. Instead of recognizing her absolute blackness, she proceeds to turn it into an accident. She learns that her grandmother was white.

I found that I was proud of it. I was certainly not the only one who had white blood, but a white grandmother was not so ordinary as a white grandfather.[5] So my mother, then, was a mixture? I should have guessed it when I looked at her light colour. I found her prettier than ever, and cleverer and more refined. If she had married a white man, do you suppose I should have been completely white? ... And life might not have been so hard for me? ... I daydreamed about this grandmother whom I had never known and who had died because she had loved a coloured man of Martinique.... How could a Canadian woman have loved a man of Martinique? I could never stop thinking of our priest and I made up my mind that I could never love anyone but a white man, a blue-eyed blond, a Frenchman.[6]

We are thus put on notice that what Mayotte wants is a kind of lactification. For, in a word, the race must be whitened; every woman in Martinique knows this, says it, repeats it. Whiten the race, save the race, but not in the sense that one might think: not to 'preserve the uniqueness of that part of the world in which they grew up', but make sure that it will be white. Every time I have made up my mind to analyse certain kinds of behaviour, I have been unable to avoid the consideration of certain nauseating phenomena. The number of sayings, proverbs, petty rules of conduct that govern the choice of a lover in the Antilles is astounding. It is always essential to avoid falling back into the pit of niggerhood, and every woman in the Antilles, whether in a casual flirtation or in a serious affair, is determined to select the least black of the men. Sometimes, in order to justify a bad investment, she is compelled to resort to such arguments as this: 'X is black, but misery is blacker.' I know a great number of girls from Martinique, students in France, who admitted to me with complete candour – completely white candour – that they would find it impossible to marry black men. (Get out of that and then deliberately go back to it? Thank you, no.) Besides, they added, it is not that we deny that blacks have any good qualities, but you know it is so much better to be white. I was talking only recently to one such woman. Breathless with anger, she stormed at me, 'If Césaire makes so much display about accepting his race, it is because he really feels it as a curse. Do the whites boast like that about theirs? Every one of us has a white potential, but some try to ignore it and others simply reverse it. As far as I am concerned, I wouldn't marry a Negro for anything in the world.' Such attitudes are not rare, and I must confess that they disturb me, for in a few years this young woman will have finished her examinations and gone off to teach in some school in the Antilles. It is not hard to guess what will come of that.

An enormous task confronts the Antillean who has begun by carefully examining the objectivity of the various prejudices prevailing in his environment. When I began this book,[7] having completed my medical studies, I thought of presenting it as my thesis. But dialectic required the constant adoption of positions. Although I had more or less concentrated on the psychic alienation of the black man, I could not remain silent about certain things which, however psychological they may be, produce consequences that extend into the domains of sciences.

Every experience, especially if it turns out to be sterile, has to become a component of reality and thus play a part in the restructuring of reality. That is to say that the patriarchal European family with its flaws, its failures, its vices, closely linked to the society that we know, produces about 30 per cent neurotics. The problem is to create, with the help of psychoanalytical, sociological, political lessons, a new family environment capable of reducing, if not of eliminating, the proportion of waste, in the asocial sense of the word.

In other words, the question is whether *basic personality* is a constant or a variable.

All these frantic women of colour in quest of white men are waiting. And one of these days, surely, they will be surprised to find that they do not want to go back, they will dream of 'a wonderful night, a wonderful lover, a white man'. Possibly, too, they will become aware, one day, that 'white men do not marry black women'. But they have consented to run this risk; what they must have is whiteness at any price. For what reason? Nothing could be simpler. Here is a story that suits their minds:

One day St Peter saw three men arrive at the gate of heaven: a white man, a mulatto and a Negro.

'What do you want most?' he asked the white man.

'Money.'

'And you?' he asked the mulatto.

'Fame.'

St Peter turned then to the Negro, who said with a wide smile:[8] 'I'm just carrying these gentlemen's bags.'

Not long ago Etiemble described one of his disillusionments: 'I was stupefied, as an adolescent, when a girl who knew me quite well jumped up in anger because I had said to her, in a situation where the word was not only appropriate but the one word that suited the occasion: "You, as a Negress – ." "Me? A Negress? Can't you see I'm practically white? I despise Negroes. Niggers stink. They're dirty and lazy. Don't ever mention niggers to me." '[9]

I knew another black girl who kept a list of Parisian dance-halls 'where-there-was-no-chance-of-running-into-niggers'.

We must see whether it is possible for the black man to overcome his feeling of insignificance, to rid his life of the compulsive quality that makes it so like the behaviour of the phobic. Affect is exacerbated in the Negro, he is full of rage because he feels small, he suffers from an inadequacy in all human communication, and all these factors chain him with an unbearable insularity.

Describing the phenomenon of ego-withdrawal, Anna Freud writes:

As a method of avoiding 'pain', ego-restriction, like the various forms of denial, does not come under the heading of the psychology of neurosis but is a normal stage in the development of the ego. When the ego is young and plastic, its withdrawal from one field of activity is sometimes compensated for by excellence in another, upon which it concentrates. But, when it has become rigid or has already acquired an intolerance of 'pain' and so is obsessionally fixated to a method of flight, such withdrawal is punished by impaired development. By abandoning one position after another it becomes one-sided, loses too many interests and can show but a meagre achievement.[10]

We understand now why the black man cannot take pleasure in his insularity. For him there is only one way out and it leads into the white world. Whence his constant preoccupation with attracting the attention of the white man, his concern with being powerful like the white man, his determined effort to acquire protective qualities – that is, the proportion of being or having that enters into the composition of an ego. As I said earlier, it is from within that the Negro will seek admittance to the white sanctuary. The attitude derives from the intention.

Ego-withdrawal as a successful defence mechanism is impossible for the Negro. He requires a white approval.

In the midst of her mystical euphoria and her rhapsodic canticles, it seems to Mayotte Capécia that she is an angel and that she soars away 'all pink and white'. Nevertheless, in the film, *Green Pastures*, God and the angels are black, but the film was a brutal shock to our author: 'How is it possible to imagine God with Negro characteristics? This is not my vision of paradise. But, after all, it was just an American film.'[11]

Indeed no, the good and merciful God cannot be black: He is a white man with bright pink cheeks. From black to white is the course of mutation. One is white as one is rich, as one is beautiful, as one is intelligent.

Meanwhile, André has departed to carry the *white message* to other Mayottes under other skies: delightful little genes with blue eyes, bicycling the whole length of the chromosome corridor. But, as a good white man, he has left instructions behind him. He is speaking of his and Mayotte's child: 'You will bring him up, you will tell him about me, you will say, "He was a superior person. You must work hard to be worthy of him." '[12]

What about dignity? He had no need now to achieve it: it was injected now into the labyrinth of his arteries, entrenched in his little pink fingernails, a solidly rooted, white dignity.

And what about the father? This is what Etiemble has to say about him:

A fine specimen of his kind; he talked about the family, work, the nation, our good Pétain and our good God, all of which allowed him to make her pregnant according to form. God has made use of us, said the handsome swine, the handsome white man, the handsome officer. After which, under the same God-fearing Pétainist proprieties, I shove her over to the next man.

Before we have finished with her whose white lord is 'like one dead' and who surrounds herself with dead men in a book crowded with deplorably dead things, we feel that we should like to ask Africa to send us a special envoy.[13]

Nor are we kept waiting. Abdoulaye Sadji, in *Nini*,[14] offers us a description of how black men can behave in contact with Europeans. I have said that Negrophobes exist. It is not hatred of the Negro, however, that motivates them; they lack the courage for that, or they have lost it. Hate is not inborn; it has to be constantly cultivated, to be brought into being, in conflict with more or less recognized guilt complexes. Hate demands existence, and he who hates has to show his hate in appropriate actions and behaviour; in a sense, he has to become hate. That is why the Americans have substituted discrimination for lynching. Each to his own side of the street. Therefore we are not surprised that in the cities of (French?) black Africa there are European quarters. Mournier's work, *L'Éveil de l'Afrique noire*, had already attracted my interest, but I was impatiently awaiting an African voice. Thanks to Alioune Diop's magazine, I have been able to coordinate the psychological motivations that govern men of colour.

There is wonder, in the most religious sense of the word, in this passage:

M. Campian is the only white man in Saint-Louis who goes regularly to the Saint-Louis Club[15] – a man of a certain social standing, for he is an engineer with the Department of Bridges and Highways, as well as deputy director of Public Works in Senegal. He is said to be very much of a Negrophile, much more so than M. Roddin, who teaches at the Lycée Faidherbe and who gave a lecture on the equality of the races in the Saint-Louis Club itself. The good character of the one or the other is a constant theme for vehement discussions. In any event, M. Campian goes to the club more often and there he has made the acquaintance of very well-behaved natives who show him much deference, who like him and who feel honoured by his presence among them.[16]

The author, who is a teacher in black Africa, feels obligated to M. Roddin for his lecture on racial equality. I call this an outrage. One can understand the complaints that Mounier heard from the young Africans whom he had occasion to meet: 'What we need here are Europeans like you.' One is constantly aware that for the black man encountering a *toubab* with understanding offers a new hope of harmony.

Analysing various passages of Abdoulaye Sadji's story, I shall attempt to grasp the living reactions of the woman of colour to the European. First of all, there are two such women: the Negress and the mulatto. The first has only one possibility and one concern: to turn white. The second wants not only to turn white but also to avoid slipping back. What indeed could be more illogical than a mulatto woman's acceptance of a Negro husband? For it must be understood once and for all that it is a question of saving the race.

Hence Nini's great problem: a Negro has had the gall to go so far as to ask her to marry him. A Negro had the gall to write to her:

The love that I offer you is pure and strong, it has nothing of a false tenderness intended to lull you with lies and illusions.... I want to see you happy, completely happy, in a setting to frame your qualities, which I believe I know how to appreciate.... I should consider it the highest of honours and the greatest of joys to have you in my house and to dedicate myself to you, body and soul. Your graces would illuminate my home and radiate light to the darkest corners.... Furthermore, I consider you too civilized and refined to reject brutally the offer of a devoted love concerned only with reassuring your happiness.[17]

This final sentence should not surprise us. Normally, the mulatto woman should refuse the presumptuous Negro without mercy. But, since she is civilized, she will not allow herself to see her lover's colour, so that she can concentrate her attention on his devotion. Describing Mactar, Abdoulaye Sadji writes: 'An idealist and a convinced advocate of unlimited progress, he still believed in the good faith of men, in their honesty, and he readily assumed that in everything merit alone must triumph.'[18]

Who is Mactar? He has passed his baccalaureate, he is an accountant in the Department of Rivers and he is pursuing a perfectly stupid little stenographer, who has, however, the least disputable quality: she is almost white. Therefore one must apologize for talking the liberty of sending her a letter: 'the utmost insolence, perhaps the first that any Negro had dared to attempt'.[19]

One must apologize for daring to offer black love to a white soul. This we encounter again in René Maran: the fear, the timorousness, the humility of the black man in his relations with the white woman, or in any case with a woman whiter than he. Just as Mayotte Capécia tolerates anything from her lord, André, Mactar makes himself the slave of Nini, the mulatto. Prepared to sell his soul. But what is waiting for this boor is the law of plea in bar. The mulatto considers his letter an insult, an outrage to her honour as a 'white lady'. This Negro is an idiot, a scoundrel, an ignoramus who needs a lesson. That lesson she is prepared to give him; she will teach him to be more courteous and less brazen; she will make him understand that 'white skins' are not for *'bougnouls'*.[20]

Having learned the circumstances, the whole mulatto 'society' plays chorus to her wrath. There is talk of taking the matter into court, of having the black man brought up on criminal charges. 'There will be letters to the head of the Department of Public Works, to the governor of the colony, to call their attention to the black man's behaviour and have him dismissed in recompense for the moral havoc that he has inflicted.'[21]

Such an offence against principle should be punished by castration. And ultimately a request is made that Mactar be formally reprimanded by the police. For, 'if he returns to his unhealthy follies, we will have him brought into line by Police Inspector Dru, whose colleagues have nick-named him the-real-bad-white-man'.[22]

We have seen here how a girl of colour reacts to a declaration of love made by one of her own. Let us inquire now what happens in the case of a white man. Once more we resort to Sadji. The long passage that he devotes to the reactions produced by the marriage of a white man and a mulatto will provide the vehicle.

For some time a rumour had been repeated all over Saint-Louis.... It was at first a little whisper that went from one to another, making the wrinkled faces of the old 'signaras' glow, putting new light into their dull eyes; then the younger women, showing the whites of their eyes and forming their heavy lips into circles, shouted the news, which caused amazement everywhere. 'Oh, it can't be! ... How do you know it's true? Can such things happen? ... It's sweet.... It's such a scream.' The news that had been running through Saint-Louis for a month was delightful, more delightful than all the promises in the world. It crowned a certain dream of grandeur, of distinction, which was common to all the mulatto women. The Ninis, the Nanas and the Nénettes live wholly outside the natural conditions of their country. The great dream that haunts every one of them is to be the bride of a white man from Europe. One could say that all their efforts are directed to this end, which is almost never attained. Their need to gesticulate, their love of ridiculous ostentation, their calculated, theatrical, revolting attitudes, are just so many effects of the same mania for grandeur. They must have white men, completely white, and nothing else will do. Almost all of them spend their entire lives waiting for this stroke of luck, which is anything but likely. And they are still waiting when old age overtakes them and forces them deep into dark refuges where the dream finally grows into a haughty resignation....

Very delightful news.... M. Darrivey, a completely white European employed in the civil service, had formally requested the hand of Dédée, a mulatto who was only half-Negro. It was unbelievable.[23]

Something remarkable must have happened on the day when the white man declared his love to the mulatto. There was recognition, incorporation into a group that had seemed hermetic. The psychological minus-value, this feeling of insignificance and its corollary, the impossibility of reaching the light, totally vanished. From one day to the next, the mulatto went from the class of slaves to that of masters.

She had been recognized through her overcompensating behaviour. She was no longer the woman who wanted to be white; she was white. She was joining the white world.

In *Magie noire*, Paul Morand described a similar phenomenon, but one has since learned to be leery of Paul Morand. From the psychological point of view, it may be interesting to consider the following problem. The educated mulatto woman, especially if she is a student, engages in doubly equivocal behaviour. She says, 'I do not like the Negro because he is savage. Not savage in a cannibal way, but lacking refinement.' An abstract point of view. And when one points out to her that in this respect some black people may be her superiors, she falls back on their 'ugliness'. A factitious point of view. Faced with the proofs of a genuine black aesthetic, she professes to be unable to understand it; one tries then to explain its canon to her, the wings of her nose flare, there is a sharp intake of breath, 'she is free to choose her own husband'. As a last resort, the appeal to subjectivity. If, as Anna Freud says, the ego is driven to desperation by the amputation of all its defence mechanisms, 'in so far as the bringing of the unconscious activities of the ego into consciousness has the effect of disclosing the defensive processes and rendering them inoperative, the result of analysis is to weaken the ego still further and to advance the pathological process'.[24]

But in Dédée's case the ego does not have to defend itself, since its claims have been officially recognized: she is marrying a white man. Every coin, however, has two sides; whole families have been made fools of. Three or four mulatto girls had acquired mulatto admirers, while all their friends had white men. 'This was looked on particularly as an insult to the family as a whole; an offence, moreover, that required amends.'[25] For these families had been humiliated in their most legitimate ambitions; the mutilation that they had suffered affected the very movement of their lives, the rhythm of their existence....

In response to a profound desire they sought to change, to 'evolve'. This right was denied to them. At any rate, it was challenged.

What is there to say, after these expositions?

Whether one is dealing with Mayotte Capécia of Martinique or with Nini of Saint-Louis, the same process is to be observed. A bilateral process, an attempt to acquire – by internalizing them – assets that were originally prohibited. It is because the Negress feels inferior that she aspires to win admittance into the white world. In this endeavour she will seek the help of a phenomenon that we shall call *affective erethism.*

This work represents the sum of the experiences and observations of seven years; regardless of the area I have studied, one thing has struck me: the Negro enslaved by his inferiority, the white man enslaved by his superiority alike behave in accordance with a neurotic orientation. Therefore I have been led to consider their alienation in terms of psychoanalytical classifications. The Negro's behaviour makes him akin to an obsessive neurotic type, or, if one prefers, he puts himself into a complete situational neurosis. In the man of colour there is a constant effort to run away from his own individuality, to annihilate his own presence. Whenever a man of colour protests, there is alienation. Whenever a man of colour rebukes, there is alienation. We shall see later, in Chapter Five ['The Negro and Psychopathology], that the Negro, having been made inferior, proceeds from humiliating insecurity through strongly voiced self-accusation to despair. The attitude of the black man toward the white, or toward his own race, often duplicates almost completely a constellation of delirium, frequently bordering on the region of the pathological.

It will be objected that there is nothing psychotic in the Negroes who are discussed here. Nevertheless I should like to cite two highly significant instances. A few years ago I knew a Negro medical student. He had an *agonizing* conviction that he was not taken at his true worth – not on the university level, he explained, but as a human being. He had an *agonizing* conviction that he would never succeed in gaining recognition as a colleague from the whites in his profession and as a physician from his European patients. In such moments of fantasy intuition,[26] the times most favourable[27] to psychosis, he would get drunk. Finally, he enlisted one day in the army as a medical officer; and, he added, not for anything in the world would he agree to go to the colonies or to serve in a colonial unit. He wanted to have white men under his command. He was a boss; as such he was to be feared or respected. That was just what he wanted, what he strove for: to make white men adopt a Negro attitude toward him. In this way he was obtaining revenge for the *imago* that had always obsessed him: the frightened, trembling Negro, abased before the white overlord.

I had another acquaintance, a customs inspector in a port on the French mainland, who was extremely severe with tourists or travellers in transit. 'Because', he explained to me, 'if you aren't a bastard they take you for a poor shit. Since I'm a Negro, you can imagine how I'm going to get it either way....'

In *Understanding Human Nature*, Adler says:

When we demonstrate cases ... it is frequently convenient to show relationships between the childhood impressions and the actual complaint ... this is best done by a graph.... We will succeed in many cases in being able to plot this graph of life, the spiritual curve along which the entire movement of an individual has taken place. The equation of the curve is the behavior pattern which this individual has followed since earliest childhood.... Actually we see this behavior pattern, whose final configuration is subject to some few changes, but whose essential contents, whose energy and meaning remain unchanged from earliest childhood, is the determining factor, even though the relations to the adult environment ... may tend to modify it in some instances.[28]

We are anticipating, and it is already clear that the individual psychology of Adler will help us to understand the conception of the world held by the man of colour. Since the black man is a former slave, we will turn to Hegel too; and, to conclude, Freud should be able to contribute to our study.

Nini and Mayotte Capécia: two types of behaviour that move us to thought.

Are there no other possibilities?

But those are pseudo-questions that do not concern us. I will say, however, that every criticism of that which is implies a solution, if indeed one can propose a solution to one's fellow – to a free being.

What I insist on is that the poison must be eliminated once and for all.

4

The Man of Colour
and the White Woman

Out of the blackest part of my soul, across the zebra striping of my mind, surges this desire to be suddenly *white*.

I wish to be acknowledged not as black but as *white*.

Now – and this is a form of recognition that Hegel had not envisaged – who but a white woman can do this for me? By loving me she proves that I am worthy of white love. I am loved like a white man.

I am a white man.

Her love takes me onto the noble road that leads to total realization....

I marry white culture, white beauty, white whiteness.

When my restless hands caress those white breasts, they grasp white civilization and dignity and make them mine.

Some thirty years ago, a coal-black Negro, in a Paris bed with a 'maddening' blonde, shouted at the moment of orgasm, 'Hurrah for Schoelcher!' When one recalls that it was Victor Schoelcher who persuaded the Third Republic to adopt the decree abolishing slavery, one understands why it is necessary to elaborate somewhat on the possible aspects of relations between black men and white women.

It will be argued that this little tale is not authenticated; but simply that it could be born and survive through the years is an indication: it is no fallacy. For the anecdote renews a conflict that, active or dormant, is always real. Its persistence attests to the black world's endorsement. To say it another way, when a story flourishes in the heart of a folklore, it is because in one way or another it expresses an aspect of 'the spirit of the group'.

In analysing *Je suis Martiniquaise* and *Nini*, we have seen how the Negress behaves with the white man. Through a novel by René Maran – which seems to be autobiographical – let us try to understand what happens when the man is black and the woman white.

The problem is admirably laid out, for the character of Jean Veneuse will make it possible for us to go much more deeply into the attitude of the black man. What are the terms of this problem? Jean Veneuse is a Negro. Born in the Antilles, he has lived in Bordeaux for years;

so he is a European. But he is black; so he is a Negro. There is the conflict. He does not understand his own race and the whites do not understand him. And, he observes, 'The Europeans in general and the French in particular, not satisfied with simply ignoring the Negro of the colonies, repudiate the one whom they have shaped into their own image.'[1]

The personality of the author does not emerge quite so easily as one might wish. An orphan sent to a provincial boarding-school, he is compelled to spend his vacations there. His friends and acquaintances scatter all over France on the slightest pretext, whereas the little Negro is forced into the habit of solitude, so that his best friends are his books. At the extreme, I should say there is a certain accusatory character, a certain resentment, an ill-disciplined aggression, in the long list – too long – of 'travelling companions' that the author offers us: at the extreme, I say, but it is exactly to the extreme that we have to go.

Unable to be assimilated, unable to pass unnoticed, he consoles himself by associating with the dead, or at least the absent. And his associations, unlike his life, ignore the barriers of centuries and oceans. He talks with Marcus Aurelius, Joinville, Pascal, Pérez Galdós, Rabindranath Tagore. If we were compelled to hang a label on Jean Veneuse, we should have to call him an introvert; others might call him a sentimentalist, but a sentimentalist who is always careful to contrive a way of winning out on the level of ideas and knowledge. As a matter of fact, his friends and schoolmates hold him in high regard: 'What a perpetual dreamer! You know, my old pal, Veneuse, is really a character. He never takes his nose out of his books except to scribble all over his notebooks.'[2]

But a sentimentalist who goes non-stop from singing Spanish songs to translating into English. Shy, but uneasy as well: 'As I was leaving them, I heard Divrande say to him: "A good kid, that Veneuse – he seems to like being sad and quiet, but he's always helpful. You can trust him. You'll see. He's the kind of Negro that a lot of white guys ought to be like." '[3]

Uneasy and anxious indeed. An anxious man who cannot escape his body. We know from other sources that René Maran cherished an affection for André Gide. It seems possible to find a resemblance between the ending of *Un homme pareil aux autres* and that of Gide's *Strait is the Gate*. This departure, this tone of emotional pain, of moral impossibility, seems an echo of the story of Jérôme and Alissa.

But there remains the fact that Veneuse is black. He is a bear who loves solitude. He is a thinker. And when a woman tries to start a flirtation with him, he says, 'Are you trying to smoke out an old bear like me? Be careful, my dear. Courage is a fine thing, but you're going to get yourself talked about if you go on attracting attention this way. A Negro? Shameful – it's beneath contempt. Associating with anybody of that race is just utterly disgracing yourself.'[4]

Above all, he wants to prove to the others that he is a man, their equal. But let us not be misled: Jean Veneuse is the man who has to be convinced. It is in the roots of his soul, as complicated as that of any European, that the doubt persists. If the expression may be allowed, Jean Veneuse is the lamb to be slaughtered. Let us make the effort.

After having quoted Stendhal and mentioned the phenomenon of 'crystallization', he declares that he loves:

... Andrée spiritually in Mme Coulanges and physically in Clarisse. It is insane. But that is how it is: I love Clarisse, I love Mme Coulanges, even though I never really think of either of them. All they are for me is an excuse that makes it possible for me to delude myself. I study Andrée in them and I begin to know her by heart.... I don't know. I know nothing. I have no wish to try to know anything; or, rather, I know nothing any more except one thing: that the Negro is a man like the rest, the equal of the others, and that his heart, which only the ignorant consider simple, can be as complicated as the heart of the most complicated of Europeans.[5]

For the simplicity of the Negro is a myth created by superficial observers. 'I love Clarisse, I love Mme Coulanges, and it is Andrée Marielle whom I really love. Only she, no one else.'[6]

Who is Andrée Marielle? You know who she is, the daughter of the poet, Louis Marielle. But now you see that this Negro, 'who has raised himself through his own intelligence and his assiduous labours to the level of the thought and the culture of Europe',[7] is incapable of escaping his race.

Andrée Marielle is white; no solution seems possible. Yet, association with Payot, Gide, Moréas and Voltaire seemed to have wiped out all that. In all good faith, Jean Veneuse:

... believed in that culture and set himself to love this new world he had discovered and conquered for his own use. What a blunder he had made! Arriving at maturity and going off to serve his adopted country in the land of his ancestors was enough to make him wonder whether he was not being betrayed by everything about him, for the white race would not accept him as one of its own and the black virtually repudiated him.[8]

Jean Veneuse, feeling that existence is impossible for him without love, proceeds to dream it into being. He proceeds to dream it alive and to produce verses:

> When a man loves he must not speak;
> Best that he hide it from himself.

Andrée Marielle has written to him that she loves him, but Jean Veneuse needs authorization. It is essential that some white man say to him, 'Take my sister.' Veneuse has put a certain number of questions to his friend, Coulanges. Here, more or less *in extenso*, is what Coulanges answers:

Old boy [Coulanges uses the English expression],

Once again you bring me your problem, once again I will give you my opinion – once and for all. Let us proceed in an orderly fashion. Your situation as you have explained it to me is as clear as it can be. Allow me nevertheless to clear the ground before me. It will be all to your good.

How old were you, anyway, when you left home to go to France? Three or four, I think. You have never seen your native island since and you have not the slightest interest in seeing it again. You have lived in Bordeaux ever since. And ever since you became a colonial official, Bordeaux is where you have spent the greatest part of your leaves. In short, you are really one of us. Perhaps you are not altogether aware of the fact. In that case, accept the fact that you are a Frenchman from Bordeaux. Get that into your thick head. You know nothing of your compatriots of the Antilles. I should be amazed, in fact, if you could even manage to communicate with them. The ones I know, furthermore, have no resemblance to you.

In fact you are like us – you are 'us'. Your thoughts are ours. You behave as we behave, as we would behave. You think of yourself – others think of you – as a Negro? Utterly mistaken! You merely look like one. As for everything else, you think as a European. And so it is natural that you love as a European. Since European men love only European women, you can hardly marry anyone but a woman of the country where you have always lived, a woman of our good old France, your real and only country. This being the case, let us get on to the subject of your latest letter. On the one hand we have one Jean Veneuse, who resembles you like a brother; on the other hand we have Mlle Andrée Marielle. Andrée Marielle, whose skin is white, loves Jean Veneuse, who is extremely brown and who adores Andrée Marielle. But that does not stop you from asking me what must be done. You magnificent idiot! …

As soon as you are back in France, rush to the father of the girl who already belongs to you in spirit and strike your fist savagely on your heart as you shout at him: 'I love her. She loves me. We love each other. She must marry me. Otherwise I will kill myself here and now.'[9]

When the question is put directly, then, the white man agrees to give his sister to the black – but on one condition: you have nothing in common with real Negroes. You are not black, you are 'extremely brown'.

This procedure is quite familiar to coloured students in France. Society refuses to consider them genuine Negroes. The Negro is a savage, whereas the student is civilized. 'You're "us",' Coulanges tells him; and if anyone thinks you are a Negro he is mistaken, because you merely look like one. But Jean Veneuse does not want this. He cannot accept it, because he knows.

He knows that, 'enraged by this degrading ostracism, mulattoes and Negroes have only one thought from the moment they land in Europe: to gratify their appetite for white women'.

The majority of them, including those of lighter skin who often go to the extreme of denying both their countries and their mothers, tend to marry in Europe not so much out of love as for the satisfaction of being the master of a European woman; and a certain tang of proud revenge enters into this.

And so I wonder whether in my case there is any difference from theirs, whether, by marrying you, who are a European, I may not appear to be making a show of contempt for the women of my own race and, above all, to be drawn on by desire for that white flesh that has been forbidden to us Negroes as long as white men have ruled the world, so that without my knowledge I am attempting to revenge myself on a European woman for everything that her ancestors have inflicted on mine throughout the centuries.[10]

What a struggle to free himself of a purely subjective conflict. I am a white man, I was born in Europe, all my friends are white. There are not eight Negroes in the city where I live. I think in French, France is my religion. I am a European, do you understand? I am not a Negro and, in order to prove it to you, I as a public employee am going to show the genuine Negroes the differences that separate me from them. Indeed, read the book again and you will be convinced:

Who knocked at the door? Ah, yes, of course.
'Is that you, Soua?'
'Yes, Major.'
'What do you want?'

'Roll call, Major. Five men guard. Seventeen men prisoners – everybody here.'
'Anything else new? Any word from the runner?'
'No, suh, major.'[11]

Monsieur Veneuse has native bearers. He has a young Negro girl in his house. And to the Negroes who seem downcast that he is leaving, he feels that the only thing for him to say is:

Please go away. Please go away. You see ... how unhappy it makes me to leave you. Please go now. I will not forget you. I am leaving you only because this is not my country and I feel too alone here, too empty, too deprived of all the comfort that I need but that you, luckily for you, do not yet require.[12]

When we read such passages we cannot help thinking of Félix Eboué, unquestionably a Negro, who saw his duty quite differently in the same circumstances. Jean Veneuse is not a Negro and does not wish to be a Negro. And yet, without his knowledge, a gulf has been created. There is something indefinable, irreversible, there is indeed the *that within* of Harold Rosenberg.[13]

Louis-T. Achille said in his report to the Interracial Conferences of 1949:

Insofar as truly interracial marriage is concerned, one can legitimately wonder to what extent it may not represent for the coloured spouse a kind of subjective consecration to wiping out in himself and in his own mind the colour prejudice from which he has suffered so long. It would be interesting to investigate this in a given number of cases and perhaps to seek in this clouded motivation the underlying reason for certain interracial marriages entered into outside the normal conditions of a happy household. Some men or some women, in effect, by choosing partners of another race, marry persons of a class or a culture inferior to their own whom they would not have chosen as spouses in their own race and whose chief asset seems to be the assurance that the partner will achieve denaturalization and (to use a loathsome word) 'deracialization'. Among certain people of colour, the fact that they are marrying someone of the white race seems to have overridden every other consideration. In this fact they find access to complete equality with that illustrious race, the master of the world, the ruler of the peoples of colour....[14]

We know historically that the Negro guilty of lying with a white woman is castrated. The Negro who has had a white woman makes himself taboo to his fellows. It is easy for the mind to formulate this drama of sexual preoccupation. And that is exactly the ultimate goal of the archetype of *Uncle Remus*: Br'er Rabbit, who represents the black man. Will he or will he not succeed in going to bed with the two daughters of Mrs Meadows? There are ups and downs, all told by a laughing, good-natured, easy-going Negro, a Negro who serves with a smile.

During the time when I was slowly being jolted alive into puberty, I had the honour of being able to look in wonder on one of my older friends who had just come back from France and who had held a Parisian girl in his arms. I shall try to analyse this problem in a special chapter.

Talking recently with several Antilleans, I found that the dominant concern among those arriving in France was to go to bed with a white woman. As soon as their ships docked in Le Havre, they were off to the houses. Once this ritual of initiation into 'authentic' manhood had been fulfilled, they took the train for Paris.

But what is important here is to examine Jean Veneuse. To this end, I shall resort in considerable measure to a study by Germaine Guex, *La Nevrose d'abandon*.

Contrasting what she calls the abandonment neurosis, which is pre-Oedipal in nature, to the real post-Oedipal conflicts described by orthodox Freudians, Dr Guex analyses two types, the first of which seems to illustrate the plight of Jean Veneuse: 'It is this tripod – the *anguish* created by every abandonment, the *aggression* to which it gives rise, and the *devaluation of self* that flows out of it – that supports the whole symptomatology of this neurosis.'[15]

We made an introvert of Jean Veneuse. We know characterologically – or, better, phenomenologically – that autistic thinking can be made dependent on a primary introversion.[16]

In a patient of the negative-aggressive type, obsession with the past and with its frustrations, its gaps, its defeats, paralyses his enthusiasm for living. Generally more inverted than the positive-loving type, he has a tendency to go back over his past and present disappointments, building up in himself a more or less secret area of bitter, disillusioned resentments that often amounts to a kind of autism. But, unlike the genuine autistic person, the abandonment-neurotic is aware of this secret zone, which he cultivates and defends against every intrusion. More egocentric than the neurotic of the second type (positive-loving), he views everything in terms of himself. He has little capacity for disinterestedness: his aggressions and a constant need for vengeance inhibit his impulses. His retreat into himself does not allow him to have any positive experience that would compensate for his past. Hence the lack of self-esteem and therefore of affective security is virtually total in such cases; and as a result there is an overwhelming feeling of impotence in relation to life and to people, as well as a complete rejection of the feeling of responsibility. Others have betrayed him and thwarted him and yet it is only from these others that he expects any improvement in his lot.[17]

A magnificent description, into which the character of Jean Veneuse fits perfectly. For, he tells us, 'arriving at maturity and going off to serve my adopted country in the land of my ancestors was enough to make me wonder *whether I was not being betrayed*[18] by everything about me, for the white race would not accept me as one of its own and the black virtually repudiated me. That is precisely my position.'[19]

The attitude is one of recrimination toward the past, devaluation of self, incapability of being understood as he would like to be. Listen again to Jean Veneuse:

Who can describe the desperation of the little *Hottentots* whose parents, in the hope of making real Frenchmen of them, transplant them to France too early? From one day to the next they are locked into boarding schools, these free, joyful children, 'for your own good', as their weeping parents tell them.

I was one of these intermittent orphans and I shall suffer for it throughout my life. At the age of seven I and my introduction to learning were turned over to a gloomy school far out in the country.... The thousand games that are supposed to enliven childhood and adolescence could not make me forget how painful mine were. It is to this schooling that my character owes its inner melancholy and that fear of social contact that today inhibits even my slightest impulses....[20]

And yet he would have liked to be surrounded, enclosed. He did not like to be *abandoned*. When school vacations came, all the other boys went home; alone – note that word *alone* – he remained in the big empty white school....

Oh, those tears of a child who had no one to wipe them.... He will never forget that he was apprenticed so young to loneliness.... A cloistered existence, a withdrawn, secluded existence in which I learned too soon to meditate and to reflect. A solitary life that in the end was profoundly moved by trifles – it has made me hypersensitive within myself, incapable of externalizing my joys or my sorrows, so that I reject everything that I love and I turn my back in spite of myself on everything that attracts me.[21]

What is going on here? Two processes. I do not want to be loved. Why not? Because once, very long ago, I attempted an object relation and I was *abandoned*. I have never forgiven my mother. Because I was abandoned, I will make someone else suffer, and desertion by me will be the direct expression of my need for revenge. I will go to Africa: I do not wish to be loved and I will flee from love-objects. That, Germaine Guex says, is called 'putting oneself to the proof in order to prove something'. I do not wish to be loved, I adopt a defensive position. And if the love-object insists, I will say plainly, 'I do not wish to be loved.'

Devaluation of self? Indeed yes.

This lack of esteem of self as an object worthy of love has grave consequences. For one thing, it keeps the individual in a state of profound inner insecurity, as a result of which it inhibits or falsifies every relation with others. It is as something that has the right to arouse sympathy or love that the individual is uncertain of himself. The lack of affective self-valuation is to be found only in persons who in their early childhood suffered from a lack of love and understanding.[22]

Jean Veneuse would like to be a man like the rest, but he knows that this position is a false one. He is a beggar. He looks for appeasement, for permission in the white man's eyes. For to him there is 'The Other'.

Affective self-rejection invariably brings the abandonment-neurotic to an extremely painful and obsessive feeling of exclusion, of having no place anywhere, of being superfluous everywhere in an affective sense.... 'I am The Other' is an expression that I have heard time and again in the language of the abandonment-neurotic. To be 'The Other' is to feel that one is always in a shaky position, to be always on guard, ready to be rejected and ... unconsciously doing everything needed to bring about exactly this catastrophe.

It would be impossible to overestimate the intensity of the suffering that accompanies such desertion states, a suffering that in one way is connected to the first experiences of rejection in childhood and that brings them back in all their strength....[23]

The abandonment-neurotic demands proofs. He is not satisfied with isolated statements. He has no confidence. Before he forms an objective relation, he exacts repeated proofs from his partner. The essence of his attitude is 'not to love in order to avoid being abandoned'. The abandonment-neurotic is insatiable. That is because he claims the right to constant amends. He wants to be loved completely, absolutely and forever. Listen:

My dearest Jean,
I got your letter of last July only today. It is completely mad. Why torture me this way? You – are you aware of the fact? – you are incomparably cruel. You give me happiness mixed with anxiety. You make me the happiest and at the same time the unhappiest of women. How many times shall I have to tell you that I love you, that I belong to you, that I am waiting for you? Come.[24]

The abandonment-neurotic has finally deserted. He is called back. He is needed. He is loved. And yet what fantasies! Does she really love me? Does she look at me objectively?

One day a man came, a great friend of Daddy Ned who had never seen Pontaponte. He came from Bordeaux. But good God, he was dirty! God, how ugly he was, this man who was such a good friend of Daddy Ned! He had a hideous black face, completely black, which showed that he must not wash very often.[25]

Looking eagerly for external reasons for his Cinderella complex, Jean Veneuse projects the entire arsenal of racial stereotypes onto a child of three or four years. And to Andrée he says, 'Tell me, Andrée darling … in spite of my colour, would you agree to marry me if I asked you?'[26]

He is frightfully full of doubt. Here is Germaine Guex on that subject:

The first characteristic seems to be the dread of showing oneself as one actually is. This is a broad field of various fears: fear of disappointing, fear of displeasing, of boring, of wearying … and consequently of losing the chance to create a bond of sympathy with others or if this bond does exist of doing damage to it. The abandonment-neurotic doubts whether he can be loved as he is, for he has had the cruel experience of being abandoned when he offered himself to the tenderness of others as a little child and hence without artifice.[27]

Jean Veneuse does not, however, lead a life devoid of compensations. He flirts with art. His reading list is impressive, his essay on Suarès is quite perceptive. That too is analysed by Germaine Guex:

Imprisoned in himself, locked into his artificial reserve, the negative-aggressive feeds his feeling of irreparable loss with everything that he continues to lose or that his passivity makes him lack…. Therefore, with the exception of such privileged sectors as *his intellectual life or his profession*,[28] he cherishes a deep-seated feeling of worthlessness.[29]

Where does this analysis lead us? To nothing short of proving to Jean Veneuse that in fact he is not like the rest. Making people ashamed of their existence, Jean-Paul Sartre said. Yes: teaching them to become aware of the potentials they have forbidden themselves, of the passivity they have paraded in just those situations in which what is needed is to hold oneself, like a sliver, to the heart of the world, to interrupt if necessary the rhythm of the world, to upset, if necessary, the chain of command, but in any case, and most assuredly, *to stand up to the world.*

Jean Veneuse is the crusader of the inner life. When he sees Andrée again, when he is face to face with this woman whom he has wanted for months and months, he takes refuge in silence, the eloquent silence of those who 'know the artificiality of words and acts'.

Jean Veneuse is a neurotic and his colour is only an attempt to explain his psychic structure. If this objective difference had not existed, he would have manufactured it out of nothing.

Jean Veneuse is one of those intellectuals who try to take a position solely on the level of ideas. Incapable of realizing any concrete contact with his fellow man. Is he treated decently, kindly, humanly? Only because he has stumbled on some servant secrets. He 'knows those people' and he is on guard against them.

My vigilance, if one can call it that, is a safety-catch. Politely and artlessly I welcome the advances that are made to me. I accept and repay the drinks that are bought for me, I take part in the little social games that are played on deck, but I do not allow myself to be taken in by the good will shown me, suspicious as I am of this excessive cordiality that has rather too quickly taken the place of the hostility in the midst of which they formerly tried to isolate me.[30]

He accepts the drinks, but he buys others in return. He does not wish to be obligated to anyone. For if he does not buy back, he is a nigger, as ungrateful as all the others.

Is someone mean? It is simply because he is a nigger. For it is impossible not to despise him. Well, it is clear to me that Jean Veneuse, alias René Maran, is neither more nor less than a black abandonment-neurotic. And he is put back into his place, his proper place. He is a neurotic who needs to be emancipated from his infantile fantasies. And I contend that Jean Veneuse represents not an example of black–white relations, but a certain mode of behaviour in a neurotic who by coincidence is black. So the purpose of our study becomes more precise: to enable the man of colour to understand, through specific examples, the psychological elements that can alienate his fellow Negroes. I will emphasize this further in the chapter devoted to phenomenological description, but let us remember that our purpose is to make possible a healthy encounter between black and white.

Jean Veneuse is ugly. He is black. What more is needed? If one re-reads the various observations of Germaine Guex, one will be convinced by the evidence: *Un homme pareil aux autres* is a sham, an attempt to make the relations between two races dependent on an organic unhealthiness. There can be no argument: in the domain of psychoanalysis as in that of philosophy, the organic, or constitutional, is a myth only for him who can go beyond it. If from a heuristic point of view one must totally deny the existence of the organic, the fact remains, and we can do nothing about it, that some individuals make every effort to fit into pre-established categories. Or, rather, yes, we can do something about it.

Earlier I referred to Jacques Lacan; it was not by accident. In his thesis, presented in 1932, he violently attacked the idea of the constitutional. Apparently I am departing from his conclusions, but my dissent will be understood when one recalls that for the idea of the constitutional as it is understood by the French school I am substituting that of structure – 'embracing unconscious psychic life, as we are able to know it in part, especially in the form of repression and inhibition, insofar as these elements take an active part in the organization peculiar to each psychic individuality'.[31]

As we have seen, on examination Jean Veneuse displays the structure of an abandonment-neurotic of the negative-aggressive type. One can attempt to explain this reactionally – that is, through the interaction of person and environment – and prescribe, for example, a new environment, 'a change of air'. It will properly be observed that in this case the structure has remained constant. The change of air that Jean Veneuse prescribed for himself was not undertaken in order to find himself as a man; he did not have as his purpose the formulation of a healthy outlook on the world; he had no striving toward the productiveness that is characteristic of psychosocial equilibrium, but sought rather to corroborate his *externalizing* neurosis.

The neurotic structure of an individual is simply the elaboration, the formation, the eruption within the ego, of conflictual clusters arising in part out of the environment and in part out of the purely personal way in which that individual reacts to these influences.

Just as there was a touch of fraud in trying to deduce from the behaviour of Nini and Mayotte Capécia a general law of the behaviour of the black woman with the white man, there would be a similar lack of objectivity, I believe, in trying to extend the attitude of Veneuse to the man of colour as such. And I should like to think that I have discouraged any endeavours to connect the defeats of Jean Veneuse with the greater or lesser concentration of melanin in his epidermis.

This sexual myth – the quest for white flesh – perpetuated by alienated psyches, must no longer be allowed to impede active understanding.

In no way should my colour be regarded as a flaw. From the moment the Negro accepts the separation imposed by the European he has no further respite, and 'is it not understandable that thenceforward he will try to elevate himself to the white man's level? To elevate himself in the range of colours to which he attributes a kind of hierarchy?'[32]

We shall see that another solution is possible. It implies a restructuring of the world.

5
The Negro and Psychopathology

Psychoanalytic schools have studied the neurotic reactions that arise among certain groups, in certain areas of civilization. In response to the requirements of dialectic, one should investigate the extent to which the conclusions of Freud or of Adler can be applied to the effort to understand the man of colour's view of the world.

It can never be sufficiently emphasized that psychoanalysis sets as its task the understanding of given behaviour patterns – within the specific group represented by the family. When the problem is a neurosis experienced by an adult, the analyst's task is to uncover in the new psychic structure an analogy with certain infantile elements, a repetition, a duplication of conflicts that owe their origin to the essence of the family constellation. In every case the analyst clings to the concept of the family as a 'psychic circumstance and object'.[1]

Here, however, the evidence is going to be particularly complicated. In Europe the family represents in effect a certain fashion in which the world presents itself to the child. There are close connections between the structure of the family and the structure of the nation. Militarization and the centralization of authority in a country automatically entail a resurgence of the authority of the father. In Europe and in every country characterized as civilized or civilizing, the family is a miniature of the nation. As the child emerges from the shadow of his parents, he finds himself once more among the same laws, the same principles, the same values. A normal child that has grown up in a normal family will be a normal man.[2] There is no disproportion between the life of the family and the life of the nation. Conversely, when one examines a closed society – that is, a society that has been protected from the flood of civilization – one encounters the same structures as those just described. Father Trilles' *L'âme du Pygmée d'Afrique*, for instance, convinces us of that; although with every word one is aware of the need to Christianize the savage Negro soul, the book's description of the whole culture – the conditions of worship, the persistence of rites, the survival of myths – has nothing of the artificial impression given by *La philosophie bantoue*.

In both cases the characteristics of the family are projected onto the social environment. It is true that the children of pickpockets or burglars, accustomed to a certain system of clan law, would be surprised to find that the rest of the world behaved differently, but a new kind of training – except in instances of perversion or arrested development (Heuyer)[3] should be able to direct them into a moralization, a socialization of outlook.

It is apparent in all such cases that the sickness lies in the family environment.

For the individual the authority of the state is a reproduction of the authority of the family by which he was shaped in his childhood. Ultimately the individual assimilates all the authorities that he meets to the authority of the parents: he perceives the present in terms of the past. Like all other human conduct, behaviour toward authority is something learned. And it is learned in the heart of a family that can be described, from the psychological point of view, by the form of organization peculiar to it – that is, by the way in which its authority is distributed and exercised.[4]

But – and this is a most important point – we observe the opposite in the man of colour. A normal Negro child, having grown up within a normal family, will become abnormal on the slightest contact with the white world. This statement may not be immediately understandable. Therefore let us proceed by going backward. Paying tribute to Dr Breuer, Freud wrote:

In almost every case, we could see that the symptoms were, so to speak, like residues of emotional experiences, to which for this reason we later gave the name of psychic traumas. Their individual characters were linked to the traumatic scenes that had provoked them. According to the classic terminology, the symptoms were determined by 'scenes' of which they were the mnemic residues, and it was no longer necessary to regard them as arbitrary and enigmatic effects of the neurosis. In contrast, however, to what was expected, it was not always a single event that was the cause of the symptom; most often, on the contrary, it arose out of multiple traumas, frequently analogous and repeated. As a result, it became necessary to reproduce chronologically this whole series of pathogenic memories, but in reverse order: the latest at the beginning and the earliest at the end; it was impossible to make one's way back to the first trauma, which is often the most forceful, if one skipped any of its successors.

It could not be stated more positively; every neurosis has its origins in specific *Erlebnisse*. Later Freud added:

This trauma, it is true, has been quite expelled from the consciousness and the memory of the patient and as a result he has apparently been saved from a great mass of suffering, but the repressed desire continues to exist in the unconscious; it is on watch constantly for an opportunity to make itself known and it soon comes back into consciousness, but in a disguise that makes it impossible to recognize; in other words, the repressed thought is replaced in consciousness by another that acts as its surrogate, its *Ersatz*, and that soon surrounds itself with all those feelings of morbidity that had been supposedly averted by the repression.

These *Erlebnisse* are repressed in the unconscious.

What do we see in the case of the black man? Unless we make use of that frightening postulate – which so destroys our balance – offered by Jung, the *collective unconscious*, we can understand absolutely nothing. A drama is enacted every day in colonized countries. How is one to explain, for example, that a Negro who has passed his baccalaureate and has gone to the Sorbonne to study to become a teacher of philosophy is already on guard before any conflictual elements have coalesced round him? René Ménil accounted for this reaction in Hegelian terms. In his view it was:

the consequence of the replacement of the repressed [African] spirit in the consciousness of the slave by an authority symbol representing the Master, a symbol implanted in the subsoil of the collective group and charged with maintaining order in it as a garrison controls a conquered city.[5]

We shall see in our section on Hegel that René Ménil has made no misjudgement. Meanwhile we have the right to put a question to ourselves: how is the persistence of this reaction in the twentieth century to be explained when in other ways there is complete identification with the white man? Very often the Negro who becomes abnormal has never had any relations with whites. Has some remote experience been repressed in his unconscious? Did the little black child see his father beaten or lynched by a white man? Has there been a real traumatism? To all of this we have to answer *no*. Well, then?

If we want to answer correctly, we have to fall back on the idea of *collective catharsis*. In every society, in every collectivity, exists – must exist – a channel, an outlet through which the forces accumulated in the form of aggression can be released. This is the purpose of games in children's institutions, of psychodramas in group therapy and, in a more general way, of illustrated magazines for children – each type of society, of course, requiring its own specific kind of catharsis. The Tarzan stories, the sagas of twelve-year-old explorers, the adventures of Mickey Mouse and all those 'comic books' serve actually as a release for collective aggression. The magazines are put together by white men for little white men. This is the heart of the problem. In the Antilles – and there is every reason to think that the situation is the same in the other colonies – these same magazines are devoured by the local children. In the magazines the Wolf, the Devil, the Evil Spirit, the Bad Man, the Savage are always symbolized by Negroes or Indians; since there is always identification with the victor, the little Negro, quite as easily as the little white boy, becomes an explorer, an adventurer, a missionary 'who faces the danger of being eaten by the wicked Negroes'. I shall be told that this is hardly important; but only because those who say it have not given much thought to the role of such magazines. Here is what G. Legman thinks of them:

With very rare exceptions, every American child who was six years old in 1938 had therefore assimilated at the very least 18,000 scenes of ferocious tortures and bloody violence.... Except the Boers, the Americans are the only modern nation that within living memory has completely driven the autochthonous population off the soil that it had occupied.[6] America alone, then, could have had an uneasy national conscience to lull by creating the myth of the 'Bad Injun',[7] in order later to be able to bring back the historic figure of the Noble Redskin vainly defending his lands against invaders armed with rifles and Bibles; the punishment that we deserve can be averted only by denying responsibility for the wrong and throwing the blame on the victim; by proving – at least to our own satisfaction – that by striking the first and only blow we were acting solely on the legitimate ground of defense.... [Anticipating the repercussions of these magazines on American culture, Legman went on:] There is still no answer to the question whether this maniacal fixation on violence and death is the substitute for a forbidden sexuality or whether it does not rather serve the purpose of channeling, along a line left open by sexual censorship, both the child's and the adult's desire for aggression against the economic and social structure which, though with their entire consent, perverts them. In both cases the root of the perversion, whether it be of a sexual or of an economic character, is of the essence; that is why, as long as we remain incapable of attacking these fundamental repressions, every attack aimed at such simple escape devices as comic books will remain futile.[8]

The black schoolboy in the Antilles, who in his lessons is forever talking about 'our ancestors, the Gauls',[9] identifies himself with the explorer, the bringer of civilization, the white man who carries truth to savages – an all-white truth. There is identification – that is, the young Negro subjectively adopts a white man's attitude. He invests the hero, who is white, with all his own aggression – at that age closely linked to sacrificial dedication, a sacrificial dedication permeated with sadism. An eight-year-old child who offers a gift, even to an adult, cannot endure a refusal. Little by little, one can observe in the young Antillean the formation and crystallization of an attitude and a way of thinking and seeing that are essentially white. When in school he has to read stories of savages told by white men, he always thinks of the Senegalese. As a schoolboy, I had many occasions to spend whole hours talking about the supposed customs of the savage Senegalese. In what was said there was a lack of awareness that was at the very least paradoxical. Because the Antillean does not think of himself as a black man; he thinks of himself as an Antillean. The Negro lives in Africa. Subjectively, intellectually, the Antillean conducts himself like a white man. But he is a Negro. That he will learn once he goes to Europe; and when he hears Negroes mentioned he will recognize that the word includes himself as well as the Senegalese. What are we to conclude on this matter?

To impose the same 'Evil Spirits' on the white man and on the black man is a major error in education. If one is willing to understand the 'Evil Spirit' in the sense of an attempt to personify the *id*, the point of view will be understood. If we are utterly honest, we must say that children's counting-out rhymes are subject to the same criticism. It will have already been noticed that I should like nothing more nor less than the establishment of children's magazines especially for Negroes, the creation of songs for Negro children and, ultimately, the publication of history texts especially for them, at least through the grammar-school grades. For, until there is evidence to the contrary, I believe that if there is a traumatism it occurs during those years. The young Antillean is a Frenchman called on at all times to live with white compatriots. One forgets this rather too often.

The white family is the agent of a certain system. The society is indeed the sum of all the families in it. The family is an institution that prefigures a broader institution: the social or the national group. Both turn on the same axes. The white family is the workshop in which one is shaped and trained for life in society. 'The family structure is internalized in the superego', Marcus says, 'and projected into political [though I would say social] behaviour.'

As long as he remains among his own people, the little black follows very nearly the same course as the little white. But if he goes to Europe, he will have to reappraise his lot. For the Negro in France, which is his country, will feel different from other people. One can hear the glib remark: the Negro makes himself inferior. But the truth is that he is made inferior. The young Antillean is a Frenchman called upon constantly to live with white compatriots. Now, the Antillean family has for all practical purposes no connection with the national – that is, the French, or European – structure. The Antillean has therefore to choose between his family and European society; in other words, the individual who *climbs up* into society – white and civilized – tends to reject his family – black and savage – on the plane of imagination, in accord with the childhood *Erlebnisse* that we discussed earlier. In this case the schema of Marcus becomes

Family ← Individual → Society

and the family structure is cast back into the *id*.

The Negro recognizes the unreality of many of the beliefs that he has adopted with reference to the subjective attitude of the white man. When he does, his real apprenticeship begins. And reality proves to be extremely resistant. But, it will be objected, you are merely describing a universal phenomenon, the criterion of maturity being in fact adaptation to society. My answer is that such a criticism goes off in the wrong direction, for I have just shown that for the Negro there is a myth to be faced. A solidly established myth. The Negro is unaware of it as long as his existence is limited to his own environment; but the first encounter with a white man oppresses him with the whole weight of his blackness.[10]

Then there is the unconscious. Since the racial drama is played out in the open, the black man has no time to 'make it unconscious'. The white man, on the other hand, succeeds in doing so to a certain extent, because a new element appears: guilt. The Negro's inferiority or superiority complex or his feeling of equality is *conscious*. These feelings forever chill him. They make his drama. In him there is none of the affective amnesia characteristic of the typical neurotic.

Whenever I have read a psychoanalytic work, discussed problems with my professors, or talked with European patients, I have been struck by the disparity between the corresponding schemas and the reality that the Negro presents. It has led me progressively to the conclusion that there is a dialectical substitution when one goes from the psychology of the white man to that of the black.

The earliest values, which Charles Odier describes,[11] are different in the white man and in the black man. The drive toward socialization does not stem from the same motivations. In cold actuality, we change worlds. A close study should be divided into two parts:

1. a psychoanalytic interpretation of the life experience of the black man;
2. a psychoanalytic interpretation of the Negro myth.

But reality, which is our only recourse, prevents such procedures. The facts are much more complicated. What are they?

The Negro is a phobogenic object, a stimulus to anxiety. From the patient treated by Sérieux and Capgras[12] to the girl who confides to me that to go to bed with a Negro would be terrifying to her, one discovers all the stages of what I shall call the Negro-phobogenesis. There has been much talk of psychoanalysis in connection with the Negro. Distrusting the ways in which it might be applied,[13] I have preferred to call this chapter 'The Negro and Psychopathology', well aware that Freud and Adler and even the cosmic Jung did not think of the Negro in all their investigations. And they were quite right not to have. It is too often forgotten that neurosis is not a basic element of human reality. Like it or not, the Oedipus complex is far from coming into being among Negroes. It might be argued, as Malinowski contends, that the matriarchal structure is the only reason for its absence. But, putting aside the question whether the ethnologists are not so imbued with the complexes of their own civilization that they are compelled to try to find them duplicated in the peoples they study, it would be relatively easy for me to show that in the French Antilles 97 per cent of the families cannot produce one Oedipal neurosis. This incapacity is one on which we heartily congratulate ourselves.[14]

With the exception of a few misfits within the closed environment, we can say that every neurosis, every abnormal manifestation, every affective erethism in an Antillean is the product of his cultural situation. In other words, there is a constellation of postulates, a series of propositions that slowly and subtly – with the help of books, newspapers, schools and their texts, advertisements, films, radio – work their way into one's mind and shape one's view of the world of the group to which one belongs.[15] In the Antilles that view of the world is white because no black voice exists. The folklore of Martinique is meagre and few children in Fort-de-France know the stories of 'Compè Lapin', twin brother of the Br'er Rabbit of Louisiana's Uncle Remus. A European familiar with the current trends of Negro poetry, for example, would be amazed to learn that as late as 1940 no Antillean found it possible to think of himself as a Negro. It was only with the appearance of Aimé Césaire that the acceptance of negritude and the statement of its claims began to be perceptible. The most concrete proof of this, furthermore, is that feeling which pervades each new generation of students arriving in Paris: it takes them several weeks to recognize that contact with Europe compels them to face a certain number of problems that until their arrival had never touched them. And yet these problems were by no means invisible.[16]

Whenever I had a discussion with my professors or talked with European patients, I became aware of the differences that might prevail between the two worlds. Talking recently to a physician who had always practised in Fort-de-France, I told him what conclusions I had arrived at; he went farther, saying that they were valid not only in psychopathology but also in general medicine. 'In the same way', he added, 'you never encounter a case of pure typhoid such as you studied in the textbooks; there is always a more or less manifest complication of malaria.' It would be interesting to study, for example, a case of schizophrenia as experienced by a Negro – if indeed that kind of malady were to be found there.

What am I getting at? Quite simply this: when the Negro makes contact with the white world, a certain sensitizing action takes place. If his psychic structure is weak, one observes a collapse of the ego. The black man stops behaving as an *actional* person. The goal of his behaviour will be The Other (in the guise of the white man), for The Other alone can give him worth. That is on the ethical level: self-esteem. But there is something else.

I have said that the Negro is phobogenic. What is phobia? I prefer to answer that question by relying on the latest work of Hesnard: 'Phobia is a neurosis characterized by the anxious fear of an object (in the broadest sense of anything outside the individual) or, by extension, of a situation.'[17] Naturally that object must have certain aspects. It must arouse, Hesnard says, both fear and revulsion. But here we encounter a difficulty. Applying the genetic method to the understanding of phobia, Charles Odier wrote that all anxiety derives from a certain subjective insecurity linked to the absence of the mother.[18] This occurs, according to Odier, sometime in the second year of life.

Investigating the psychic structure of the phobic, he comes to this conclusion: 'Before attacking the adult beliefs, all the elements of the infantile structure which produced them must be analysed.'[19]

The choice of the phobic object is therefore *overdetermined*. This object does not come at random out of the void of nothingness; in some situation it has previously evoked an affect in the patient. His phobia is the latent presence of this affect at the root of his world; there is an organization that has been given a form. For the object, naturally, need not be there, it is enough that somewhere it *exists*: it is a possibility. This object is endowed with evil intentions and with all the attributes of a malefic power.[20] In the phobic, affect has a priority that defies all rational thinking. As we can see, the phobic is a person who is governed by the laws of rational pre-logic and affective pre-logic: methods of thinking and feeling that go back to the age at which he experienced the event that impaired his security. The difficulty indicated here is this: was there a trauma harmful to security in the case of the young woman whom we mentioned a little earlier? In the majority of Negrophobic men has there been an attempt at rape? An attempt at *fellatio*? Proceeding with complete orthodoxy, we should be led by the application of analytic conclusions to this: if an extremely frightening object, such as a more or less imaginary attacker, arouses terror, this is also – for most often such cases are those of women – and especially a terror mixed with sexual revulsion. 'I'm afraid of men' really means, at the bottom of the motivation of the fear, because they might do all kinds of things to me, but not commonplace cruelties: sexual abuses – in other words, immoral and shameful things.[21]

'*Contact* alone is enough to evoke anxiety. For contact is at the same time the basic schematic type of initiating sexual action (touching, caresses-sexuality).'[22] Since we have learned to know all the tricks the ego uses in order to defend itself, we know too that its denials must in no case be taken literally. Are we not now observing a complete inversion? Basically, does this fear of rape not itself cry out for rape? Just as there are faces that ask to be slapped, can one not speak of women who ask to be raped? In *If He Hollers Let Him Go*, Chester Himes describes this type very well. The big blonde trembles whenever the Negro goes near her. Yet she has nothing to fear, since the factory is full of white men. In the end, she and the Negro go to bed together.

When I was in military service I had the opportunity to observe the behaviour of white women from three or four European countries when they were among Negroes at dances. Most of the time the women made involuntary gestures of flight, of withdrawing, their faces filled with a fear that was not feigned. And yet the Negroes who asked them to dance would have been utterly unable to commit any act at all against them, even if they had wished to do so. The behaviour of these women is clearly understandable from the standpoint of imagination. That is because the Negrophobic woman is in fact nothing but a putative sexual partner – just as the Negrophobic man is a repressed homosexual.

In relation to the Negro, everything takes place on the genital level. A few years ago, I remarked to some friends during a discussion that in a general sense the white man behaves toward the Negro as an elder brother reacts to the birth of a younger. I have since learnt that Richard Sterba arrived at the same conclusion in America.

On the phenomenological level there would be a double reality to be observed. The Jew is feared because of his potential for acquisitiveness. 'They' are everywhere. The banks, the stock exchanges, the government are infested with 'them'. 'They' control everything. Soon the whole country will belong to 'them'. 'They' do better in examinations than the 'real' Frenchmen. Soon 'they' will be making the laws for us. Not long ago, an acquaintance studying for the civil service said to me, 'Say what you want, "they" take good care of one another. When Moch was in power, for instance, the number of kikes in government jobs was appalling.' In the medical profession the situation is no different. Every Jewish student who wins a prize in a competition does it through 'pull'. As for the Negroes, they have tremendous sexual powers. What do you expect, with all the freedom they have in their jungles! They copulate at all times and in all places. They are really genital. They have so many children that they cannot even count them. Be careful, or they will flood us with little mulattoes.

Things are indeed going to hell....

The government and the civil service are at the mercy of the Jews.

Our women are at the mercy of the Negroes.

For the sexual potency of the Negro is hallucinating. That is indeed the word: This potency *must be* hallucinating. Psychoanalysts who study the problem soon enough find the mechanisms of every neurosis. Sexual anxiety is predominant here. All the Negrophobic women I have known had abnormal sex lives. Their husbands had left them; or they were widows and they were afraid to find a substitute for the dead husband; or they were divorced and they had doubts at the thought of a new object investment. All of them endowed the Negro with powers that other men (husband, transient lovers) did not have. And besides there was also an element of perversion, the persistence of infantile formations: God knows how they make love! It must be terrifying.[23]

There is one expression that through time has become singularly eroticized: the black athlete. There is something in the mere idea, one young woman confided to me, that makes the heart skip a beat. A prostitute told me that in her early days the mere thought of going to bed with a Negro brought on an orgasm. She went in search of Negroes and never asked them for money. But, she added, 'going to bed with them was no more remarkable than going to bed with white men. It was before I did it that I had the orgasm. I used to think about (imagine) all the things they might do to me: and that was what was so terrific.'

Still on the genital level, when a white man hates black men, is he not yielding to a feeling of impotence or of sexual inferiority? Since his ideal is an infinite virility, is there not a phenomenon of diminution in relation to the Negro, who is viewed as a penis symbol? Is the lynching of the Negro not a sexual revenge? We know how much of sexuality there is in all cruelties, tortures, beatings. One has only to re-read a few pages of the Marquis de Sade to be easily convinced of the fact. Is the Negro's superiority real? Everyone *knows* that it is not. But that is not what matters. The pre-logical thought of the phobic has decided that such is the case.[24] Another woman developed a Negrophobia after she had read *J'irai cracher sur vos tombes*. I tried to demonstrate the irrationality of her position by pointing out to her that victimized white women were as sick as the Negro. Besides, I added, this was no case of black vengeance, as the title of the book might seem to imply, because the author was a white man, Boris Vian. I had to accept the futility of all such efforts. That young woman did not want to listen. Anyone who has read the book will understand at once the ambivalence her phobia revealed. I knew a Negro medical student who would not dare to make a vaginal examination of any patient in the gynaecological clinic. He told me that one day he had heard one of them say, 'There's a nigger in there. If he touches me, I'll slap his face. You never know with them. He must have great big hands; and besides he's sure to be rough.'

If one wants to understand the racial situation psychoanalytically, not from a universal viewpoint but as it is experienced by individual consciousnesses, considerable importance must be given to sexual phenomena. In the case of the Jew, one thinks of money and its cognates. In that of the Negro, one thinks of sex. Anti-Semitism can be rationalized on a basic level. It is because he takes over the country that the Jew is a danger. An acquaintance told me recently that although he was not an anti-Semite he had been constrained to admit that the majority of Jews whom he had known during the war had behaved very badly. I tried in vain to get him to concede that such a statement was the fruit of a determined desire to find the essence of the Jew wherever it might exist.

On a clinical level, I am reminded of the story of the young woman who suffered from a kind of tactile delirium, constantly washing her hands and arms ever since the day a Jew had been introduced to her.

Jean-Paul Sartre has made a masterful study of the problem of anti-Semitism; let us try to determine what are the constituents of Negrophobia. This phobia is to be found on an instinctual, biological level. At the extreme, I should say that the Negro, because of his body, impedes the closing of the postural schema of the white man – at the point, naturally, at which the black man makes his entry into the phenomenal world of the white man. This is not the place in which to state the conclusions I drew from studying the influence exerted on the body by the appearance of another body. (Let us assume, for example, that four fifteen-year-old boys, all more or less athletic, are doing the high jump. One of them wins by jumping four feet ten inches. Then a fifth boy arrives and tops the mark by a half-inch. The four other bodies experience a destructuration.) What is important to us here is to show that with the Negro the cycle of the *biological* begins.[25]

No anti-Semite, for example, would ever conceive of the idea of castrating the Jew. He is killed or sterilized. But the Negro is castrated. The penis, the symbol of manhood, is annihilated, which is to say that it is denied. The difference between the two attitudes is apparent. The Jew is attacked in his religious identity, in his history, in his race, in his relations with his ancestors and with his posterity; when one sterilizes a Jew, one cuts off the source; every time that a Jew is persecuted, it is the whole race that is persecuted in his person. But it is in his corporeality that the Negro is attacked. It is as a concrete personality that he is lynched. It is as an actual being that he is a threat. The Jewish menace is replaced by the fear of the sexual potency of the Negro. O. Mannoni said:

An argument widely used by racialists against those who do not share their convictions is worthy of mention for its revealing character. 'What', they say, 'if you had a daughter, do you mean to say that you would marry her to a negro?' I have seen people who appeared to have no racialist bias lose all critical sense when confronted with this kind of question. The reason is that such an argument disturbs certain uneasy feelings in them (more exactly *incestuous* feelings) and they turn to racialism as a defence reaction.[26]

Before we go further, it seems important to make this point: granted that unconscious tendencies toward incest exist, why should these tendencies emerge more particularly with respect to the Negro? In what way, taken as an absolute, does a black son-in-law differ from a white son-in-law? Is there not a reaction of unconscious tendencies in both cases? Why not, for instance, conclude that the father revolts because in his opinion the Negro will introduce his daughter into a sexual universe for which the father does not have the key, the weapons, or the attributes?

Every intellectual gain requires a loss in sexual potential. The civilized white man retains an irrational longing for unusual eras of sexual license, of orgiastic scenes, of unpunished rapes, of unrepressed incest. In one way these fantasies respond to Freud's life instinct. Projecting his own desires onto the Negro, the white man behaves 'as if' the Negro really had them. When it is a question of the Jew, the problem is clear: He is suspect because he wants to own the wealth or take over the positions of power. But the Negro is fixated at the genital; or at any rate he has been fixated there. Two realms: the intellectual and the sexual. An erection on Rodin's *Thinker* is a shocking thought. One cannot decently 'have a hard on' everywhere. The Negro symbolizes the biological danger; the Jew, the intellectual danger.

To suffer from a phobia of Negroes is to be afraid of the biological. For the Negro is only biological. The Negroes are animals. They go about naked. And God alone knows.... Mannoni said further: 'In his urge to identify the anthropoid apes, Caliban, the Negroes, even the Jews with the mythological figures of the satyrs, man reveals that there are sensitive spots in the human soul at a level[27] where thought becomes confused and where sexual excitement is strangely linked with violence and aggressiveness.'[28] Mannoni includes the Jew in his scale. I see nothing inappropriate there. But here the Negro is the master. He is the specialist of this matter: Whoever says *rape* says *Negro*.

Over three or four years I questioned some 500 members of the white race – French, German, English, Italian. I took advantage of a certain air of trust, of relaxation; in each instance I waited until my subject no longer hesitated to talk to me quite openly – that is, until he was sure that he would not offend me. Or else, in the midst of associational tests, I inserted the word *Negro* among some twenty others. Almost 60 per cent of the replies took this form:

Negro brought forth biology, penis, strong athletic, potent, boxer, Joe Louis, Jesse Owens, Senegalese troops, savage, animal, devil, sin.

Senegalese soldier, used as the stimulus, evoked dreadful, bloody, tough, strong.

It is interesting to note that one in fifty reacted to the word *Negro* with *Nazi* or *SS*; when one knows the emotional meaning of the SS image, one recognizes that the difference from the other answers is negligible. Let me add that some Europeans helped me by giving the test to their acquaintances: in such cases the proportion went up notably. From this result one must acknowledge the effect of my being a Negro: unconsciously there was a certain reticence.

The Negro symbolizes the biological. First of all, he enters puberty at the age of nine and is a father at the age of ten; he is hot-blooded and his blood is strong; he is tough. As a white man remarked to me not long ago, with a certain bitterness: 'You all have strong constitutions.' What a beautiful race – look at the Senegalese.... Weren't they called *our Black Devils* during the war? ... But they must be brutal ... I just can't see them putting those big hands of theirs on my shoulders. I shudder at the mere thought of it. ... Well aware that in certain cases one must interpret by opposites, I understand this extra-fragile woman: at bottom what she wants most is to have the powerful Negro bruise her frail shoulders. Sartre says that when one speaks the phrase 'a young Jewess', there is an imaginary reek of rape and pillage.... Conversely, we might say that the expression 'a handsome Negro' contains a 'possible' allusion to similar phenomena. I have always been struck by the speed with which 'handsome young Negro' turns into 'young colt' or 'stallion'. In the film *Mourning Becomes Electra*, a good part of the plot is based on sexual rivalry. Orin rebukes his sister, Vinnie, because she admired the splendid naked natives of the South Seas. He cannot forgive her for it.[29]

Analysis of the real is always difficult. An investigator can choose between two attitudes toward his subject. First, he can be satisfied only to describe, in the manner of those anatomists who are all surprised when, in the midst of a description of the tibia, they are asked how many fibular depressions *they* have. That is because in their researches there is never a question of themselves but of others.

In the beginning of my medical studies, after several nauseating sessions in the dissection room, I asked an older hand how I could prevent such reactions. 'My friend, pretend you're dissecting a cat and everything will be all right....' Second, once he has described reality, the investigator can make up his mind to change it. In principle, however, the decision to describe seems naturally to imply a critical approach and therefore a need to go farther toward some solution. Both authorized and anecdotal literature have created too many stories about Negroes to be suppressed. But putting them all together does not help us in our real task, which is to disclose their mechanics. What matters for us is not to collect facts and behaviour, but to find their meaning. Here we can refer to Jaspers, when he wrote:

Comprehension in depth of a single instance will often enable us, phenomenologically, to apply this understanding in general to innumerable cases. Often what one has once grasped is soon met again. What is important in phenomenology is less the study of a large number of instances than the intuitive and deep understanding of a few individual cases.[30]

The question that arises is this: can the white man behave healthily toward the black man and can the black man behave healthily toward the white man?

A pseudo-question, some will say. But when we assert that European culture has an *imago* of the Negro which is responsible for all the conflicts that may arise, we do not go beyond reality. In the chapter on language we saw that on the screen the Negro faithfully reproduces that *imago*. Even serious writers have made themselves its spokesmen. So it was that Michel Cournot could write:

The black man's sword is a sword. When he has thrust it into your wife, she has really felt something. It is a revelation. In the chasm that it has left, your little toy is lost. Pump away until the room is awash with your sweat, you might as well just be singing. This is *good-bye*.... Four Negroes with their penises exposed would fill a cathedral. They would be unable to leave the building until their erections had subsided; and in such close quarters that would not be a simple matter.

To be comfortable without problems, they always have the open air. But then they are faced with a constant insult: the palm tree, the breadfruit tree and so many other proud growths that would not slacken for an empire, erect as they are for all eternity, and piercing heights that are not easily reached at any price.[31]

When one reads this passage a dozen times and lets oneself go – that is, when one abandons oneself to the movement of its images – one is no longer aware of the Negro but only of a penis; the Negro is eclipsed. He is turned into a penis. He *is* a penis. It is easy to imagine what such descriptions can stimulate in a young girl in Lyon. Horror? Lust? Not indifference, in any case. Now, what is the truth? The average length of the penis among the black men of Africa, Dr Palès says, rarely exceeds 120 millimetres (4.6244 inches). Testut, in his *Traité d'anatomie humaine*, offers the same figure for the European. But these are facts that persuade no one. The white man is convinced that the Negro is a beast; if it is not the length of the penis, then it is the sexual potency that impresses him. Face to face with this man who is 'different from himself', he needs to defend himself. In other words, to personify The Other. The Other will become the mainstay of his preoccupations and his desires.[32] The prostitute whom I mentioned earlier told me that her hunt for Negroes dated from the time when she had been told this story: one night a woman who was in bed with a Negro went mad; she remained insane for two years, but then, when she had been cured, refused to go to bed with anyone else. The prostitute did not know what had driven the other woman mad. But she sought furiously to reproduce the same situation, to discover this secret which was part of the ineffable. One must recognize that what she wanted was the destruction, the dissolution, of her being on a sexual level. Every experiment that she made with a Negro reinforced her limitations. This delirium of orgasm was unattainable. She could not experience it, so she avenged herself by losing herself in speculation.

One thing must be mentioned in this connection: a white woman who has had a Negro lover finds it difficult to return to white men. Or so at least it is believed, particularly by white men: 'Who knows what "they" can give a woman?' Who indeed does know? Certainly 'they' do not. On this subject I cannot overlook this comment by Etiemble:

Racial jealousy produces the crimes of racism: to many white men, the black is simply that marvellous sword which, once it has transfixed their wives, leaves them forever transfigured. My statistical sources have been able to provide me with no documentation on this point. I have, however, known some Negroes; some white women who have had Negroes; and, finally, some Negro women who have had white lovers. I have heard enough confidences from all of them to be able to deplore the fact that M. Cournot applies his talents to the rejuvenation of a fable in which the white man will always be able to find a specious argument: shameful, dubious and thus doubly effective.[33]

An endless task, the cataloguing of reality. We accumulate facts, we discuss them, but with every line that is written, with every statement that is made, one has the feeling of incompleteness. Attacking J.-P. Sartre, Gabriel d'Arbousier wrote:

This anthology, which puts Antilleans, Guianans, Senegalese and Malagasies on the same footing, creates a deplorable confusion. In this way it states the cultural problem of the overseas countries by detaching it from the historical and social reality of each of them, from the national characteristics and the varying conditions imposed on each of them by imperialist exploitation and oppression. Thus, when Sartre wrote, 'Simply by plunging into the depths of his memory as a former slave, the black man asserts that suffering is the lot of man and that it is no less undeserved on that account', did he take into consideration what that might mean for a Hova, a Moor, a Touareg, a Peul, or a Bantu of the Congo or the Ivory Coast?[34]

The objection is valid. It applies to me as well. In the beginning I wanted to confine myself to the Antilles. But, regardless of consequences, dialectic took the upper hand and I was compelled to *see* that the Antillean is first of all a Negro. Nevertheless, it would be impossible to overlook the fact that there are Negroes whose nationality is Belgian, French, English; there are also Negro republics. How can one claim to have got hold of an essential when such facts as these demand one's recognition? The truth is that the Negro race has been scattered, that it can no longer claim unity. When Il Duce's troops invaded Ethiopia, a movement of solidarity arose among men of colour. But, though one or two airplanes were sent from America to the invaded country, not a single black man made any practical move. The Negro has a country, he takes his place in a Union or a Commonwealth. Every description should be put on the level of the discrete phenomenon, but here again we are driven out to infinite perspectives. In the universal situation of the Negro there is an ambiguity, which is, however, resolved in his concrete existence. This in a way places him beside the Jew. Against all the arguments I have just cited, I come back to one fact: *wherever he goes, the Negro remains a Negro.*

In some countries the Negro has entered into the culture. As we have already indicated, it would be impossible to ascribe too much importance to the way in which white children establish contact with the reality of the Negro. In the United States, for example, even if he does not live in the South, where he naturally encounters Negroes concretely, the white child is introduced to them through the myth of Uncle Remus. (In France there is the parallel of *La Case de l'Oncle Tom – Uncle Tom's Cabin*.) Miss Sally's and Marse John's little boy listens with a mixture of fear and admiration to the tales of Br'er Rabbit. To Bernard Wolfe this ambivalence in the white man is the dominant factor in the white American psychology. Relying on the life of Joel Chandler Harris, Wolfe goes so far as to show that the admiration corresponds to a certain identification of the white man with the black. It is perfectly obvious what these stories are all about. Br'er Rabbit gets into conflicts with almost all the other animals in creation and naturally he is always the winner. These stories belong to the oral tradition of the plantation Negroes. Therefore it is relatively easy to recognize the Negro in his remarkably ironic and wary disguise as a rabbit. In order to protect themselves against their own unconscious masochism, which impels them to rapturous admiration of the (black) rabbit's prowess, the whites have tried to drain these stories of their aggressive potential. This is how they have been able to tell themselves that 'the black man makes all the animals behave *like a lower order of human intelligence, the kind that the Negro himself can understand. The black man naturally feels that he is in closer touch with the "lower animals" than with the white man, who is so far superior to him in every respect.*' Others have advanced the theory, with straight faces, that these stories are not reactions to the conditions imposed on the Negro in the United States but are simply *survivals of Africa.* Wolfe gives us the clue to such interpretations:

On the basis of all the evidence, Br'er Rabbit is an animal because the Negro must be an animal; the rabbit is an outlander because the Negro must be branded as an outlander down to his chromosomes. Ever since slavery began, his Christian and democratic guilt as a slave-owner has led the southerner to describe the Negro as an animal, an unchangeable African whose nature was determined as protoplasm by his 'African' genes. If the black man found himself relegated to the Limbo of mankind, he was the victim not of Americans but of the organic inferiority of his jungle ancestors.

So the southerner refused to see in these stories the aggression that the Negro infused into them. But, Wolfe says, their compiler, Harris, was a psychopath:

He was especially adept at this task because he was filled to the bursting point with pathological racial obsessions over and above those that tormented the South and, to a lesser degree, all of white America.... Indeed, for Harris as well as for many other white Americans, the Negro seemed to be in every respect the opposite of his own anxious self: unworried, gregarious, voluble, muscularly relaxed, never a victim of boredom, or passive, unashamedly exhibitionistic, devoid of self-pity in his condition of concentrated suffering, exuberant....

But Harris always had the feeling of being handicapped. Therefore Wolfe sees him as frustrated – but not after the classic schema: it was the very essence of the man that made it impossible for him to exist in the 'natural' way of the Negro. No one had barred him from it; it was just impossible for him. Not prohibited, but unrealizable. And it is because the white man feels himself frustrated by the Negro that he seeks in turn to frustrate the black, binding him with prohibitions of all kinds. And here again the white man is the victim of his unconscious. Let us listen again to Wolfe:

The Remus stories are a monument to the ambivalence of the South. Harris, the archetype of the southerner, went in search of the Negro's love and claimed that he had won it (the grin of Uncle Remus).[35] But at the same time he was striving for the Negro's hatred (Br'er Rabbit) and he revelled in it, in an unconscious orgy of masochism – very possibly punishing himself for not being the black man, the stereotype of the black man, the prodigious 'giver'. Is it not possible that the white South, and perhaps the majority of white America, often behave in the same way in their relations with the Negro?

There is a quest for the Negro, the Negro is in demand, one cannot get along without him, he is needed, but only if he is made palatable in a certain way. Unfortunately, the Negro knocks down the system and breaks the treaties. Will the white man rise in resistance? No, he will adjust to the situation. This fact, Wolfe says, explains why many books dealing with racial problems become best-sellers.[36]

Certainly no one is *compelled* to read stories of Negroes who make love to white women (*Deep are the Roots*, *Strange Fruit*, *Uncle Remus*), of whites who learn that they are Negroes (*Kingsblood Royal*, *Lost Boundaries*, *Uncle Remus*), of white men strangled by black men (*Native Son*, *If He Hollers Let Him Go*, *Uncle Remus*).... We can package the Negro's grin and market it on a grand scale in our popular culture as a cloak for this masochism: The caress sweetens the blow. And, as *Uncle Remus* shows, here the interplay of the races is in large part unconscious. The white man is no more aware of his masochism when he is being titillated by the subtle content of the stereotyped grin than the

Negro is aware of his sadism when he transforms the stereotype into a cultural bludgeon. Perhaps less.[37]

In the United States, as we can see, the Negro makes stories in which it becomes possible for him to work off his aggression; the white man's unconscious justifies this aggression and gives it worth by turning it on himself, thus reproducing the classic schema of masochism.[38]

We can now stake out a marker. For the majority of white men the Negro represents the sexual instinct (in its raw state). The Negro is the incarnation of a genital potency beyond all moralities and prohibitions. The women among the whites, by a genuine process of induction, invariably view the Negro as the keeper of the impalpable gate that opens into the realm of orgies, of bacchanals, of delirious sexual sensations.... We have shown that reality destroys all these beliefs. But they all rest on the level of the imagined, in any case on that of a paralogism. The white man who ascribes a malefic influence to the black is regressing on the intellectual level, since, as we have shown, his perception is based on a mental age of eight years (the comic books). Is there not a concurrent regression to and fixation at pregenital levels of sexual development? Self-castration? (The Negro is taken as a terrifying penis.) Passivity justifying itself by the recognition of the superiority of the black man in terms of sexual capacity? It is obvious what a variety of questions it would be interesting to raise. There are, for instance, men who go to 'houses' in order to be beaten by Negroes; passive homosexuals who insist on black partners.

Another solution might be this: there is first of all a sadistic aggression toward the black man, followed by a guilt complex because of the sanction against such behaviour by the democratic culture of the country in question. This aggression is then tolerated by the Negro: whence masochism. But, I shall be told, your schema is invalid: it does not contain the elements of classic masochism. Perhaps, indeed, this situation is not classic. In any event, it is the only way in which to explain the masochistic behaviour of the white man.

From a heuristic point of view, without attributing any reality to it, I should like to propose an explanation of the fantasy: *a Negro is raping me*. From the work of Helene Deutsch[39] and Marie Bonaparte,[40] both of whom took up and in a way carried to their ultimate conclusions Freud's ideas on female sexuality, we have learned that, alternatively clitoral and clitoral-vaginal and finally purely vaginal, a woman –

having retained, more or less commingled, her libido in a passive conception and her aggression, having surmounted her double Oedipus complex – proceeds through her biological and psychological growth and arrives at the assumption of her role, which is achieved by neuropsychic integration. We cannot, however, ignore certain failures or certain fixations.

Corresponding to the clitoral stage there is an active Oedipus complex, although, according to Marie Bonaparte, it is not a sequence but a coexistence of the active and the passive. The desexualization of aggression in a girl is less complete than in a boy.[41] The clitoris is perceived as a diminished penis, but, going beyond the concrete, the girl clings only to the quality. She apprehends reality in qualitative terms. In her, as in the little boy, there will be impulses directed at the mother; she too would like to disembowel the mother.

Our question, then, is whether, side by side with the final achievement of femininity, there is not some survival of this infantile fantasy. 'Too strong an aversion in a woman against the rough games of men is, furthermore, a suspicious indication of male protest and excessive bisexuality. It is possible that such a woman will be clitoral.'[42] Here is my own view of the matter. First the little girl sees a sibling rival beaten by the father, a libidinal aggressive. At this stage (between the ages of five and nine), the father, who is now the pole of her libido, refuses in a way to take up the aggression that the little girl's unconscious demands of him. At this point, lacking support, this free-floating aggression requires an investment. Since the girl is at the age in which the child begins to enter the folklore and the culture along roads that we know, the Negro becomes the predestined depository of this aggression. If we go farther into the labyrinth, we discover that when a woman lives the fantasy of rape by a Negro, it is in some way the fulfilment of a private dream, of an inner wish. Accomplishing the phenomenon of turning against self, it is the woman who rapes herself. We can find clear proof of this in the fact that it is commonplace for women, during the sexual act, to cry to their partners: 'Hurt me!' They are merely expressing this idea: hurt me as I would hurt me if I were in your place. The fantasy of rape by a Negro is a variation of this emotion: 'I wish the Negro would rip me open as I would have ripped a woman open.' Those who grant our conclusions on the psychosexuality of the white woman may ask what we have to say about the woman of colour.

I know nothing about her. What I can offer, at the very least, is that for many women in the Antilles – the type that I shall call the all-but-whites – the aggressor is symbolized by the Senegalese type, or in any event by an inferior (who is so considered).

The Negro is the genital. Is this the whole story? Unfortunately not. The Negro is something else. Here again we find the Jew. He and I may be separated by the sexual question, but we have one point in common. Both of us stand for Evil. The black man more so, for the good reason that he is black. Is not whiteness in symbols always ascribed in French to Justice, Truth, Virginity? I knew an Antillean who said of another Antillean, 'His body is black, his language is black, his soul must be black too.' This logic is put into daily practice by the white man. The black man is the symbol of Evil and Ugliness.

Henri Baruk, in a recent work on psychiatry,[43] described what he termed the anti-Semitic psychoses.

In one of my patients the vulgarity and the obscenity of his ravings transcended all that the French language could furnish and took the form of obvious pederastic[44] allusions with which the patient deflected his inner hatred in transferring it to the scapegoat of the Jews, calling for them to be slaughtered. Another patient, suffering from a fit of delirium aggravated by the events of 1940, had such violent anti-Semitic feelings that one day in a hotel, suspecting the man in the next room to be a Jew, he broke into his room during the night to murder him....

A third patient, with a physically weak constitution – he suffered from chronic colitis – was humiliated by his poor health and ultimately ascribed it to poisoning by means of a 'bacterial injection' given to him by one of the male nurses in an institution where he had been earlier – nurses who were anticlerical and Communists, he said, and who had wanted to punish him for his Catholic convictions and utterances. Now that he was in our hospital and safe from 'a crew of union men', he felt that he was between Scylla and Charybdis, since he was in the hands of a Jew. By definition this Jew could be only a thief, a monster, a man capable of any and all crimes.

Confronted by such a tide of aggression, this Jew will have to take a stand. Here is all the ambiguity that Sartre describes. Certain pages of *Anti-Semite and Jew* are the finest that I have ever read. The finest, because the problem discussed in them grips us in our guts.[45]

The Jew, authentic or inauthentic, is struck down by the fist of the *'salaud'*. His situation is such that everything he does is bound to turn against him. For naturally the Jew prefers himself, and it happens that he forgets his Jewishness, or hides it, hides himself from it. That is because he has then admitted the validity of the Aryan system. There are Good and Evil. Evil is Jewish. Everything Jewish is ugly. Let us no longer be Jews. I am no longer a Jew. Down with the Jews. In such circumstances, these are the most aggressive. Like that patient of Baruk who had a persecution complex and who, seeing the doctor one day wearing his yellow star, grabbed him by the lapel and shouted: 'I, sir, am a Frenchman.' Or this woman:

Making rounds in the ward of my colleague, Dr Daday, I encountered a Jewish patient who had been the target of taunts and insults from her fellow-patients. A non-Jewish patient had gone to her defence. The Jewish patient thereupon turned on the woman who had defended the Jews, hurling every possible anti-Semitic calumny at her and demanding that that Jewess be got rid of.[46]

This is a fine example of a reactional phenomenon. In order to react against anti-Semitism, the Jew turns himself into an anti-Semite. This is what Sartre presents in *The Reprieve*, in which Birnenschatz finally acts out his disavowal with an intensity that borders on delirium. We shall see that the word is not too strong. Americans who go to Paris are amazed to see so many white women accompanied by Negroes. In New York, Simone de Beauvoir went for a walk with Richard Wright and was rebuked in the street by an old lady. Sartre said: here it is the Jew, somewhere else it is the Negro. What is essential is a scapegoat. Baruk says nothing different: 'Release from hate complexes will be accomplished only if mankind learns to renounce the scapegoat complex.'

Fault, guilt, refusal of guilt, paranoia – one is back in homosexual territory. In sum, what others have described in the case of the Jew applies perfectly in that of the Negro.[47]

Good-Evil, Beauty-Ugliness, White-Black: such are the characteristic pairings of the phenomenon that, making use of an expression of Dide and Guiraud, we shall call 'manicheism delirium'.[48]

Seeing only one type of Negro, assimilating anti-Semitism to Negrophobia, these seem to be the errors of analysis being committed here. Someone to whom I was talking about this book asked me what I expected to come of it. Ever since Sartre's decisive essay, *What Is Literature?*, originally in *Situations II*, literature has been committed more and more to its sole really *contemporary* task, which is to persuade the group to progress to reflection and mediation: this book, it is hoped, will be a mirror with a progressive infrastructure, in which it will be possible to discern the Negro on the road to disalienation.

When there is no longer a 'human minimum', there is no culture. It matters very little to me to know that 'Muntu means Power' among the Bantu[49] – or at least it might have interested me if certain details had not held me back. What use are reflections on Bantu ontology when one reads elsewhere:

When 75,000 black miners went on strike in 1946, the state police forced them back to work by firing on them with rifles and charging with fixed bayonets. Twenty-five were killed and thousands were wounded.

At that time Smuts was the head of the government and a delegate to the Peace Conference. On farms owned by white men, the black labourers live almost like serfs. They may have their families with them, but no man is allowed to leave the farm without the permission of his master. If he does so, the police are notified and he is brought back by force and whipped....

Under the Act for Native Administration, the governor-general, as the supreme authority, has autocratic powers over the Africans. By proclamation he may arrest and detain any African deemed dangerous to public order. He may forbid meetings of more than ten persons in any native residential area. The writ of *habeas corpus* is not available to Africans. Mass arrests without warrants are made constantly.

The non-white populations of South Africa are at an impasse. All the modern modes of slavery make it impossible for them to flee from this scourge. In the case of the African especially, white society has smashed his old world without giving him a new one. It has destroyed the traditional tribal foundations of his existence and it blocks the road of the future after having closed the road of the past....

Apartheid aspires to banish the Negro from participating in modern history as a free and independent force.[50]

I apologize for this long quotation, but it permits me to bring out some possibilities of black men's mistakes. Alioune Diop, for example, in his introduction to *La Philosophie bantoue*, remarks that Bantu ontology knows nothing of the metaphysical misery of Europe. The inference that he draws from this is none the less dangerous:

The double question that arises is to determine whether the genius of the black man should cultivate what constitutes his individuality, that youth of spirit, that innate respect for man and creation, that joy in living, that peace which is not a disfigurement of man imposed and suffered through moral hygiene, but a natural harmony with the happy majesty of life.... One wonders too what the Negro can contribute to the modern world.... What we can say is that the very idea of culture conceived as a revolutionary will is as contrary to our genius as the very idea of progress. Progress would have haunted our consciousness only if we had grievances against life, which is a gift of nature.

Be careful! It is not a matter of finding Being in Bantu thought, when Bantu existence subsists on the level of non-being, of the imponderable.[51] It is quite true that Bantu philosophy is not going to open itself to understanding through a revolutionary will: but it is precisely in that degree in which Bantu society, being a closed society, does not contain that substitution of the exploiter for the ontological relations of Forces. Now we know that Bantu society no longer exists. And there is nothing ontological about segregation. Enough of this rubbish.

For some time there has been much talk about the Negro. A little too much. The Negro would like to be dropped, so that he may regroup his forces, his authentic forces.

One day he said: 'My negritude is neither a tower....'

And someone came along to Hellenize him, to make an Orpheus of him ... this Negro who is looking for the universal. He is looking for the universal! But in June, 1950, the hotels of Paris refused to rent rooms to Negro pilgrims. Why? Purely and simply because their Anglo-Saxon customers (who are rich and who, as everyone knows, hate Negroes) threatened to move out.

The Negro is aiming for the universal, but on the screen his Negro essence, his Negro 'nature', is kept intact:

> always a servant
> always obsequious and smiling
> me never steal, me never lie
> eternally 'sho' good eatin'....

The Negro is universalizing himself, but at the Lycée Saint-Louis, in Paris, one was thrown out: He had had the impudence to read Engels.

There is a drama there, and the black intellectuals are running the risk of being trapped by it.

What? I have barely opened eyes that had been blindfolded and someone already wants to drown me in the universal? What about the others? Those who 'have no voice', those who 'have no spokesman'. ... I need to lose myself in my negritude, to see the fires, the segregations, the repressions, the rapes, the discriminations, the boycotts. We need to put our fingers on every sore that mottles the black uniform.

One can already imagine Alioune Diop wondering what place the black genius will have in the universal chorus. It is my belief that a true culture cannot come to life under present conditions. It will be time enough to talk of the black genius when the man has regained his rightful place.

Once again I come back to Césaire; I wish that many black intellectuals would turn to him for their inspiration. I must repeat to myself too:

And more than anything, my body, as well as my soul, do not allow yourself to cross your arms like a sterile spectator, for life is not a spectacle, for a sea of sorrows is not a stage, for a man who cries out is not a dancing bear....

Continuing to take stock of reality, endeavouring to ascertain the instant of symbolic crystallization, I very naturally found myself on the threshold of Jungian psychology. European civilization is characterized by the presence, at the heart of what Jung calls the collective unconscious, of an archetype: an expression of the bad instincts, of the darkness inherent in every ego, of the uncivilized savage, the Negro who slumbers in every white man. And Jung claims to have found in uncivilized peoples the same psychic structure that his diagram portrays. Personally, I think that Jung has deceived himself. Moreover, all the peoples that he has known – whether the Pueblo Indians of Arizona or the Negroes of Kenya in British East Africa – have had more or less traumatic contacts with the white man. I said earlier that in his Salavinizations[52] the young Antillean is never black; and I have tried to show what this phenomenon corresponds to. Jung locates the collective unconscious in the inherited cerebral matter. But the collective unconscious, without our having to fall back on the genes, is purely and simply the sum of prejudices, myths, collective attitudes of a given group. It is taken for granted, to illustrate, that the Jews who have settled in Israel will produce in less than a hundred years a collective unconscious different from the ones that they had had before 1945 in the countries which they were forced to leave.

On the level of philosophic discussion, this would be the place to bring up the old problem of instinct and habit: instinct, which is inborn (we know how we must view this 'innateness') invariable, specific; habit, which is acquired. On this level one would have only to demonstrate that Jung has confused instinct and habit. In his view, in fact, the collective unconscious is bound up with the cerebral structure, the myths and archetypes are permanent engrams of the race. I hope I have shown that nothing of the sort is the case and that in fact the collective unconscious is cultural, which means acquired. Just as a young mountaineer of the Carpathians, under the physicochemical conditions of his country, is likely to develop a myxoedema, so a Negro like René Maran, who has lived in France and breathed and eaten the myths and prejudices of racist Europe, and assimilated the collective unconscious of that Europe, will be able, if he stands outside himself, to express only his hatred of the Negro. One must move softly, and there is a whole drama in having to lay bare, little by little, the workings of processes that are seen in their totality. Will this statement be susceptible of understanding? *In Europe, the black man is the symbol of Evil.* One must move softly, I know, but it is not easy. The torturer is the black man, Satan is black, one talks of shadows, when one is dirty one is black – whether one is thinking of physical dirtiness or of moral dirtiness. It would be astonishing, if the trouble were taken to bring them all together, to see the vast number of expressions that make the black man the equivalent of sin. In Europe, whether concretely or symbolically, the black man stands for the bad side of the character. As long as one cannot understand this fact, one is doomed to talk in circles about the 'black problem'. Blackness, darkness, shadow, shades, night, the labyrinths of the earth, abysmal depths, blacken someone's reputation; and, on the other side, the bright look of innocence, the white dove of peace, magical, heavenly light. A magnificent blond child – how much peace there is in that phrase, how much joy and, above all, how much hope! There is no comparison with a magnificent black child: literally, such a thing is unwonted. Just the same, I shall not go back into the stories of black angels. In Europe, that is to say, in every civilized and civilizing country, the Negro is the symbol of sin. The archetype of the lowest values is represented by the Negro. And it is exactly the same antinomy that is encountered in Desoille's *waking dreams.* How else is one to explain, for example, that the unconscious representing the base and inferior traits is coloured black? With Desoille, in whose work the situation is (without any intention of a pun) clearer, it is always a matter of descending or climbing. When I descend I see caverns, grottoes where savages dance. Let there be no mistake, above all. For example, in one of the waking-dream sessions that Desoille describes for us, we find Gauls in a cave. But, it must be pointed out, the Gaul is a simple fellow. A Gaul in a cave, it is almost like a family picture – a result, perhaps, of 'our ancestors, the Gauls'. I believe it is necessary to become a child again in order to grasp certain psychic realities. This is where Jung was an innovator: he wanted to go back to the childhood of the world, but he made a remarkable mistake; he went back only to the childhood of Europe.

In the remotest depth of the European unconscious an inordinately black hollow has been made in which the most moral impulses, the most shameful desires lie dormant. And as every man climbs up toward whiteness and light, the European has tried to repudiate this uncivilized self, which has attempted to defend itself. When European civilization came into contact with the black world, with those savage peoples, everyone agreed: those Negroes were the principle of evil.

Jung consistently identifies the foreign with the obscure, with the tendency to evil: he is perfectly right. This mechanism of projection – or, if one prefers, transference – has been described by classic psychoanalysis. In the degree to which I find in myself something unheard-of, something reprehensible, only one solution remains for me: to get rid of it, to ascribe its origin to someone else. In this way I eliminate a short circuit that threatens to destroy my equilibrium. One must be careful with waking dreams in the early sessions, because it is not good if the obscenity emerges too soon. The patient must come to understand the workings of sublimation before he makes any contact with the unconscious. If a Negro comes up in the first session, he must be removed at once; to that end, suggest a stairway or a rope to the patient, or propose that he let himself be carried off in a helicopter. Infallibly, the Negro will stay in his hole. In Europe the Negro has one function: that of symbolizing the lower emotions, the baser inclinations, the dark side of the soul. In the collective unconscious of *homo occidentalis*, the Negro – or, if one prefers, the colour black – symbolizes evil, sin, wretchedness, death, war, famine. All birds of prey are black. In Martinique, whose collective unconscious makes it a European country, when a 'blue' Negro – a coal-black one – comes to visit, one reacts at once: 'What bad luck is he bringing?'

The collective unconscious is not dependent on cerebral heredity; it is the result of what I shall call the unreflected imposition of a culture. Hence there is no reason to be surprised when an Antillean exposed to waking-dream therapy relives the same fantasies as a European. It is because the Antillean partakes of the same collective unconscious as the European.

If what has been said thus far is grasped, this conclusion may be stated: it is normal for the Antillean to be anti-Negro. Through the collective unconscious the Antillean has taken over all the archetypes belonging to the European. The *anima* of the Antillean Negro is almost always a white woman. In the same way, the *animus* of the Antilleans is always a white man. That is because in the works of

Anatole France, Balzac, Bazin, or any of the rest of 'our' novelists, there is never a word about an ethereal yet ever present black woman or about a dark Apollo with sparkling eyes.... But I too am guilty, here I am talking of Apollo! There is no help for it: I am a white man. For unconsciously I distrust what is black in me, that is, the whole of my being.

I am a Negro – but of course I do not know it, simply because I am one. When I am at home my mother sings me French love songs in which there is never a word about Negroes. When I disobey, when I make too much noise, I am told to 'Stop acting like a nigger.'

Somewhat later I read white books and little by little I take into myself the prejudices, the myths, the folklore that have come to me from Europe. But I will not accept them all, since certain prejudices do not apply in the Antilles. Anti-Semitism, for instance, does not exist there, for there are no Jews, or virtually none. Without turning to the idea of collective catharsis, it would be easy for me to show that, without thinking, the Negro selects himself as an object capable of carrying the burden of original sin. The white man chooses the black man for this function, and the black man who is white also chooses the black man. The black Antillean is the slave of this cultural imposition. After having been the slave of the white man, he enslaves himself. The Negro is in every sense of the word a victim of white civilization. It is not surprising that the artistic creations of Antillean poets bear no special watermark: these men are white. To come back to psycho-pathology, let us say that the Negro lives an ambiguity that is extraordinarily neurotic. At the age of twenty – at the time, that is, when the collective unconscious has been more or less lost, or is resistant at least to being raised to the conscious level – the Antillean recognizes that he is living an error. Why is that? Quite simply because – and this is very important – the Antillean has recognized himself as a Negro, but, by virtue of an ethical transit, he also feels (collective unconscious) that one is a Negro to the degree to which one is wicked, sloppy, malicious, instinctual. Everything that is the opposite of these Negro modes of behaviour is white. This must be recognized as the source of Negrophobia in the Antillean. In the collective unconscious, black = ugliness, sin, darkness, immorality. In other words, he is Negro who is immoral. If I order my life like that of a moral man, I simply am not a Negro. Whence the Martinican custom of saying of a worthless white man that he has 'a nigger soul'. Colour is nothing, I do not even notice it, I know only one thing, which is the purity of my conscience and the whiteness of my soul. 'Me white like snow', the other said.

Cultural imposition is easily accomplished in Martinique. The ethical transit encounters no obstacle. But the real white man is waiting for me. As soon as possible he will tell me that it is not enough to try to be white, but that a white totality must be achieved. It is only then that I shall recognize the betrayal. – Let us conclude. An Antillean is made white by the collective unconscious, by a large part of his individual unconscious, and by the virtual totality of his mechanism of individuation. The colour of his skin, of which there is no mention in Jung, is black. All the inabilities to understand are born of this blunder.

While he was in France, studying for his degree in literature, Césaire 'discovered his cowardice'. He knew that it was cowardice, but he could never say why. He felt that it was ridiculous, idiotic, I might say even unhealthy, but in none of his writings can one trace the mechanism of that cowardice. That is because what was necessary was to shatter the current situation and to try to apprehend reality with the soul of a child. The Negro in the streetcar was funny and ugly. Certainly Césaire laughed at him. That was because there was nothing in common between himself and this authentic Negro. A handsome Negro is introduced to a group of white Frenchmen. If it is a group of intellectuals, we can be sure that the Negro will try to assert himself. He will insist that attention be paid not to the colour of his skin but to the force of his intellect. There are many people in Martinique who at the age of twenty or thirty begin to steep themselves in Montesquieu or Claudel for the sole purpose of being able to quote them. That is because, through their knowledge of these writers, they expect their colour to be forgotten.

Moral consciousness implies a kind of scission, a fracture of consciousness into a bright part and an opposing black part. In order to achieve morality, it is essential that the black, the dark, the Negro vanish from consciousness. Hence a Negro is forever in combat with his own image.

If in like manner one allows M. Hesnard his scientific conception of the moral life, and if the world of moral sickness is to be understood by starting from Fault and Guilt, a normal person will be one who has freed himself of this guilt, or who in any case has managed not to submit to it. More directly, each individual has to charge the blame for his baser drives, his impulses, to the account of an evil genius, which is that of the culture to which he belongs (we have seen that this is the Negro). This collective guilt is borne by what is conventionally called the scapegoat. Now the scapegoat for white society – which is based on myths of progress, civilization, liberalism, education, enlightenment, refinement – will be precisely the force that opposes the expansion and the triumph of these myths. This brutal opposing force is supplied by the Negro.

In the society of the Antilles, where the myths are identical with those of the society of Dijon or Nice, the young Negro, identifying himself with the civilizing power, will make the nigger the scapegoat of his moral life.

I was fourteen years old when I began to understand the meaning of what I now call cultural imposition. I had an acquaintance, now dead, whose father, an Italian, had married a Martinican. This man had lived in Fort-de-France for more than twenty years. He was considered an Antillean, but, underneath, his origin was always remembered. Now, in France, from a military point of view, an Italian is despised; one Frenchmen is the equal of ten Italians; the Italians have no guts.... My acquaintance had been born in Martinique and he associated only with Martinicans. On the day Montgomery routed the Italian army at Bengazi, I wanted to mark the Allies' victory on my map. Measuring the substantial advance of the lines, I could not help exulting: 'We really murdered them!' My acquaintance, who was not unaware of his father's origin, was extremely embarrassed. For that matter, so was I. Both of us were victims of a cultural imposition. I am convinced that anyone who has grasped this phenomenon and all its consequences will know exactly in what direction to look for the solution. Listen to the Rebel of Césaire:

It is rising ... it is rising from the depths of the earth ... the black tide is rising ... waves of cries ... bogs of animal odours ... the raging storm of naked feet ... and the paths of the cliffs are teeming with more, they clamber down the sides of ravines where obscene savage torrents pour impregnation into chaotic rivers, seas of corruption, oceans in convulsion, amid a black laughter of knives and bad alcohol....

Do you understand? Césaire has *come down*. He is ready to see what is happening at the very depths, and he can go up. He is ripe for the dawn. But he does not leave the black man down there. He lifts him to his own shoulders and raises him to the clouds. Earlier, in *Cahier d'un retour au pays natal*, he had prepared us. What he has chosen is, to use the expression of Gaston Bachelard,[53] a psyche of ascent:

and for this, O lord with white teeth, men
with fragile necks
receive and collect fatal calm triangular
and for me my dances
my bad-nigger dances
for me my dances
break-the-yoke dance
jail-break dance
it-is-fine-and-good-and-right-to-be-a-Negro dance
For me my dances and let the sun bounce off the racket
        of my hands
no the unjust sun is no longer enough for me
twist yourself, wind, round my new growth
touch my spaced fingers
I give you my conscience and its rhythm of flesh
I give you the flames that char my weakness
I give you the chain-gang
I give you the swamp
I give you the Intourist with the three-cornered journey
devour wind
I give you my rugged lips
devour and twist yourself
and twisting clasp me in a greater shiver
embrace me into the fury of us
embrace, embrace US
but biting us as well
into the blood of our blood bitten
embrace, my purity has no bond but your
purity
but then embrace
like a field of measured *filaos*
the evening
our many-coloured purities
and bind, bind me without remorse
bind me with your great arms to the glowing clay
bind my black vibration to the very navel
of the world
bind, bind me bitter brotherhood
then, strangling me with your lasso of stars
rise, Dove
rise

rise
rise
I follow you who are imprinted on my ancestral
white cornea
rise glutton of the sky
and the vast black hole where I wanted to drown myself
the other moon
there now I want to haul out the evil tongue
of the night in its moveless glaze![54]

One can understand why Sartre views the adoption of a Marxist position by black poets as the logical conclusion of Negrohood. In effect, what happens is this: as I begin to recognize that the Negro is the symbol of sin, I catch myself hating the Negro. But then I recognize that I am a Negro. There are two ways out of this conflict. Either I ask others to pay no attention to my skin, or else I want them to be aware of it. I try then to find value for what is bad – since I have unthinkingly conceded that the black man is the colour of evil. In order to terminate this neurotic situation, in which I am compelled to choose an unhealthy, conflictual solution, fed on fantasies, hostile, inhuman in short, I have only one solution: to rise above this absurd drama that others have staged round me, to reject the two terms that are equally unacceptable, and, through one human being, to reach out for the universal. When the Negro dives – in other words, goes under – something remarkable occurs.

Listen again to Césaire:

Ho ho
Their power is well anchored
Gained
Needed
My hands bathe in bright heather
In swamps of annatto trees
My gourd is heavy with stars
But I am weak. Oh I am weak.
Help me.
And here I am on the edge of metamorphosis
Drowned blinded
Frightened of myself, terrified of myself
Of the gods ... you are no gods. I am free.
THE REBEL: I have a pact with this night, for twenty years
I have heard it calling softly for me....[55]

Having again discovered that night, which is to say the sense of his identity, Césaire learned first of all that 'it is no use painting the foot of the tree white, the strength of the bark cries out from beneath the paint....'

Then, once he had laid bare the white man in himself, he killed him:

We broke down the doors. The master's room was wide open. The master's room was brilliantly lighted, and the master was there, quite calm ... and we stopped.... He was the master.... I entered. 'It is you', he said to me, quite calmly.... It was I. It was indeed I, I told him, the good slave, the faithful slave, the slavish slave, and suddenly his eyes were two frightened cockroaches on a rainy day ... I struck, the blood flowed: That is the only *baptism* that I remember today.[56]

'After an unexpected and salutary internal revolution, he now paid tribute to his own revolting ugliness.'[57]

What more is there to add? After having driven himself to the limit of self-destruction, the Negro is about to leap, whether deliberately or impetuously, into the 'black hole' from which will come 'the great Negro cry with such force that the pillars of the world will be shaken by it'.

The European knows and he does not know. On the level of reflection, a Negro is a Negro; but in the unconscious there is the firmly fixed image of the nigger-savage. I could give not a dozen but a thousand illustrations. Georges Mounin said in *Présence Africaine*: 'I had the good luck not to discover the Negroes through Lévy-Bruhl's *Mentalité primitive* read in a sociology course; more broadly, I had the good luck to discover the Negroes otherwise than through books – and I am grateful for it every day....'[58]

Mounin, whom it would be impossible to take for an average Frenchman, added, and thus rose inestimably in my opinion:

I profited perhaps by learning, at an age when one's mind has not yet been prejudiced, that Negroes are men like ourselves.... I as a white man thus gained, perhaps, the possibility of always being natural with a Negro – and never, in his presence, to fall stupidly and imperceptibly into that attitude of ethnographic investigator that is still too often our unbearable manner of *putting them in their place....*

In the same issue of *Présence Africaine*, Émile Dermenghem, who cannot be accused of Negrophobia, said:

One of my childhood memories is of a visit to the World's Fair of 1900, during which my chief enthusiasm was to see a Negro. My imagination had naturally been stimulated by my reading: *Capitaine de quinze ans* (A Captain at Fifteen), *Les Aventures de Robert* (Robert's Adventures), *Les Voyages de Livingstone* (Livingstone's Travels).

Dermenghem tells us that this was the manifestation of his taste for the exotic. While I may be prepared to put my two hands into his and believe the Dermenghem who wrote the article, I ask his permission to entertain doubts about the Dermenghem of the 1900 Fair.

I should be annoyed with myself if I were simply picking up old subjects that had been worked dry for fifty years. To write about the chances for Negro friendship is an unselfish undertaking, but unfortunately the Negrophobes and the other princes consort are impregnable to unselfishness. When we read, 'The Negro is a savage, and to lead savages there is only one method: a kick in the butt', we sit at our desks and we like to think that 'all such idiocies will have to die out'. But everyone is in agreement on that. To quote *Présence Africaine* (No. 5) again, Jacques Howlett wrote there:

Two things, furthermore, it seems, contributed to the aversion toward the Negro in the world of the other, which are impossible for me to comprehend: the colour of his skin and his nakedness, for I pictured the Negro naked. Certainly, superficial factors (although one cannot be sure to what extent they continue to haunt our new ideas and our altered conceptions) could sometimes mask that remote black and naked being, almost nonexistent; such as the nice Negro with the red army tarboosh and the infinite Fernandel-like grin, the symbol of some chocolate confection; or the brave Senegalese *pioupiou*, 'a slave to his orders', a Don Quixote without glory, 'a good-fellow hero' with all that stems from the 'epic of empire'; or the Negro 'waiting for salvation', the 'submissive child' of a bearded missionary.

Farther on, Jacques Howlett tells us that as a reaction he made the Negro his symbol of innocence. He tells us the reason why, but we have to remember that he was no longer eight years old, for he speaks of 'a bad conscience about sexuality' and about 'solipsism'. I am convinced, however, as far as that 'innocence for a grown man' is concerned, that Jacques Howlett has left it far, far behind him.

Beyond all question the most interesting testimony is presented by Michel Salomon. Although he defends himself against the charge, he stinks of racism. He is a Jew, he has a 'millennial experience of anti-Semitism', and yet he is a racist. Listen to him:

But to say that the mere fact of his skin, of his hair, of that aura of sensuality that he [the Negro] gives off, does not spontaneously give rise to a certain embarrassment, whether of attraction or of revulsion, is to reject the facts in the name of a ridiculous prudery that has never solved anything....

Later he goes to the extreme of telling us about the 'prodigious vitality of the black man'.

M. Salomon's study informs us that he is a physician. He should be wary of those literary points of view that are unscientific. The Japanese and the Chinese are ten times more prolific than the Negro: does that make them sensual? And in addition, M. Salomon, I have a confession to make to you: I have never been able, without revulsion, to hear a *man* say of another man: 'He is so sensual!' I do not know what the sensuality of a man is. Imagine a woman saying of another woman: 'She's so terribly desirable – she's darling....' The Negro, M. Salomon, gives off no aura of sensuality either through his skin or through his hair. It is just that over a series of long days and long nights the image of the biological-sexual-sensual-genital-nigger has imposed itself on you and you do not know how to get free of it. The *eye* is not merely a mirror, but a correcting mirror. The *eye* should make it possible for us to correct cultural errors. I do not say the *eyes*, I say the *eye*, and there is no mystery about what that eye refers to; not to the crevice in the skull but to that very uniform light that wells out of the reds of Van Gogh, that glides through a concerto of Tchaikovsky, that fastens itself desperately to Schiller's *Ode to Joy*, that allows itself to be conveyed by the worm-ridden bawling of Césaire.

The Negro problem does not resolve itself into the problem of Negroes living among white men but rather of Negroes exploited, enslaved, despised by a colonialist, capitalist society that is only accidentally white. You wonder, M. Salomon, what you would do 'if you had 800,000 Negroes in France'; because for you there is a problem, the problem of the increase of Negroes, the problem of the Black Peril. The Martinican is a Frenchman, he wants to remain part of the French Union; he asks only one thing, he wants the idiots and the exploiters to give him the chance to live like a human being. I can imagine myself lost, submerged in a white flood composed of men like Sartre or Aragon, I should like nothing better. You say, M. Salomon, that there is nothing to be gained by caution, and I share your view. But I do not feel that I should be abandoning my personality by marrying a European, whoever she might be; I can tell you that I am making no 'fool's bargains'. If my children are suspected, if the crescents of their fingernails are inspected, it will be simply because society will not have changed, because, as you so well put it, society will have kept its mythology intact. For my part, I refuse to consider the problem from the standpoint of *either-or*....

What is all this talk of a black people, of a Negro nationality? I am a Frenchman. I am interested in French culture, French civilization, the French people. We refuse to be considered 'outsiders', we have full part in the French drama. When men who were not basically bad, only deluded, invaded France in order to subjugate her, my position as a Frenchman made it plain to me that my place was not outside but in the very heart of the problem. I am personally interested in the future of France, in French values, in the French nation. What have I to do with a black empire?

Georges Mounin, Dermenghem, Howlett, Salomon have all tried to find answers to the question of the origin of the myth of the Negro. All of them have convinced us of one thing. It is that an authentic grasp of the reality of the Negro could be achieved only to the detriment of the cultural crystallization.

Recently, in a children's paper, I read a caption to a picture in which a young black Boy Scout was showing a Negro village to three or four white scouts: 'This is the kettle where my ancestors cooked yours.' One will gladly concede that there are no more Negro cannibals, but we should not allow ourselves to forget.... Quite seriously, however, I think that the writer of that caption has done a genuine service to Negroes without knowing it. For the white child who reads it will not form a mental picture of the Negro in the act of eating the white man, but rather as having eaten him. Unquestionably, this is progress.

Before concluding this chapter, I should like to abstract a case study, for access to which I must thank the medical director of the women's division of the psychiatric hospital of Saint-Ylie. The case clarifies the point of view that I am defending here. It proves that, at its extreme, the myth of the Negro, the idea of the Negro, can become the decisive factor of an authentic alienation.

Mlle B. was nineteen years old when she entered the hospital in March. Her admission sheet reads:

The undersigned, Dr P., formerly on the staff of the Hospitals of Paris, certifies that he has examined Mlle B., who is afflicted with a nervous disease consisting of periods of agitation, motor instability, tics and spasms which are conscious but which she cannot control. These symptoms have been increasing and prevent her from leading a normal social life. Her commitment for observation is required under the provisions laid down by the law of 1838 regarding voluntary commitments.

Twenty-four hours later the chief physician found these facts:

Afflicted with neurotic tics that began at the age of ten and became aggravated at the onset of puberty, and further when she began going to work away from home. Intermittent depressions with anxiety, accompanied by a recrudescence of these symptoms. Obesity. Requests treatment. Feels reassured in company. Assigned to an open ward. Should remain institutionalized.

Her immediate family had no history of pathological manifestations. Puberty occurred at the age of sixteen. A physical examination showed nothing except adiposity and a minimal epidermal indication of a slight endocrine insufficiency. Her menstrual periods were regular.

An interview made it possible to isolate these details: 'It's especially when I'm working that the tics come.' (The patient was working at a job that entailed her living away from home.) The tics affected the eyes and the forehead; she panted and yelped. She slept quite well, without nightmares, and ate well. She was not out of sorts during menstruation. When she went to bed, the facial tics were constant until she fell asleep.

The observations of the ward nurse:

It is worst when she is alone. When she is talking with others, or is merely with them, it is less noticeable. The tic depends on what she is doing. She begins by tapping both her feet and then goes on to raise her feet, her legs, her arms, her shoulders symmetrically.

She uttered sounds. It was never possible to understand what she was saying. This manifestation ended in quite loud, inarticulate cries. As soon as she was spoken to, these stopped.

The psychiatrist in charge decided to employ waking-dream therapy. A preliminary interview had brought out the existence of hallucinations in the form of terrifying circles and the patient had been asked to describe them. Here is an excerpt from the notes on the first session:

Deep and concentric, the circles expanded and contracted to the rhythm of a Negro tom-tom. This tom-tom made the patient think of the danger of losing her parents, especially her mother.

I then asked her to make the sign of the cross over these circles, but they did not disappear. I told her to take a cloth and rub them out, and they vanished.

She turned in the direction of the tom-tom. She was surrounded by half-naked men and women dancing in a frightening way. I told her not to be afraid to join the dance. She did so. Immediately the appearance of the dancers changed. It was a splendid party. The men and women were well dressed and they were dancing a waltz, *The Snow Star*.

I told her to go closer to the circles; she could no longer see them. I told her to think of them; they appeared, but they were broken. I told her to go in through the opening. 'I'm not completely surrounded any more', she said spontaneously, 'I can get out again.' The circle broke into two pieces and then into several. Soon there were only two pieces, and then they disappeared. There were frequent throat and eye tics while she was talking.

A succession of such sessions will bring about the sedation of the motor disturbance.

Here are notes on another session:

I told her to bring back the circles. She could not see them at first; then they came. They were broken. She entered them. They broke, rose again, then gently, one after another, fell away into the void. I told her to listen to the tom-tom. She did not hear it. She called to it. She heard it on the left.

I suggested to her that an angel would go with her to the tom-tom: she wanted to go all alone. But someone was coming down from the sky. It was an angel. He was smiling; he took her close to the tom-tom. There were only black men there, and they were dancing round a large fire and looked evil. The angel asked her what they were going to do; she said they were going to burn a white man. She looked for him everywhere. She could not see him.

'Ah, I see him! He's a white man about fifty years old. He's half undressed.'

The angel began to negotiate with the black chief (for she was afraid). The black chief said that this white man was not from their country and so they were going to burn him. But he had done nothing wrong.

They set him free and went back to their dancing, joyfully. She refused to take part in the dance.

I sent her to talk to the chief. He was dancing alone. The white man had disappeared. She wanted to go away and seemed to have no desire to know the Negroes. She wanted to go away with her angel, somewhere where she would really be at home, with her mother, her brothers and her sisters.

When the tics had ceased, the treatment was dropped. A few days later the patient was seen again because she had had a relapse. These are the notes of that session:

The circles kept coming closer. She hit them with a stick. They broke into fragments. The stick was a magic wand. It changed these bits of iron into something shining and beautiful.

She turned toward a fire. It was the fire round which the Negroes were dancing. She wanted to know the chief, and she approached him.

One Negro who had stopped dancing started again, but in a new rhythm. She danced round the fire and let the Negroes take her hands.

These sessions have clearly improved her condition. She writes to her parents, receives visits, goes to the film showings in the hospital. She takes part in group games. Now, when some other patient plays a waltz on the piano in the day rooms, this patient asks others to dance with her. She is popular and respected among the other patients.

I take this passage from the notes of another session:

She began to think about the circles again. Each was broken into a single piece, on the right of which something was missing. The smaller circles remained intact. She wanted to break them. She took them in her hands and bent them, and then they broke. One, however, was still left. She went through it. On the other side she found she was in darkness. But she was not afraid. She called someone and her guardian angel came down, friendly and smiling. He led her to the right, back into the daylight.

In this case, the waking-dream therapy produced appreciable results. But as soon as the patient was once more *alone* the tics returned.

I do not want to elaborate on the infrastructure of this psychoneurosis. The questions put by the chief psychiatrist had brought out a fear of imaginary Negroes – a fear first experienced at the age of twelve.

I had a great many talks with this patient. When she was ten or twelve years old, her father, 'an old-timer in the Colonial Service', liked to listen to programmes of Negro music. The tom-tom echoed through their house every evening, long after she had gone to bed. Besides, as we have pointed out, it is at this age that the savage-cannibal-Negro makes his appearance. The connection was easily discernible.

In addition, her brothers and sisters, who had discovered her weak point, amused themselves by scaring her. Lying in bed and hearing the tom-toms, she virtually *saw* Negroes. She fled under the covers, trembling. Then smaller and smaller circles appeared, blurring the Negroes. These circles are easily recognizable as a kind of defence mechanism against her hallucinosis. Later, the circles appeared without the Negroes – the defence mechanism had taken over without reference to what had brought it on.

I talked with the girl's mother, who corroborated what the patient had said. The girl was very emotional and, at the age of twelve, she had often been observed to tremble in her bed. My presence on her ward made no perceptible difference in her mental state. By now it was the circles *alone* that produced the motor reactions: outcries, facial tics, random gesticulation.

Even when one concedes a constitutional factor here, it is clear that her alienation is the result of a fear of the Negro, a fear aggravated by determining circumstances. Although the patient had made considerable progress, it was doubtful whether she would soon be able to resume a normal life in society.

6
Algeria Unveiled

The way people clothe themselves, together with the traditions of dress and finery that custom implies, constitutes the most distinctive form of a society's uniqueness, that is to say the one that is the most immediately perceptible. Within the general pattern of a given costume, there are of course always modifications of detail, innovations which in highly developed societies are the mark of fashion. But the effect as a whole remains homogeneous and great areas of civilization, immense cultural regions, can be grouped together on the basis of original, specific techniques of men's and women's dress.

It is by their apparel that types of society first become known, whether through written accounts and photographic records or motion pictures. Thus, there are civilizations without neckties, civilizations with loin-cloths, and others without hats. The fact of belonging to a given cultural group is usually revealed by clothing traditions. In the Arab world, for example, the veil worn by women is at once noticed by the tourist. One may remain for a long time unaware of the fact that a Moslem does not eat pork or that he denies himself daily sexual relations during the month of Ramadan, but the veil worn by the women appears with such constancy that it generally suffices to characterize Arab society.

In the Arab Maghreb, the veil belongs to the clothing traditions of the Tunisian, Algerian, Moroccan and Libyan national societies. For the tourist and the foreigner, the veil demarcates both Algerian society and its feminine component.[1] In the case of the Algerian man, on the other hand, regional modifications can be noted: the *fez* in urban centres, turbans and *djellabas*[2] in the countryside. The masculine garb allows a certain margin of choice, a modicum of heterogeneity. The woman seen in her white veil unifies the perception that one has of Algerian feminine society. Obviously what we have here is a uniform that tolerates no modification, no variant.[3]

The *haïk*[4] very clearly demarcates the Algerian colonized society. It is of course possible to remain hesitant before a little girl, but all uncertainty vanishes at the time of puberty. With the veil, things become well-defined and ordered. The Algerian woman, in the eyes of the observer, is unmistakably 'she who hides behind a veil'.

We shall see that this veil, one of the elements of the traditional Algerian garb, was to become the bone of contention in a grandiose battle, on account of which the occupation forces were to mobilize their most powerful and most varied resources, and in the course of which the colonized were to display a surprising force of inertia. Taken as a whole, colonial society, with its values, its areas of strength and its philosophy, reacts to the veil in a rather homogeneous way. The decisive battle was launched before 1954, more precisely during the early 1930s. The officials of the French administration in Algeria, committed to destroying the people's originality and under instructions to bring about the disintegration, at whatever cost, of forms of existence likely to evoke a national reality directly or indirectly, were to concentrate their efforts on the wearing of the veil, which was looked upon at this juncture as a symbol of the status of the Algerian woman. Such a position is not the consequence of a chance intuition. It is on the basis of the analyses of sociologists and ethnologists that the specialists in so-called native affairs and the heads of the Arab Bureaux coordinated their work. At an initial stage, there was a pure and simple adoption of the well-known formula, 'Let's win over the women and the rest will follow.' This definition of policy merely gave a scientific coloration to the 'discoveries' of the sociologists.[5]

Beneath the patrilineal pattern of Algerian society, the specialists described a structure of matrilineal essence. Arab society has often been presented by Westerners as a formal society in which outside appearances are paramount. The Algerian woman, an intermediary between obscure forces and the group, appeared in this perspective to assume a primordial importance. Behind the visible, manifest patriarchy, the more significant existence of a basic matriarchy was affirmed. The role of the Algerian mother, that of the grandmother, the aunt and the 'old woman', were inventoried and defined.

This enabled the colonial administration to define a precise political doctrine: 'If we want to destroy the structure of Algerian society, its capacity for resistance, we must first of all conquer the women; we must go and find them behind the veil where they hide themselves and in the houses where the men keep them out of sight.' It is the situation of woman that was accordingly taken as the theme of action. The dominant administration solemnly undertook to defend this woman, pictured as humiliated, sequestered, cloistered.... It described the immense possibilities of woman, unfortunately transformed by the Algerian man into an inert, demonetized, indeed dehumanized object. The behaviour of the Algerian was very firmly denounced and described as medieval and barbaric. With infinite science, a blanket indictment against the 'sadistic and vampirish' Algerian attitude toward women was prepared and drawn up. Around the family life of the Algerian, the occupier piled up a whole mass of judgements, appraisals, reasons, accumulated anecdotes and edifying examples, thus attempting to confine the Algerian within a circle of guilt.

Mutual aid societies and societies to promote solidarity with Algerian women sprang up in great number. Lamentations were organized. 'We want to make the Algerian ashamed of the fate that he metes out to women.' This was a period of effervescence, of putting into application a whole technique of infiltration, in the course of which droves of social workers and women directing charitable works descended on the Arab quarters.

The indigent and famished women were the first to be besieged. Every kilo of semolina distributed was accompanied by a dose of indignation against the veil and the cloister. The indignation was followed up by practical advice. Algerian women were invited to play 'a functional, capital role' in the transformation of their lot. They were pressed to say no to a centuries-old subjection. The immense role they were called upon to play was described to them. The colonial administration invested great sums in this combat. After it had been posited that the woman constituted the pivot of Algerian society, all efforts were made to obtain control over her. The Algerian, it was assured, would not stir, would resist the task of cultural destruction undertaken by the occupier, would oppose assimilation, so long as his woman had not reversed the stream. In the colonialist programme, it was the woman who was given the historic mission of shaking up the Algerian man. Converting the woman, winning her over to the foreign values, wrenching her free from her status, was at the same time achieving a real power over the man and attaining a practical, effective means of destructuring Algerian culture.

Still today, in 1959, the dream of a total domestication of Algerian society by means of 'unveiled women aiding and sheltering the occupier' continues to haunt the colonial authorities.[6]

The Algerian men, for their part, are a target of criticism for their European comrades, or more officially for their bosses. There is not a European worker who does not sooner or later, in the give and take of relations on the job site, the shop or the office, ask the Algerian the ritual questions: 'Does your wife wear the veil? Why don't you take your wife to the movies, to the fights, to the café?'

European bosses do not limit themselves to the disingenuous query or the glancing invitation. They use 'Indian cunning' to corner the Algerian and push him to painful decisions. In connection with a holiday – Christmas or New Year, or simply a social occasion with the firm – the boss will invite *the Algerian employee and his wife.* The invitation is not a collective one. Every Algerian is called in to the director's office and invited by name to come with 'your little family'. 'The firm being one big family, it would be unseemly for some to come without their wives, you understand? ...' Before this formal summons, the Algerian sometimes experiences moments of difficulty. If he comes with his wife, it means admitting defeat; it means 'prostituting his wife', exhibiting her, abandoning a mode of resistance. On the other hand, going alone means refusing to give satisfaction to the boss; it means running the risk of being out of a job. The study of a case chosen at random – a description of the traps set by the European in order to bring the Algerian to expose himself, to declare: 'My wife wears a veil, she shall not go out,' or else to betray: 'Since you want to see her, here she is' – would bring out the sadistic and perverse character of these contacts and relationships and would show in microcosm the tragedy of the colonial situation on the psychological level, the way the two systems directly confront each other, the epic of the colonized society, with its specific ways of existing, in the face of the colonialist hydra.

With the Algerian intellectual, the aggressiveness appears in its full intensity. The *fellah,* 'the passive slave of a rigidly structured group', is looked upon with a certain indulgence by the conqueror.[7] The lawyer and the doctor, on the other hand, are severely frowned upon. These intellectuals, who keep their wives in a state of semi-slavery, are literally pointed to with an accusing finger. Colonial society blazes up vehemently against this inferior status of the Algerian woman. Its members worry and show concern for those unfortunate women, doomed 'to produce brats', kept behind walls, banned.

Before the Algerian intellectual, racialist arguments spring forth with special readiness. For all that he is a doctor, people will say, he still remains an Arab. 'You can't get away from nature.' Illustrations of this kind of race prejudice can be multiplied indefinitely. Clearly, the intellectual is reproached for limiting the extension of learned Western habits, for not playing his role as an active agent of upheaval of the colonized society, for not giving his wife the benefit of the privileges of a more worthy and meaningful life.... In the large population centres it is altogether commonplace to hear a European confess acidly that he has never seen the wife of an Algerian he has known for twenty years. At a more diffuse, but highly revealing, level of apprehension, we find the bitter observation that 'we work in vain' ... that 'Islam holds its prey.'

The method of presenting the Algerian as a prey fought over with equal ferocity by Islam and France with its Western culture reveals the whole approach of the occupier, his philosophy and his policy. This expression indicates that the occupier, smarting from his failures, presents in a simplified and pejorative way the system of values by means of which the colonized person resists his innumerable offensives. What is in fact the assertion of a distinct identity, concern with keeping intact a few shreds of national existence, is attributed to religious, magical, fanatical behaviour.

This rejection of the conqueror assumes original forms, according to circumstances or to the type of colonial situation. On the whole, these forms of behaviour have been fairly well studied in the course of the past twenty years; it cannot be said, however, that the conclusions that have been reached are wholly valid. Specialists in basic education for underdeveloped countries or technicians for the advancement of retarded societies would do well to understand the sterile and harmful character of any endeavour that illuminates preferentially a given element of the colonized society. Even within the framework of a newly independent nation, one cannot attack this or that segment of the cultural whole without endangering the work undertaken (leaving aside the question of the native's psychological balance). More precisely, the phenomena of counter-acculturation must be understood as the organic impossibility of a culture to modify any one of its customs without at the same time re-evaluating its deepest values, its most stable models. To speak of counter-acculturation in a colonial situation is an absurdity. The phenomena of resistance observed in the colonized must be related to an attitude of counter-assimilation, of maintenance of a cultural, hence national, originality.

The occupying forces, in applying their maximum psychological attention to the veil worn by Algerian women, were obviously bound to achieve some results. Here and there it thus happened that a woman was 'saved', and symbolically unveiled.

These test-women, with bare faces and free bodies, henceforth circulated like sound currency in the European society of Algeria. These women were surrounded by an atmosphere of newness. The Europeans, over-excited and wholly given over to their victory, carried away in a kind of trance, would speak of the psychological phenomena of conversion. And in fact, in the European society, the agents of this conversion were held in esteem. They were envied. The benevolent attention of the administration was drawn to them.

After each success, the authorities were strengthened in their conviction that the Algerian woman would support Western penetration into the native society. Every rejected veil disclosed to the eyes of the colonialists horizons until then forbidden, and revealed to them, piece by piece, the flesh of Algeria laid bare. The occupier's aggressiveness, and hence his hopes, multiplied ten-fold each time a new face was uncovered. Every new Algerian woman unveiled announced to the occupier an Algerian society whose systems of defence were in the process of dislocation, open and breached. Every veil that fell, every body that became liberated from the traditional embrace of the *haïk*, every face that offered itself to the bold and impatient glance of the occupier, was a negative expression of the fact that Algeria was beginning to deny herself and was accepting the rape of the colonizer. Algerian society with every abandoned veil seemed to express its willingness to attend the master's school and to decide to change its habits under the occupier's direction and patronage.

We have seen how colonial society, the colonial administration, perceives the veil, and we have sketched the dynamics of the efforts undertaken to fight it as an institution and the resistances developed by the colonized society. At the level of the individual, of the private European, it may be interesting to follow the multiple reactions provoked by the existence of the veil, which reveal the original way in which the Algerian woman manages to be present or absent.

For a European not directly involved in this work of conversion, what reactions are there to be recorded?

The dominant attitude appears to us to be a romantic exoticism, strongly tinged with sensuality.

And, to begin with, the veil hides a beauty.

A revealing reflection – among others – of this state of mind was communicated to us by a European visiting Algeria who, in the exercise of his profession (he was a lawyer), had had the opportunity of seeing a few Algerian women without the veil. These men, he said, speaking of the Algerians, are guilty of concealing so many strange beauties. It was his conclusion that a people with a cache of such prizes, of such perfections of nature, owes it to itself to show them, to exhibit them. If worst came to worst, he added, it ought to be possible to force them to do so.

A strand of hair, a bit of forehead, a segment of an 'overwhelmingly beautiful' face glimpsed in a streetcar or on a train, may suffice to keep alive and strengthen the European's persistence in his irrational conviction that the Algerian woman is the queen of all women.

But there is also in the European the crystallization of an aggressiveness, the strain of a kind of violence before the Algerian woman. Unveiling this woman is revealing her beauty; it is baring her secret, breaking her resistance, making her available for adventure. Hiding the face is also disguising a secret; it is also creating a world of mystery, of the hidden. In a confused way, the European experiences his relation with the Algerian woman at a highly complex level. There is in it the will to bring this woman within his reach, to make her a possible object of possession.

This woman who sees without being seen frustrates the colonizer. There is no reciprocity. She does not yield herself, does not give herself, does not offer herself. The Algerian has an attitude toward the Algerian woman which is on the whole clear. He does not see her. There is even a permanent intention not to perceive the feminine profile, not to pay attention to women. In the case of the Algerian, therefore, there is not, in the street or on a road, that behaviour characterizing a sexual encounter that is described in terms of the glance, of the physical bearing, the muscular tension, the signs of disturbance to which the phenomenology of encounters has accustomed us.

The European faced with an Algerian woman wants to see. He reacts in an aggressive way before this limitation of his perception. Frustration and aggressiveness, here too, evolve apace. Aggressiveness comes to light, in the first place, in structurally ambivalent attitudes and in the dream material that can be revealed in the European, whether he is normal or suffers from neuropathological disturbances.[8]

In a medical consultation, for example, at the end of the morning, it is common to hear European doctors express their disappointment. The women who remove their veils before them are commonplace, vulgar; there is really nothing to make such a mystery of. One wonders what they are hiding.

European women settle the conflict in a much less roundabout way. They bluntly affirm that no one hides what is beautiful and discern in this strange custom an 'altogether feminine' intention of disguising imperfections. And they proceed to compare the strategy of the European woman, which is intended to correct, to embellish, to bring out (beauty treatments, hairdos, fashion), with that of the Algerian woman, who prefers to veil, to conceal, to cultivate the man's doubt and desire. On another level, it is claimed that the intention is to mislead the customer, and that the wrapping in which the 'merchandise' is presented does not really alter its nature, or its value.

The content of the dreams of Europeans brings out other special themes. Jean-Paul Sartre, in his *Réflections sur la question juive*, has shown that on the level of the unconscious, the Jewish woman almost always has an aura of rape about her.

The history of the French conquest in Algeria, including the overrunning of villages by the troops, the confiscation of property and the raping of women, the pillaging of a country, has contributed to the birth and the crystallization of the same dynamic image. At the level of the psychological strata of the occupier, the evocation of this freedom given to the sadism of the conqueror, to his eroticism, creates faults, fertile gaps through which both dreamlike forms of behaviour and, on certain occasions, criminal acts can emerge.

Thus the rape of the Algerian woman in the dream of a European is always preceded by a rending of the veil. We here witness a double deflowering. Likewise, the woman's conduct is never one of consent or acceptance, but of abject humility.

Whenever, in dreams having an erotic content, a European meets an Algerian woman, the specific features of his relations with the colonized society manifest themselves. These dreams evolve neither on the same erotic plane, nor at the same tempo, as those that involve a European woman.

With an Algerian woman, there is no progressive conquest, no mutual revelation. Straight off, with the maximum of violence, there is possession, rape, near-murder. The act assumes a para-neurotic brutality and sadism, even in a normal European. This brutality and this sadism are in fact emphasized by the frightened attitude of the Algerian woman. In the dream, the woman-victim screams, struggles like a doe, and, as she weakens and faints, is penetrated, martyrized, ripped apart.

Attention must likewise be drawn to a characteristic of this dream content that appears important to us. The European never dreams of an Algerian woman taken in isolation. On the rare occasions when the encounter has become a binding relationship that can be regarded as a couple, it has quickly been transformed by the desperate flight of the woman who, inevitably, leads the male 'among women'. The European always dreams of a group of women, of a field of women, suggestive of the gynaeceum, the harem – exotic themes deeply rooted in the unconscious.

The European's aggressiveness will express itself likewise in contemplation of the Algerian woman's morality. Her timidity and her reserve are transformed in accordance with the commonplace laws of conflictual psychology into their opposite, and the Algerian woman becomes hypocritical, perverse and even a veritable nymphomaniac.

We have seen that on the level of individuals the colonial strategy of destructuring Algerian society very quickly came to assign a prominent place to the Algerian woman. The colonialist's relentlessness, his methods of struggle were bound to give rise to reactionary forms of behaviour on the part of the colonized. In the face of the violence of the occupier, the colonized found himself defining a principled position with respect to a formerly inert element of the native cultural configuration. It was the colonialist's frenzy to unveil the Algerian woman, it was his gamble on winning the battle of the veil at whatever cost, that were to provoke the native's bristling resistance. The deliberately aggressive intentions of the colonialist with respect to the *haïk* gave a new life to this dead element of the Algerian cultural stock – dead because stabilized, without any progressive change in form or colour. We here recognize one of the laws of the psychology of colonization. In an initial phase, it is the action, the plans of the occupier that determine the centres of resistance around which a people's will to survive becomes organized.

It is the white man who creates the Negro. But it is the Negro who creates negritude. To the colonialist offensive against the veil, the colonized opposes the cult of the veil. What was an undifferentiated element in a homogeneous whole acquires a taboo character, and the attitude of a given Algerian woman with respect to the veil will be constantly related to her overall attitude with respect to the foreign occupation. The colonized, in the face of the emphasis given by the colonialist to this or that aspect of his traditions, reacts very violently. The attention devoted to modifying this aspect, the emotion the conqueror puts into his pedagogical work, his prayers, his threats, weave a whole universe of resistances around this particular element of the culture. Holding out against the occupier on this precise element means inflicting upon him a spectacular setback; it means more particularly maintaining 'coexistence' as a form of conflict and latent warfare. It means keeping up the atmosphere of an armed truce.

Upon the outbreak of the struggle for liberation, the attitude of the Algerian woman, or of native society in general, with regard to the veil was to undergo important modifications. These innovations are of particular interest in view of the fact that they were at no time included in the programme of the struggle. The doctrine of the Revolution, the strategy of combat, never postulated the necessity for a revision of forms of behaviour with respect to the veil. We are able to affirm even now that when Algeria has gained her independence such questions will not be raised, for in the practice of the Revolution the people have understood that problems are resolved in the very movement that raises them.

Until 1955, the combat was waged exclusively by the men. The revolutionary characteristics of this combat, the necessity for absolute secrecy, obliged the militant to keep his woman in absolute ignorance. As the enemy gradually adapted himself to the forms of combat, new difficulties appeared which required original solutions. The decision to involve women as active elements of the Algerian Revolution was not reached lightly. In a sense, it was the very conception of the combat that had to be modified. The violence of the occupier, his ferocity, his delirious attachment to the national territory, induced the leaders no longer to exclude certain forms of combat. Progressively, the urgency of a total war made itself felt. But involving the women was not solely a response to the desire to mobilize the entire nation. The women's entry into the war had to be harmonized with respect for the revolutionary nature of the war. In other words, the women had to show as much spirit of sacrifice as the men. It was therefore necessary to have the same confidence in them as was required from seasoned militants who had served several prison sentences. A moral elevation and a strength of character that were altogether exceptional would therefore be required of the women. There was no lack of hesitations. The revolutionary wheels had assumed such proportions; the mechanism was running at a given rate. The machine would have to be complicated; in other words its network would have to be extended without affecting its efficiency. The women could not be conceived of as a replacement product, but as an element capable of adequately meeting the new tasks.

In the mountains, women helped the *guerrilla* during halts or when convalescing after a wound or a case of typhoid contracted in the *djebel*.[9] But deciding to incorporate women as essential elements, to have the Revolution depend on their presence and their action in this or that sector, was obviously a wholly revolutionary step. To have the Revolution rest at any point on their activity was an important choice.

Such a decision was made difficult for several reasons. During the whole period of unchallenged domination, we have seen that Algerian society, and particularly the women, had a tendency to flee from the occupier. The tenacity of the occupier in his endeavour to unveil the women, to make of them an ally in the work of cultural destruction, had the effect of strengthening the traditional patterns of behaviour. These patterns, which were essentially positive in the strategy of resistance to the corrosive action of the colonizer, naturally had negative effects. The woman, especially the city woman, suffered a loss of ease and of assurance. Having been accustomed to confinement, her body did not have the normal mobility before a limitless horizon of avenues, of unfolded sidewalks, of houses, of people dodged or bumped into. This relatively cloistered life, with its known categorized, regulated comings and goings, made any immediate revolution seem a dubious proposition. The political leaders were perfectly familiar with these problems, and their hesitations expressed their consciousness of their responsibilities. They were entitled to doubt the success of this measure. Would not such a decision have catastrophic consequences for the progress of the Revolution?

To this doubt there was added an equally important element. The leaders hesitated to involve the women, being perfectly aware of the ferocity of the colonizer. The leaders of the Revolution had no illusions as to the enemy's criminal capacities. Nearly all of them had passed through their jails or had had sessions with survivors from the camps or the cells of the French judicial police. No one of them failed to realize that any Algerian woman arrested would be tortured to death. It is relatively easy to commit oneself to this path and to accept among different eventualities that of dying under torture. The matter is a little more difficult when it involves designating someone who manifestly runs the risk of certain death. But the decision as to whether or not the women were to participate in the Revolution had to be made; the inner oppositions became massive and each decision gave rise to the same hesitations, produced the same despair.

In the face of the extraordinary success of this new form of popular combat, observers have compared the action of the Algerian women to that of certain women resistance fighters or even secret agents of the specialized services. It must be constantly borne in mind that the committed Algerian woman learns both her role as 'a woman alone in the street' and her revolutionary mission instinctively. The Algerian woman is not a secret agent. It is without apprenticeship, without briefing, without fuss, that she goes out into the street with three grenades in her handbag or the activity report of an area in her bodice. She does not have the sensation of playing a role she has read about ever so many times in novels, or seen in motion pictures. There is not that coefficient of play, of imitation, almost always present in this form of action when we are dealing with a Western woman.

What we have here is not the bringing to light of a character known and frequented a thousand times in imagination or in stories. It is an authentic birth in a pure state, without preliminary instruction. There is no character to imitate. On the contrary, there is an intense dramatization, a continuity between the woman and the revolutionary. The Algerian woman rises directly to the level of tragedy.[10]

The growth in number of the FLN cells,[11] the range of new tasks – finance, intelligence, counter-intelligence, political training – the necessity to provide for one active cell three or four replacement cells to be held in reserve, ready to become active at the slightest alert concerning the front cell, obliged the leaders to seek other avenues for the carrying out of strictly individual assignments. After a final series of meetings among leaders, and especially in view of the urgency of the daily problems that the Revolution faced, the decision to concretely involve women in the national struggle was reached.

The revolutionary character of this decision must once again be emphasized. At the beginning, it was the married women who were contacted. But rather soon these restrictions were abandoned. The married women whose husbands were militants were the first to be chosen. Later, widows or divorced women were designated. In any case, there were never any unmarried girls – first of all, because a girl of even twenty or twenty-three hardly ever has occasion to leave the family domicile unaccompanied. But the woman's duties as mother or spouse, the desire to limit to the minimum the possible consequences of her arrest and her death, and also the more and more numerous volunteering of unmarried girls, led the political leaders to make another leap, to remove all restrictions, to accept indiscriminately the support of all Algerian women.

Meanwhile the woman who might be acting as a liaison agent, as a bearer of tracts, as she walked some hundred or two hundred metres ahead of the man under whose orders she was working, still wore a veil; but after a certain period the pattern of activity that the struggle involved shifted in the direction of the European city. The protective mantle of the Kasbah, the almost organic curtain of safety that the Arab town weaves round the native, withdrew, and the Algerian woman, exposed, was sent forth into the conqueror's city. Very quickly she adopted an absolutely unbelievable offensive tactic. When colonized people undertake an action against the oppressor, and when this oppression is exercised in the form of exacerbated and continuous violence as in Algeria, they must overcome a considerable number of taboos. The European city is not the prolongation of the native city. The colonizers have not settled in the midst of the natives. They have surrounded the native city; they have laid siege to it. Every exit from the Kasbah of Algiers opens on enemy territory. And so it is in Constantine, in Oran, in Blida, in Bone.

The native cities are deliberately caught in the conqueror's vice. To get an idea of the rigour with which the immobilizing of the native city, of the autochthonous population, is organized, one must have in one's hands the plans according to which a colonial city has been laid out and compare them with the comments of the general staff of the occupation forces.

Apart from the charwomen employed in the conquerors' homes, those whom the colonizer indiscriminately calls the 'Fatmas', the Algerian women, especially the young Algerian women, rarely venture into the European city. Their movements are almost entirely limited to the Arab city. And even in the Arab city their movements are reduced to the minimum. The rare occasions on which the Algerian woman abandons the city are almost always in connection with some event, either of an exceptional nature (the death of a relative residing in a nearby locality), or, more often, traditional family visits for religious feasts, or a pilgrimage. In such cases, the European city is crossed in a car, usually early in the morning. The Algerian woman, the young Algerian woman – except for a very few students (who, besides, never have the same ease as their European counterparts) – must overcome a multiplicity of inner resistances, of subjectively organized fears, of emotions. She must at the same time confront the essentially hostile world of the occupier and the mobilized, vigilant and efficient police forces. Each time she ventures into the European city, the Algerian woman must achieve a victory over herself, over her childish fears. She must consider the image of the occupier lodged somewhere in her mind and in her body, remodel it, initiate the essential work of eroding it, make it inessential, remove something of the shame that is attached to it, devalidate it.

Initially subjective, the breaches made in colonialism are the result of a victory of the colonized over their old fear and over the atmosphere of despair distilled day after day by a colonialism that has incrusted itself with the *prospect of enduring forever.*

The young Algerian woman, whenever she is called upon, establishes a link. Algiers is no longer the Arab city, but the autonomous area of Algiers, the nervous system of the enemy apparatus. Oran, Constantine develop their dimensions. In launching the struggle, the Algerian is loosening the vice that was tightening around the native cities. From one area of Algiers to another, from the Ruisseau to Hussein-Dey, from El-Biar to the rue Michelet, the Revolution creates new links. More and more, it is the Algerian woman, the Algerian girl, who will be assuming these tasks.

Among the tasks entrusted to the Algerian woman is the bearing of messages, of complicated verbal orders learned by heart, sometimes despite complete absence of schooling. But she is also called upon to stand watch, for an hour and often more, before a house where district leaders are conferring.

During those interminable minutes when she must avoid standing still, so as not to attract attention, and avoid venturing too far since she is responsible for the safety of the brothers within, incidents that are at once funny and pathetic are not infrequent. An unveiled Algerian girl who 'walks the street' is very often noticed by young men who behave like young men all over the world, but who use a special approach as the result of the idea people habitually have of one who has discarded the veil. She is treated to unpleasant, obscene, humiliating remarks. When such things happen, she must grit her teeth, walk away a few steps, elude the passers-by who draw attention to her, who give other passers-by the desire either to follow their example, or to come to her defence. Or it may be that the Algerian woman is carrying in her bag or in a small suitcase twenty, thirty, forty million francs, money belonging to the Revolution, money which is to be used to take care of the needs of the families of prisoners, or to buy medicine and supplies for the guerrillas.

This revolutionary activity has been carried on by the Algerian woman with exemplary constancy, self-mastery and success. Despite the inherent, subjective difficulties and notwithstanding the sometimes violent incomprehension of a part of the family, the Algerian woman assumes all the tasks entrusted to her.

But things were gradually to become more complicated. Thus the unit leaders who go into the town and who avail themselves of the women-scouts, of the girls whose function it is to lead the way, are no longer new to political activity, are no longer unknown to the police. Authentic military chiefs have now begun to pass through the cities. These are known, and are being looked for. There is not a police superintendent who does not have their pictures on his desk.

These soldiers on the move, these fighters, always carry their weapons – automatic pistols, revolvers, grenades, sometimes all three. The political leader must overcome much resistance in order to induce these men, who under no circumstance would allow themselves to be taken prisoner, to entrust their weapon to the girl who is to walk ahead of them, it being up to them, if things go badly, to recover the arms immediately. The group accordingly makes its way into the European city. A hundred metres ahead, a girl may be carrying a suitcase and behind her are two or three ordinary-looking men. This girl who is the group's lighthouse and barometer gives warning in case of danger. The file makes its way by fits and starts; police cars and patrols cruise back and forth.

There are times, as these soldiers have admitted after completing such a mission, when the urge to recover their weapons is almost irresistible because of the fear of being caught short and not having time to defend themselves. With this phase, the Algerian woman penetrates a little further into the flesh of the Revolution.

But it was from 1956 on that her activity assumed really gigantic dimensions. Having to react in rapid succession to the massacre of Algerian civilians in the mountains and in the cities, the revolutionary leadership found that if it wanted to prevent the people from being gripped by terror it had no choice but to adopt forms of terror which until then it had rejected. This phenomenon has not been sufficiently analysed; not enough attention has been given to the reasons that lead a revolutionary movement to choose the weapon that is called terrorism.

During the French Resistance, terrorism was aimed at soldiers, at Germans of the Occupation, or at strategic enemy installations. The technique of terrorism is the same. It consists of individual or collective attempts by means of bombs or by the derailing of trains. In Algeria, where European settlers are numerous and where the territorial militias lost no time in enrolling the postman, the nurse and the grocer in the repressive system, the men who directed the struggle faced an absolutely new situation.

The decision to kill a civilian in the street is not an easy one and no one comes to it lightly. No one takes the step of placing a bomb in a public place without a battle of conscience.

The Algerian leaders who, in view of the intensity of the repression and the frenzied character of the oppression, thought they could answer the blows received without any serious problems of conscience, discovered that the most horrible crimes do not constitute a sufficient excuse for certain decisions.

The leaders in a number of cases cancelled plans or even in the last moment called off the *fidaï*[12] assigned to place a given bomb. To explain these hesitations there was, to be sure, the memory of civilians killed or frightfully wounded. There was the political consideration not to do certain things that could compromise the cause of freedom. There was also the fear that the Europeans working with the Front might be hit in these attempts. There was thus a threefold concern: not to pile up possibly innocent victims, not to give a false picture of the Revolution and, finally, the anxiety to have the French democrats on their side, as well as the democrats of all the countries of the world and the Europeans of Algeria who were attracted by the Algerian national ideal.

Now the massacres of Algerians, the raids in the countryside, strengthened the assurance of the European civilians, seemed to consolidate the colonial status and injected hope into the colonialists. The Europeans who, as a result of certain military actions on the part of the Algerian National Army in favour of the struggle of the Algerian people, had soft-pedalled their race prejudice and their insolence, recovered their old arrogance, their traditional contempt.

I remember a woman clerk in Birtouta who, on the day of the interception of the plane transporting the five members of the National Liberation Front, waved their photographs in front of her shop, shrieking: 'They've been caught! They're going to get their what-you-call'ems cut off!'

Every blow dealt the Revolution, every massacre perpetrated by the adversary, intensified the ferocity of the colonialists and hemmed in the Algerian civilian on all sides.

Trains loaded with French soldiers, the French Navy on manoeuvers and bombarding Algiers and Philippeville, the jet planes, the militiamen who descended on the *douars*[13] and decimated uncounted Algerians, all this contributed to giving the people the impression that they were not defended, that they were not protected, that nothing had changed and that the Europeans could do what they wanted. This was the period when one heard Europeans announcing in the streets: 'Let's each one of us take ten of them and bump them off and you'll see the problem solved in no time.' And the Algerian people, especially in the cities, witnessed this boastfulness which added insult to injury and noted the impunity of these criminals who did not even take the trouble to hide. Any Algerian man or woman in a given city could in fact name the torturers and murderers of the region.

A time came when some of the people allowed doubt to enter their minds, and they began to wonder whether it was really possible, quantitatively and qualitatively, to resist the occupant's offensives. Was freedom worth the consequences of penetrating into that enormous circuit of terrorism and counter-terrorism? Did this disproportion not express the impossibility of escaping oppression?

Another part of the people, however, grew impatient and conceived the idea of putting an end to the advantage the enemy derived by pursuing the path of terror. The decision to strike the adversary individually and by name could no longer be eluded. All the prisoners 'shot and killed while trying to escape', and the cries of the tortured, demanded that new forms of combat be adopted.

Members of the police and the meeting places of the colonialists (cafés in Algiers, Oran, Constantine) were the first to be singled out. From this point on the Algerian woman became wholly and deliberately immersed in the revolutionary action. It was she who would carry in her bag the grenades and the revolvers that a *fidaï* would take from her at the last moment, before the bar, or as a designated criminal passed. During this period Algerians caught in the European city were pitilessly challenged, arrested, searched.

This is why we must watch the parallel progress of this man and this woman, of this couple that brings death to the enemy, life to the Revolution. The one supporting the other, but apparently strangers to each other. The one radically transformed into a European woman, poised and unconstrained, whom no one would suspect, completely at home in the environment, and the other, a stranger, tense, moving toward his destiny.

The Algerian *fidaï*, unlike the unbalanced anarchists made famous in literature, does not take dope. The *fidaï* does not need to be unaware of danger, to befog his consciousness, or to forget. The 'terrorist', from the moment he undertakes an assignment, allows death to enter into his soul. He has a rendezvous with death. The *fidaï*, on the other hand, has a rendezvous with the life of the Revolution, and with his own life. The *fidaï* is not one of the sacrificed. To be sure, he does not shrink before the possibility of losing his life for the independence of his country, but at no moment does he choose death.

If it has been decided to kill a given police superintendent responsible for tortures, or a given colonialist leader, it is because these men constitute an obstacle to the progress of the Revolution. Froger, for example, symbolized a colonialist tradition and a method inaugurated at Sétif and at Guelma in 1954.[14] Moreover, Froger's apparent power crystallized the colonization and gave new life to the hopes of those who were beginning to have doubts as to the real solidity of the system. It was around people like Froger that the robbers and murderers of the Algerian people would meet and encourage one another. This was something the *fidaï* knew, and that the woman who accompanied him, his woman-arsenal, likewise knew.

Carrying revolvers, grenades, hundreds of false identity cards or bombs, the unveiled Algerian woman moves like a fish in the Western waters. The soldiers, the French patrols, smile to her as she passes, compliments on her looks are heard here and there, but no one suspects that her suitcases contain the automatic pistol which will presently mow down four or five members of one of the patrols.

We must come back to that young girl, unveiled only yesterday, who walks with sure steps down the streets of the European city teeming with policemen, parachutists, militiamen. She no longer slinks along the walls as she tended to do before the Revolution. Constantly called upon to efface herself before a member of the dominant society, the Algerian woman avoided the middle of the sidewalk which in all countries in the world belongs rightfully to those who command.

The shoulders of the unveiled Algerian woman are thrust back with easy freedom. She walks with a graceful, measured stride, neither too fast nor too slow. Her legs are bare, not confined by the veil, given back to themselves, and her hips are free.

The body of the young Algerian woman, in traditional society, is revealed to her by its coming to maturity and by the veil. The veil covers the body and disciplines it, tempers it, at the very time when it experiences its phase of greatest effervescence. The veil protects, reassures, isolates. One must have heard the confessions of Algerian women or have analysed the dream content of certain recently unveiled women to appreciate the importance of the veil for the body of the woman. Without the veil she has an impression of her body being cut up into bits, put adrift; the limbs seem to lengthen indefinitely. When the Algerian woman has to cross a street, for a long time she commits errors of judgement as to the exact distance to be negotiated. The unveiled body seems to escape, to dissolve. She has an impression of being improperly dressed, even of being naked. She experiences a sense of incompleteness with great intensity. She has the anxious feeling that something is unfinished, and along with this a frightful sensation of disintegrating. The absence of the veil distorts the Algerian woman's corporal pattern. She quickly has to invent new dimensions for her body, new means of muscular control. She has to create for herself an attitude of unveiled-woman-outside. She must overcome all timidity, all awkwardness (for she must pass for a European), and at the same time be careful not to overdo it, not to attract notice to herself. The Algerian woman who walks stark naked into the European city relearns her body, re-establishes it in a totally revolutionary fashion. This new dialectic of the body and of the world is primary in the case of one revolutionary woman.[15]

But the Algerian woman is not only in conflict with her body. She is a link, sometimes an essential one, in the revolutionary machine. She carries weapons, knows important points of refuge. And it is in terms of the concrete dangers that she faces that we must gauge the insurmountable victories that she has had to win in order to be able to say to her chief, on her return: 'Mission accomplished ... R.A.S.' [16]

Another difficulty to which attention deserves to be called appeared during the first months of feminine activity. In the course of her comings and goings, it would happen that the unveiled Algerian woman was seen by a relative or a friend of the family. The father was sooner or later informed. He would naturally hesitate to believe such allegations. Then more reports would reach him. Different persons would claim to have seen 'Zohra or Fatima unveiled, walking like a ... My Lord, protect us! ...' The father would then decide to demand explanations. He would hardly have begun to speak when he would stop. From the young girl's look of firmness the father would have understood that her commitment was of long standing. The old fear of dishonour was swept away by a new fear, fresh and cold – that of death in battle or of torture of the girl. Behind the girl, the whole family – even the Algerian father, the authority for all things, the founder of every value – following in her footsteps, becomes committed to the new Algeria.

Removed and reassumed again and again, the veil has been manipulated, transformed into a technique of camouflage, into a means of struggle. The virtually taboo character assumed by the veil in the colonial situation disappeared almost entirely in the course of the liberating struggle. Even Algerian women not actively integrated into the struggle formed the habit of abandoning the veil. It is true that under certain conditions, especially from 1957 on, the veil reappeared. The missions in fact became increasingly difficult. The adversary now knew, since certain militant women had spoken under torture, that a number of women very Europeanized in appearance were playing a fundamental role in the battle. Moreover, certain European women of Algeria were arrested, to the consternation of the adversary who discovered that his own system was breaking down. The discovery by the French authorities of the participation of Europeans in the liberation struggle marks a turning point in the Algerian Revolution.[17] From that day, the French patrols challenged every person. Europeans and Algerians were equally suspect. All historic limits crumbled and disappeared. Any person carrying a package could be required to open it and show its contents. Anyone was entitled to question anyone as to the nature of a parcel carried in Algiers, Philippeville or Batna. Under those conditions it became urgent to conceal the package from the eyes of the occupier and again to cover oneself with the protective *haïk*.

Here again, a new technique had to be learned: how to carry a rather heavy object dangerous to handle under the veil and still give the impression of having one's hands free, that there was nothing under this *haïk* except a poor woman or an insignificant young girl. It was not enough to be veiled. One had to look so much like a 'fatma' that the soldier would be convinced that this woman was quite harmless.

Very difficult. Three metres ahead of you the police challenge a veiled woman who does not look particularly suspect. From the anguished expression of the unit leader you have guessed that she is carrying a bomb, or a sack of grenades, bound to her body by a whole system of strings and straps. For the hands must be free, exhibited bare, humbly and abjectly presented to the soldiers so that they will look no further. Showing empty and apparently mobile and free hands is the sign that disarms the enemy soldier.

The Algerian woman's body, which in an initial phase was pared down, now swelled. Whereas in the previous period the body had to be made slim and disciplined to make it attractive and seductive, it now had to be squashed, made shapeless and even ridiculous. This, as we have seen, is the phase during which she undertook to carry bombs, grenades, machine-gun clips.

The enemy, however, was alerted, and in the streets one witnessed what became a commonplace spectacle of Algerian women glued to the wall, on whose bodies the famous magnetic detectors, the 'frying pans', would be passed. Every veiled woman, every Algerian woman became suspect. There was no discrimination. This was the period during which men, women, children, the whole Algerian people, experienced at one and the same time their national vocation and the recasting of the new Algerian society.

Ignorant or feigning to be ignorant of these new forms of conduct, French colonialism, on the occasion of 13 May, re-enacted its old campaign of Westernizing the Algerian woman. Servants under the threat of being fired, poor women dragged from their homes, prostitutes, were brought to the public square and *symbolically* unveiled to the cries of '*Vive l'Algérie française!*' Before this new offensive old reactions reappeared. Spontaneously and without being told, the Algerian women who had long since dropped the veil once again donned the *haïk,* thus affirming that it was not true that woman liberated herself at the invitation of France and of General de Gaulle.

Behind these psychological reactions, beneath this immediate and almost unanimous response, we again see the overall attitude of rejection of the values of the occupier, even if these values objectively may be worth choosing. It is because they fail to grasp this intellectual reality, this characteristic feature (the famous sensitivity of the colonized), that the colonizers rage at always 'doing them good in spite of themselves'. Colonialism wants everything to come from it. But the dominant psychological feature of the colonized is to withdraw before any invitation of the conqueror's. In organizing the famous cavalcade of 13 May, colonialism has obliged Algerian society to go back to methods of struggle already outmoded. In a certain sense, the different ceremonies have caused a turning back, a regression.

Colonialism must accept the fact that things happen without its control, without its direction. We are reminded of the words spoken in an international assembly by an African political figure. Responding to the standard excuse of the immaturity of colonial peoples and their incapacity to administer themselves, this man demanded for the underdeveloped peoples 'the right to govern themselves badly'. The doctrinal assertions of colonialism in its attempt to justify the maintenance of its domination almost always push the colonized to the position of making uncompromising, rigid, static counter-proposals.

After 13 May, the veil was resumed, but stripped once and for all of its exclusively traditional dimension.

There is thus a historic dynamism of the veil that is very concretely perceptible in the development of colonization in Algeria. In the beginning, the veil was a mechanism of resistance, but its value for the social group remained very strong. The veil was worn because tradition demanded a rigid separation of the sexes, but also because the occupier was *bent on unveiling Algeria.* In a second phase, the mutation occurred in connection with the Revolution and under special circumstances. The veil was abandoned in the course of revolutionary action. What had been used to block the psychological or political offensives of the occupier became a means, an instrument. The veil helped the Algerian woman to meet the new problems created by the struggle.

The colonialists are incapable of grasping the motivations of the colonized. It is the necessities of combat that give rise in Algerian society to new attitudes, to new modes of action, to new ways.

APPENDIX[18]

On the Algerian earth which is freeing itself day by day from the colonialist's grip, we witness a dislocation of the old myths.

Among things that are 'incomprehensible' to the colonial world the case of the Algerian woman has been all too frequently mentioned. The studies of sociologists, Islam specialists and jurists are full of observations on the Algerian woman.

Described by turns as the man's slave or as the unchallenged sovereign of the home, Algerian woman and her status absorb the attention of theoreticians.

Others, of equal authority, affirm that the Algerian woman 'dreams of being free', but that a retrograde and ferocious patriarchy opposes this legitimate aspiration. The most recent debates in the French National Assembly indicate the interest attached to a coherent approach to this 'problem'. The majority of the speakers describe the fate of the Algerian woman and demand an improvement in her status. This, it is added, is the only means of disarming the rebellion. Colonialist intellectuals consistently use the 'sociological case study' approach to the colonial system. Such and such a country, they will say, called for, was crying for conquest. Thus, to take a famous example, the Madagascan was described as having a dependency complex.

As for the Algerian woman, she is 'inaccessible, ambivalent, with a masochistic component'. Specific behaviours are described which illustrate these different characteristics. The truth is that the study of an occupied people, militarily subject to an implacable domination, requires documentation and checking difficult to combine. It is not the soil that is occupied. It is not the ports or the aerodromes. French colonialism has settled itself in the very centre of the Algerian individual and has undertaken a sustained work of clean-up, of expulsion of self, of rationally pursued mutilation.

There is not occupation of territory, on the one hand, and independence of persons on the other. It is the country as a whole, its history, its daily pulsation that are contested, disfigured, in the hope of a final destruction. Under these conditions, the individual's breathing is an observed, an occupied breathing. It is a combat breathing.

From this point on, the real values of the occupied quickly tend to acquire a clandestine form of existence. In the presence of the occupier, the occupied learns to dissemble, to resort to trickery. To the scandal of military occupation, he opposes a scandal of contact. Every contact between the occupied and the occupier is a falsehood.

In forty-eight hours the Algerian woman has knocked down all the pseudo-truths that years of 'field studies' were believed to have amply confirmed. To be sure, the Algerian Revolution has brought about an objective modification of attitudes and outlook. But the Algerian people had never disarmed. 1 November 1954 was not the awakening of the people, but the signal it was waiting for in order to get into motion, in order to put into practice in full daylight a tactic acquired, and solidly reinforced, in the heyday of the Franco-Moslem period.

The Algerian woman, like her brothers, had minutely built up defence mechanisms which enable her today to play a primary role in the struggle for liberation.

To begin with, there is the much-discussed status of the Algerian woman – her alleged confinement, her lack of importance, her humility, her silent existence bordering on quasi-absence. And 'Moslem society' has made no place for her, amputating her personality, allowing her neither development nor maturity, maintaining her in a perpetual infantilism.

Such affirmations, illuminated by 'scientific works', are today receiving the only valid challenge: the experience of revolution.

The Algerian woman's ardent love of the home is not a limitation imposed by the universe. It is not hatred of the sun or the streets or spectacles. It is not a flight from the world.

What is true is that under normal conditions, an interaction must exist between the family and society at large. The home is the basis of the truth of society, but society authenticates and legitimizes the family. The colonial structure is the very negation of this reciprocal justification. The Algerian woman, in imposing such a restriction on herself, in choosing a form of existence limited in scope, was deepening her consciousness of struggle and preparing for combat.

This withdrawal, this rejection of an imposed structure, this falling back upon the fertile kernel that a restricted but coherent existence represents, constituted for a long time the fundamental strength of the occupied. All alone, the woman, by means of conscious techniques, presided over the setting up of the system. What was essential was that the occupier should constantly come up against a unified front. This accounts for the aspect of sclerosis that tradition must assume.

In reality, the effervescence and the revolutionary spirit have been kept alive by the woman in the home. For revolutionary war is not a war of men.

It is not a war waged with an active army and reserves. Revolutionary war, as the Algerian people is waging it, is a total war in which the woman does not merely knit for or mourn the soldier. The Algerian woman is at the heart of the combat. Arrested, tortured, raped, shot down, she testifies to the violence of the occupier and to his inhumanity.

As a nurse, a liaison agent, a fighter, she bears witness to the depth and the density of the struggle.

We shall speak also of the woman's fatalism, of her absence of reaction in the face of adversity, of her inability to measure the gravity of events. The constant smile, the persistence of an apparently unfounded hope, the refusal to go down on her knees, is likened to an inability to grasp reality.

The humour, which is a rigorous appraisal of events, is unperceived by the occupier. And the courage that the Algerian woman manifests in the struggle is not an unexpected creation or the result of a mutation. It is the insurrectional phase of that same humour.

The woman's place in Algerian society is indicated with such vehemence that the occupier's confusion is readily understandable. This is because Algerian society reveals itself not to be the womanless society that had been so convincingly described.

Side by side with us, our sisters do their part in further breaking down the enemy system and in liquidating the old mystifications once and for all.

Section Three:

On Negritude
and National Culture

7
The Fact of Blackness

'Dirty nigger!' Or simply, 'Look, a Negro!'

I came into the world imbued with the will to find a meaning in things, my spirit filled with the desire to attain to the source of the world, and then I found that I was an object in the midst of other objects.

Sealed into that crushing objecthood, I turned beseechingly to others. Their attention was a liberation, running over my body suddenly abraded into non-being, endowing me once more with an agility that I had thought lost, and by taking me out of the world, restoring me to it. But just as I reached the other side, I stumbled, and the movements, the attitudes, the glances of the other fixed me there, in the sense in which a chemical solution is fixed by a dye. I was indignant; I demanded an explanation. Nothing happened. I burst apart. Now the fragments have been put together again by another self.

As long as the black man is among his own, he will have no occasion, except in minor internal conflicts, to experience his being through others. There is of course the moment of 'being for others', of which Hegel speaks, but every ontology is made unattainable in a colonized and civilized society. It would seem that this fact has not been given sufficient attention by those who have discussed the question. In the *Weltanschauung* of a colonized people there is an impurity, a flaw that outlaws any ontological explanation. Someone may object that this is the case with every individual, but such an objection merely conceals a basic problem. Ontology – once it is finally admitted as leaving existence by the wayside – does not permit us to understand the being of the black man. For not only must the black man be black; he must be black in relation to the white man. Some critics will take it on themselves to remind us that this proposition has a converse. I say that this is false. The black man has no ontological resistance in the eyes of the white man. Overnight the Negro has been given two frames of reference within which he has had to place himself. His metaphysics, or, less pretentiously, his customs and the sources on which they were based, were wiped out because they were in conflict with a civilization that he did not know and that imposed itself on him.

The black man among his own in the twentieth century does not know at what moment his inferiority comes into being through the other. Of course I have talked about the black problem with friends, or, more rarely, with American Negroes. Together we protested, we asserted the equality of all men in the world. In the Antilles there was also that little gulf that exists among the almost-white, the mulatto and the nigger. But I was satisfied with an intellectual understanding of these differences. It was not really dramatic. And then....

And then the occasion arose when I had to meet the white man's eyes. An unfamiliar weight burdened me. The real world challenged my claims. In the white world the man of colour encounters difficulties in the development of his bodily schema. Consciousness of the body is solely a negating activity. It is a third-person consciousness. The body is surrounded by an atmosphere of certain uncertainty. I know that if I want to smoke, I shall have to reach out my right arm and take the pack of cigarettes lying at the other end of the table. The matches, however, are in the drawer on the left, and I shall have to lean back slightly. And all these movements are made not out of habit but out of implicit knowledge. A slow composition of my *self* as a body in the middle of a spatial and temporal world – such seems to be the schema. It does not impose itself on me; it is, rather, a definitive structuring of the self and of the world – definitive because it creates a real dialectic between my body and the world.

For several years certain laboratories have been trying to produce a serum for 'denegrification'; with all the earnestness in the world, laboratories have sterilized their test tubes, checked their scales and embarked on researches that might make it possible for the miserable Negro to whiten himself and thus to throw off the burden of that corporeal malediction. Below the corporeal schema I had sketched a historico-racial schema. The elements that I used had been provided for me not by 'residual sensations and perceptions primarily of a tactile, vestibular, kinesthetic and visual character',[1] but by the other, the white man, who had woven me out of a thousand details, anecdotes, stories. I thought that what I had in hand was to construct a physiological self, to balance space, to localize sensations, and here I was called on for more.

'Look, a Negro!' It was an external stimulus that flicked over me as I passed by. I made a tight smile.

'Look, a Negro!' It was true. It amused me.

'Look, a Negro!' The circle was drawing a bit tighter. I made no secret of my amusement.

'Mama, see the Negro! I'm frightened!' Frightened! Frightened! Now they were beginning to be afraid of me. I made up my mind to laugh myself to tears, but laughter had become impossible.

I could no longer laugh, because I already knew that there were legends, stories, history and, above all, *historicity*, which I had learned about from Jaspers. Then, assailed at various points, the corporeal schema crumbled, its place taken by a racial epidermal schema. In the train it was no longer a question of being aware of my body in the third person but in a triple person. In the train I was given not one but two, three places. I had already stopped being amused. It was not that I was finding febrile coordinates in the world. I existed triply: I occupied space. I moved toward the other ... and the evanescent other, hostile but not opaque, transparent, not there, disappeared. Nausea....

I was responsible at the same time for my body, for my race, for my ancestors. I subjected myself to an objective examination, I discovered my blackness, my ethnic characteristics; and I was battered down by tom-toms, cannibalism, intellectual deficiency, fetishism, racial defects, slave-ships and, above all else, above all: 'Sho' good eatin'.'

On that day, completely dislocated, unable to be abroad with the other, the white man, who unmercifully imprisoned me, I took myself far off from my own presence, far indeed, and made myself an object. What else could it be for me but an amputation, an excision, a haemorrhage that spattered my whole body with black blood? But I did not want this revision, this thematization. All I wanted was to be a man among other men. I wanted to come, lithe and young, into a world that was ours and to help to build it together.

But I rejected all immunization of the emotions. I wanted to be a man, nothing but a man. Some identified me with ancestors of mine who had been enslaved or lynched: I decided to accept this. It was on the universal level of the intellect that I understood this inner kinship – I was the grandson of slaves in exactly the same way in which President Lebrun was the grandson of tax-paying, hard-working peasants. In the main, the panic soon vanished.

In America, Negoes are segregated. In South America, Negroes are whipped in the streets, and Negro strikers are cut down by machine-guns. In West Africa, the Negro is an animal. And there beside me, my neighbour in the university, who was born in Algeria, told me: 'Unless the Arab is treated like a man, no solution is possible.'

Understand, my dear boy, colour prejudice is something I find utterly foreign....
But of course, come in, sir, there is no colour prejudice among us.... Quite, the
Negro is a man like ourselves.... It is not because he is black that he is less
intelligent than we are.... I had a Senegalese buddy in the army who was really
clever....

Where am I to be classified? Or, if you prefer, tucked away?
'A Martinican, a native of "our" old colonies.'
Where shall I hide?
'Look at the nigger! ... Mama, a Negro! ... Hell, he's getting mad....
Take no notice, sir, he does not know that you are as civilized as
we. ...'

My body was given back to me sprawled out, distorted, recoloured,
clad in mourning in that white winter day. The Negro is an animal,
the Negro is bad, the Negro is mean, the Negro is ugly; look, a nigger,
it's cold, the nigger is shivering, the nigger is shivering because he
is cold, the little boy is trembling because he is afraid of the nigger,
the nigger is shivering with cold, that cold that goes through your
bones, the handsome little boy is trembling because he thinks that
the nigger is quivering with rage, the little white boy throws himself
into his mother's arms: Mama, the nigger's going to eat me up.

All around me the white man, above the sky tears at its navel, the
earth rasps under my feet, and there is a white song, a white song.
All this whiteness that burns me....

I sit down at the fire and I become aware of my uniform. I had
not seen it. It is indeed ugly. I stop there, for who can tell me what
beauty is?

Where shall I find shelter from now on? I felt an easily identifiable
flood mounting out of the countless facets of my being. I was about
to be angry. The fire was long since out, and once more the nigger
was trembling.

'Look how handsome that Negro is! ...'
'Kiss the handsome Negro's ass, madame!'
Shame flooded her face. At last I was set free from my rumination. At
the same time I accomplished two things: I identified my enemies and
I made a scene. A grand slam. Now one would be able to laugh.

The field of battle having been marked out, I entered the lists.

What? While I was forgetting, forgiving and wanting only to love,
my message was flung back in my face like a slap. The white world,
the only honourable one, barred me from all participation. A man
was expected to behave like a man. I was expected to behave like a

black man – or at least like a nigger. I shouted a greeting to the world and the world slashed away my joy. I was told to stay within bounds, to go back where I belonged.

They would see, then! I had warned them, anyway. Slavery? It was no longer even mentioned, that unpleasant memory. My supposed inferiority? A hoax that it was better to laugh at. I forgot it all, but only on condition that the world not protect itself against me any longer. I had incisors to test. I was sure they were strong. And besides....

What! When it was I who had every reason to hate, to despise, I was rejected? When I should have been begged, implored, I was denied the slightest recognition? I resolved, since it was impossible for me to get away from an *inborn complex*, to assert myself as a BLACK MAN. Since the other hesitated to recognize me, there remained only one solution: to make myself known.

In *Anti-Semite and Jew* (p. 95), Sartre says:

They [the Jews] have allowed themselves to be poisoned by the stereotype that others have of them, and they live in fear that their acts will correspond to this stereotype.... We may say that their conduct is perpetually overdetermined from the inside.

All the same, the Jew can be unknown in his Jewishness. He is not wholly what he is. One hopes, one waits. His actions, his behaviour are the final determinant. He is a white man, and, apart from some rather debatable characteristics, he can sometimes go unnoticed. He belongs to the race of those who, since the beginning of time, have never known cannibalism. What an idea, to eat one's father! Simple enough, one has only not to be a nigger. Granted, the Jews are harassed – what am I thinking of? They are hunted down, exterminated, cremated. But these are little family quarrels. The Jew is disliked from the moment he is tracked down. But in my case everything takes on a *new* guise. I am given no chance. I am overdetermined from without. I am the slave not of the 'idea' that others have of me but of my own appearance.

I move slowly in the world, accustomed now to seek no longer for upheaval. I progress by crawling. And already I am being dissected under white eyes, the only real eyes. I am *fixed*. Having adjusted their microtomes, they objectively cut away slices of my reality. I am laid bare. I feel, I see in those white faces that it is not a new man who has come in, but a new kind of man, a new genus. Why, it's a Negro!

I slip into corners, and my long antennae pick up the catch-phrases strewn over the surface of things – nigger underwear smells of nigger

– nigger teeth are white – nigger feet are big – the nigger's barrel chest – I slip into corners, I remain silent, I strive for anonymity, for invisibility. Look, I will accept the lot, as long as no one notices me!

'Oh, I want you to meet my black friend.... Aimé Césaire, a black man and a university graduate.... Marian Anderson, the finest of Negro singers.... Dr Cobb, who invented white blood, is a Negro.... Here, say hello to my friend from Martinique (be careful, he's extremely sensitive)....'

Shame. Shame and self-contempt. Nausea. When people like me, they tell me it is in spite of my colour. When they dislike me, they point out that it is not because of my colour. Either way, I am locked into the infernal circle.

I turn away from these inspectors of the Ark before the Flood and I attach myself to my brothers, Negroes like myself. To my horror, they too reject me. They are almost white. And besides they are about to marry white women. They will have children faintly tinged with brown. Who knows, perhaps little by little....

I had been dreaming.

'I want you to understand, sir, I am one of the best friends the Negro has in Lyon.'

The evidence was there, unalterable. My blackness was there, dark and unarguable. And it tormented me, pursued me, disturbed me, angered me.

Negroes are savages, brutes, illiterates. But in my own case I knew that these statements were false. There was a myth of the Negro that had to be destroyed at all costs. The time had long since passed when a Negro priest was an occasion for wonder. We had physicians, professors, statesmen. Yes, but something out of the ordinary still clung to such cases. 'We have a Senegalese history teacher. He is quite bright.... Our doctor is coloured. He is very gentle.'

It was always the Negro teacher, the Negro doctor; brittle as I was becoming, I shivered at the slightest pretext. I knew, for instance, that if the physician made a mistake it would be the end of him and of all those who came after him. What could one expect, after all, from a Negro physician? As long as everything went well, he was praised to the skies, but look out, no nonsense, under any conditions! The black physician can never be sure how close he is to disgrace. I tell you, I was walled in: no exception was made for my refined manners, or my knowledge of literature, or my understanding of the quantum theory.

I requested, I demanded explanations. Gently, in the tone that one uses with a child, they introduced me to the existence of a certain view that was held by certain people, but, I was always told, 'We must hope that it will very soon disappear.' What was it? Colour prejudice.

It [colour prejudice] is nothing more than the unreasoning hatred of one race for another, the contempt of the stronger and richer peoples for those whom they consider inferior to themselves, and the bitter resentment of those who are kept in subjection and are so frequently insulted. As colour is the most obvious outward manifestation of race it has been made the criterion by which men are judged, irrespective of their social or educational attainments. The light-skinned races have come to despise all those of a darker colour, and the dark-skinned peoples will no longer accept without protest the inferior position to which they have been relegated.[2]

I had read it rightly. It was hate; I was hated, despised, detested, not by the neighbour across the street or my cousin on my mother's side, but by an entire race. I was up against something unreasoned. The psychoanalysts say that nothing is more traumatizing for the young child than his encounters with what is rational. I would personally say that for a man whose only weapon is reason there is nothing more neurotic than contact with unreason.

I felt knife blades open within me. I resolved to defend myself. As a good tactician, I intended to rationalize the world and to show the white man that he was mistaken.

In the Jew, Jean-Paul Sartre says, there is:

... a sort of impassioned imperialism of reason: for he wishes not only to convince others that he is right; his goal is to persuade them that there is an absolute and unconditioned value to rationalism. He feels himself to be a missionary of the universal; against the universality of the Catholic religion, from which he is excluded, he asserts the 'catholicity' of the rational, an instrument by which to attain to the truth and establish a spiritual bond among men.[3]

And, the author adds, though there may be Jews who have made intuition the basic category of their philosophy, their intuition:

... has no resemblance to the Pascalian subtlety of spirit, and it is this latter – based on a thousand imperceptible perceptions – which to the Jew seems his worst enemy. As for Bergson, his philosophy offers the curious appearance of an anti-intellectualist doctrine constructed entirely by the most rational and most critical of intelligences. It is through argument that he establishes the existence of pure duration, of philosophic intuition; and that very intuition which discovers duration or life, is itself universal, since anyone may practice it, and it leads toward the universal, since its objects can be named and conceived.[4]

With enthusiasm I set to cataloguing and probing my surroundings. As times changed, one had seen the Catholic religion at first justify and then condemn slavery and prejudices. But by referring everything to the idea of the dignity of man, one had ripped prejudice to shreds. After much reluctance, the scientists had conceded that the Negro was a human being; *in vivo* and *in vitro* the Negro had been proved analogous to the white man: the same morphology, the same histology. Reason was confident of victory on every level. I put all the parts back together. But I had to change my tune.

That victory played cat and mouse; it made a fool of me. As the other put it, when I was present, it was not; when it was there, I was no longer. In the abstract there was agreement: The Negro is a human being. That is to say, amended the less firmly convinced, that like us he has his heart on the left side. But on certain points the white man remained intractable. Under no conditions did he wish any intimacy between the races, for it is a truism that 'crossings between widely different races can lower the physical and mental level.... Until we have a more definite knowledge of the effect of race-crossings we shall certainly do best to avoid crossings between widely different races.'[5]

For my own part, I would certainly know how to react. And in one sense, if I were asked for a definition of myself, I would say that I am one who waits; I investigate my surroundings, I interpret everything in terms of what I discover, I become sensitive.

In the first chapter of the history that the others have compiled for me, the foundation of cannibalism has been made eminently plain in order that I may not lose sight of it. My chromosomes were supposed to have a few thicker or thinner genes representing cannibalism. In addition to the *sex-linked*, the scholars had now discovered the *racial-linked*.[6] What a shameful science!

But I understand this 'psychological mechanism'. For it is a matter of common knowledge that the mechanism is only psychological. Two centuries ago I was lost to humanity, I was a slave forever. And then came men who said that it all had gone on far too long. My tenaciousness did the rest; I was saved from the civilizing deluge. I have gone forward.

Too late. Everything is anticipated, thought out, demonstrated, made the most of. My trembling hands take hold of nothing; the vein has been mined out. Too late! But once again I want to understand.

Since the time when someone first mourned the fact that he had arrived too late and everything had been said, a nostalgia for the past has seemed to persist. Is this that lost original paradise of which Otto Rank speaks? How many such men, apparently rooted to the womb of the world, have devoted their lives to studying the Delphic oracles or exhausted themselves in attempts to plot the wanderings of Ulysses! The pan-spiritualists seek to prove the existence of a soul in animals by using this argument: A dog lies down on the grave of his master and starves to death there. We had to wait for Janet to demonstrate that the aforesaid dog, in contrast to man, simply lacked the capacity to liquidate the past. We speak of the glory of Greece, Artaud says; but, he adds, if modern man can no longer understand the *Choephoroi* of Aeschylus, it is Aeschylus who is to blame. It is tradition to which the anti-Semites turn in order to ground the validity of their 'point of view'. It is tradition, it is that long historical past, it is that blood relation between Pascal and Descartes, that is invoked when the Jew is told, 'There is no possibility of your finding a place in society.' Not long ago, one of those good Frenchmen said in a train where I was sitting: 'Just let the real French virtues keep going and the race is safe. Now more than ever, national union must be made a reality. Let's have an end of internal strife! Let's face up to the foreigners (here he turned toward my corner) no matter who they are.'

It must be said in his defence that he stank of cheap wine; if he had been capable of it, he would have told me that my emancipated-slave blood could not possibly be stirred by the name of Villon or Taine.

An outrage!

The Jew and I: since I was not satisfied to be racialized, by a lucky turn of fate I was humanized. I joined the Jew, my brother in misery.

An outrage!

At first thought it may seem strange that the anti-Semite's outlook should be related to that of the Negrophobe. It was my philosophy professor, a native of the Antilles, who recalled the fact to me one day: 'Whenever you hear anyone abuse the Jews, pay attention, because he is talking about you.' And I found that he was universally right – by which I meant that I was answerable in my body and in my heart for what was done to my brother. Later I realized that he meant, quite simply, an anti-Semite is inevitably anti-Negro.

You come too late, much too late. There will always be a world
– a white world – between you and us.... The other's total inability
to liquidate the past once and for all. In the face of this affective
ankylosis of the white man, it is understandable that I could have
made up my mind to utter my Negro cry. Little by little, putting out
pseudopodia here and there, I secreted a race. And that race staggered
under the burden of a basic element. What was it? *Rhythm*! Listen to
our singer, Léopold Senghor:

It is the thing that is most perceptible and least material. It is the archetype of the
vital element. It is the first condition and the hallmark of Art, as breath is of life:
breath, which accelerates or slows, which becomes even or agitated according
to the tension in the individual, the degree and the nature of his emotion. This
is rhythm in its primordial purity, this is rhythm in the masterpieces of Negro
art, especially sculpture. It is composed of a theme – sculptural form – which
is set in opposition to a sister theme, as inhalation is to exhalation, and that is
repeated. It is not the kind of symmetry that gives rise to monotony; rhythm
is alive, it is free.... This is how rhythm affects what is least intellectual in us,
tyrannically, to make us penetrate to the spirituality of the object; and that
character of abandon which is ours is itself rhythmic.[7]

Had I read that right? I read it again with redoubled attention.
From the opposite end of the white world a magical Negro culture
was hailing me. Negro sculpture! I began to flush with pride. Was
this our salvation?

I had rationalized the world and the world had rejected me on
the basis of colour prejudice. Since no agreement was possible on
the level of reason, I threw myself back toward unreason. It was up
to the white man to be more irrational than I. Out of the necessities
of my struggle I had chosen the method of regression, but the fact
remained that it was an unfamiliar weapon; here I am at home; I am
made of the irrational; I wade in the irrational. Up to the neck in the
irrational. And now how my voice vibrates!

> Those who invented neither gunpowder nor the compass
> Those who never learned to conquer steam or electricity
> Those who never explored the seas or the skies
> But they know the farthest corners of the land of anguish
> Those who never knew any journey save that of abduction
> Those who learned to kneel in docility
> Those who were domesticated and Christianized
> Those who were injected with bastardy....

Yes, all those are my brothers – a 'bitter brotherhood' imprisons all of us alike. Having stated the minor thesis, I went overboard after something else.

> ... But those without whom the earth would not be
> >   the earth
> Tumescence all the more fruitful
> than
> the empty land
> still more the land
> Storehouse to guard and ripen all
> on earth that is most earth
> My blackness is no stone, its deafness
> hurled against the clamour of the day
> My blackness is no drop of lifeless water
> on the dead eye of the world
> My blackness is neither a tower nor a cathedral
> It thrusts into the red flesh of the sun
> It thrusts into the burning flesh of the sky
> It hollows through the dense dismay of its own
> >   pillar of patience.[8]

Eyah! the tom-tom chatters out the cosmic message. Only the Negro has the capacity to convey it, to decipher its meaning, its import. Astride the world, my strong heels spurring into the flanks of the world, I stare into the shoulders of the world as the celebrant stares at the midpoint between the eyes of the sacrificial victim.

> But they abandon themselves, possessed, to the essence of all things,
> knowing nothing of externals but possessed by the movement of all things
> >   uncaring to subdue but playing the play of the world
> >   truly the eldest sons of the world
> open to all the breaths of the world
> meeting-place of all the winds of the world
> undrained bed of all the waters of the world
> spark of the sacred fire of the World
> flesh of the flesh of the world, throbbing with the
> >   very movement of the world![9]

Blood! Blood! ... Birth! Ecstasy of becoming! Three-quarters engulfed in the conclusions of the day, I feel myself redden with blood. The arteries of all the world, convulsed, torn away, uprooted, have turned toward me and fed me.

'Blood! Blood! All our blood stirred by the male heart of the sun.'[10]

Sacrifice was a middle point between the creation and myself – now I went back no longer to sources but to The Source. Nevertheless, one had to distrust rhythm, earth-mother love, this mystic, carnal marriage of the group and the cosmos.

In *La vie sexuelle en Afrique noire*, a work rich in perceptions, De Pédrals implies that always in Africa, no matter what field is studied, it will have a certain magico-social structure. He adds:

All these are the elements that one finds again on a still greater scale in the domain of secret societies. To the extent, moreover, to which persons of either sex, subjected to circumcision during adolescence, are bound under penalty of death not to reveal to the uninitiated what they have experienced, and to the extent to which initiation into a secret society always excites to acts of *sacred love*, there is good ground to conclude by viewing both male and female circumcision and the rites that they embellish as constitutive of minor secret societies.[11]

I walk on white nails. Sheets of water threaten my soul on fire. Face to face with these rites, I am doubly alert. Black magic! Orgies, witches' sabbaths, heathen ceremonies, amulets. Coitus is an occasion to call on the gods of the clan. It is a sacred act, pure, absolute, bringing invisible forces into action. What is one to think of all these manifestations, all these initiations, all these acts? From very direction I am assaulted by the obscenity of dances and of words. Almost at my ear there is a song:

> First our hearts burned hot
> Now they are cold
> All we think of now is Love
> When we return to the village
> When we see the great phallus
> Ah how then we will make Love
> For our parts will be dry and clean.[12]

The soil, which only a moment ago was still a tamed steed, begins to revel. Are these virgins, these nymphomaniacs? Black magic, primitive mentality, animism, animal eroticism, it all floods over me. All of it is typical of peoples that have not kept pace with the evolution of the human race. Or, if one prefers, this is humanity at its lowest. Having reached this point, I was long reluctant to commit

myself. Aggression was in the stars. I had to choose. What do I mean?
I had no choice....

Yes, we are – we Negroes – backward, simple, free in our behaviour.
That is because for us the body is not something opposed to what you
call the mind. We are in the world. And long live the couple, Man and
Earth! Besides, our men of letters helped me to convince you; your
white civilization overlooks subtle riches and sensitivity. Listen:

Emotive sensitivity. *Emotion is completely Negro as reason is Greek*.[13] Water
rippled by every breeze? Unsheltered soul blown by every wind, whose fruit often
drops before it is ripe? Yes, in one way, the Negro today is richer *in gifts than in
works*.[14] But the tree thrusts its roots into the earth. The river runs deep, carrying
precious seeds. And, the Afro-American poet, Langston Hughes, says:

> I have known rivers
> ancient dark rivers
> my soul has grown deep
> like the deep rivers.

The very nature of the Negro's emotion, of his sensitivity, furthermore,
explains his attitude toward the object perceived with such basic intensity.
It is an abandon that becomes need, an active state of communion, indeed of
identifications, however negligible the action – I almost said the personality – of
the object. A rhythmic attitude: The adjective should be kept in mind.[15]

So here we have the Negro rehabilitated, 'standing before the bar',
ruling the world with his intuition, the Negro recognized, set on his
feet again, sought after, taken up, and he is a Negro – no, he is not
a Negro but the Negro, exciting the fecund antennae of the world,
placed in the foreground of the world, raining his poetic power on
the world, 'open to all the breaths of the world'. I embrace the world!
I am the world! The white man has never understood this magic
substitution. The white man wants the world; he wants it for himself
alone. He finds himself predestined master of this world. He enslaves
it. An acquisitive relation is established between the world and him.
But there exist other values that fit only my forms. Like a magician,
I robbed the white man of 'a certain world', forever after lost to
him and his. When that happened, the white man must have been
rocked backward by a force that he could not identify, so little used
as he is to such reactions. Somewhere beyond the objective world
of farms and banana trees and rubber trees, I had subtly brought
the real world into being. The essence of the world was my fortune.
Between the world and me a relation of coexistence was established.
I had discovered the primeval One. My 'speaking hands' tore at the

hysterical throat of the world. The white man had the anguished
feeling that I was escaping from him and that I was taking something
with me. He went through my pockets. He thrust probes into the least
circumvolution of my brain. Everywhere he found only the obvious.
So it was obvious that I had a secret. I was interrogated; turning away
with an air of mystery, I murmured:

> Tokowaly, uncle, do you remember the nights gone by
> When my head weighed heavy on the back of your patience
>> or
> Holding my hand your hand led me by shadows and signs
> The fields are flowers of glowworms, stars hang on the
>> bushes, on the trees
> Silence is everywhere
> Only the scents of the jungle hum, swarms of reddish
>> bees that overwhelm the crickets' shrill sounds,
> And covered tom-tom, breathing in the distance of the
>> night.
> You, Tokowaly, you listen to what cannot be heard, and
>> you explain to me what the ancestors are saying in the
>> liquid calm of the constellations,
> The bull, the scorpion, the leopard, the elephant
>> and the fish we know,
> And the white pomp of the Spirits in the heavenly shell
>> that has no end,
> But now comes the radiance of the goddess Moon
>> and the veils of the shadows fall.
> Night of Africa, my black night, mystical and bright, black
>> and shining.[16]

I made myself the poet of the world. The white man had found
a poetry in which there was nothing poetic. The soul of the white
man was corrupted, and, as I was told by a friend who was a teacher
in the United States, 'The presence of the Negroes beside the whites
is in a way an insurance policy on humanness. When the whites
feel that they have become too mechanized, they turn to the men
of colour and ask them for a little human sustenance.' At last I had
been recognized, I was no longer a zero.

I had soon to change my tune. Only momentarily at a loss, the
white man explained to me that, genetically, I represented a stage
of development: 'Your properties have been exhausted by us. We
have had earth mystics such as you will never approach. Study our

history and you will see how far this fusion has gone.' Then I had the feeling that I was repeating a cycle. My originality had been torn out of me. I wept a long time, and then I began to live again. But I was haunted by a galaxy of erosive stereotypes: the Negro's *sui generis* odour ... the Negro's *sui generis* good nature ... the Negro's *sui generis* gullibility....

I had tried to flee myself through my kind, but the whites had thrown themselves on me and hamstrung me. I tested the limits of my essence; beyond all doubt there was not much of it left. It was here that I made my most remarkable discovery. Properly speaking, this discovery was a rediscovery.

I rummaged frenetically through all the antiquity of the black man. What I found there took away my breath. In his book *L'Abolition de l'esclavage* Schoelcher presented us with compelling arguments. Since then Frobenius, Westermann, Delafosse – all of them white – had joined the chorus: Ségou, Djenné, cities of more than a hundred thousand people; accounts of learned blacks (doctors of theology who went to Mecca to interpret the Koran). All of that, exhumed from the past, spread with its insides out, made it possible for me to find a valid historic place. The white man was wrong, I was not a primitive, not even a half-man, I belonged to a race that had already been working in gold and silver two thousand years ago. And there was something else as well, something else that the white man could not understand. Listen:

What sort of men were these, then, who had been torn away from their families, their countries, their religions, with a savagery unparalleled in history?

Gentle men, polite, considerate, unquestionably superior to those who tortured them – that collection of adventurers who slashed and violated and spat on Africa to make the stripping of her the easier.

The men they took away knew how to build houses, govern empires, erect cities, cultivate fields, mine for metals, weave cotton, forge steel.

Their religion had its own beauty, based on mystical connections with the founder of the city. Their customs were pleasing, built on unity, kindness, respect for age.

No coercion, only mutual assistance, the joy of living, a free acceptance of discipline.

Order – Earnestness – Poetry and Freedom.

From the untroubled private citizen to the almost fabulous leader there was an unbroken chain of understanding and trust. No science? Indeed yes; but also, to protect them from fear, they possessed great myths in which the most subtle observation and the most daring imagination were balanced and blended. No art? They had their magnificent sculpture, in which human feeling erupted so unrestrained yet always followed the obsessive laws of rhythm in its organization of the major elements of a material called upon to capture, in order to redistribute, the most secret forces of the universe....[17]

Monuments in the very heart of Africa? Schools? Hospitals? Not a single good burgher of the twentieth century, no Durand, no Smith, no Brown even suspects that such things existed in Africa before the Europeans came. ...

But Schoelcher reminds us of their presence, discovered by Caillé, Mollien, the Cander brothers. And, though he nowhere reminds us that when the Portuguese landed on the banks of the Congo in 1498, they found a rich and flourishing state there and that the courtiers of Ambas were dressed in robes of silk and brocade, at least he knows that Africa had brought itself up to a juridical concept of the state, and he is aware, living in the very flood of imperialism, that European civilization, after all, is only one more civilization among many – and not the most merciful.[18]

I put the white man back into his place; growing bolder, I jostled him and told him point-blank, 'Get used to me, I am not getting used to anyone.' I shouted my laughter to the stars. The white man, I could see, was resentful. His reaction time lagged interminably.... I had won. I was jubilant.

'Lay aside your history, your investigations of the past, and try to feel yourself into our rhythm. In a society such as ours, industrialized to the highest degree, dominated by scientism, there is no longer room for your sensitivity. One must be tough if one is to be allowed to live. What matters now is no longer playing the game of the world but subjugating it with integers and atoms. Oh, certainly, I will be told, now and then, when we are worn out by our lives in big buildings, we will turn to you as we do to our children – to the innocent, the ingenuous, the spontaneous. We will turn to you as to the childhood of the world. You are so real in your life – so funny, that is. Let us run away for a little while from our ritualized, polite civilization and let us relax, bend to those heads, those adorably expressive faces. In a way, you reconcile us with ourselves.'

Thus my unreason was countered with reason, my reason with 'real reason'. Every hand was a losing hand for me. I analysed my heredity. I made a complete audit of my ailment. I wanted to be typically Negro – it was no longer possible. I wanted to be white – that was a joke. And, when I tried, on the level of ideas and intellectual activity, to reclaim my negritude, it was snatched away from me. Proof was presented that my effort was only a term in the dialectic:

But there is something more important: the Negro, as we have said, creates an anti-racist racism for himself. In no sense does he wish to rule the world: he seeks the abolition of all ethnic privileges, wherever they come from; he asserts his solidarity with the oppressed of all colours. At once the subjective, existential, ethnic idea of *negritude* 'passes', as Hegel puts it, into the objective, positive, exact idea of *proletariat*. 'For Césaire', Senghor says, 'the white man is the symbol of capital as the Negro is that of labour.... Beyond the black-skinned men of his race it is the battle of the world proletariat that is his song.'

That is easy to say, but less easy to think out. And undoubtedly it is no coincidence that the most ardent poets of negritude are at the same time militant Marxists.

But that does not prevent the idea of race from mingling with that of class: the first is concrete and particular, the second is universal and abstract; the one stems from what Jaspers calls understanding and the other from intellection; the first is the result of a psychobiological syncretism and the second is a methodical construction based on experience. In fact, negritude appears as the minor term of a dialectical progression: the theoretical and practical assertion of the supremacy of the white man is its thesis; the position of negritude as an antithetical value is the moment of negativity. But this negative moment is insufficient by itself, and the Negroes who employ it know this very well; they know that it is intended to prepare the synthesis or realization of the human in a society without races. Thus negritude is the root of its own destruction, it is a transition and not a conclusion, a means and not an ultimate end.[19]

When I read that page, I felt that I had been robbed of my last chance. I said to my friends, 'The generation of the younger black poets has just suffered a blow that can never be forgiven.' Help had been sought from a friend of the coloured peoples, and that friend had found no better response than to point out the relativity of what they were doing. For once, that born Hegelian had forgotten that consciousness has to lose itself in the night of the absolute, the only condition to attain to consciousness of self. In opposition to rationalism, he summoned up the negative side, but he forgot that this negativity draws its worth from an almost substantive absoluteness. A consciousness committed to experience is ignorant, has to be ignorant, of the essences and the determination of its being.

Orphée noir is a date in the intellectualization of the *experience* of being black. And Sartre's mistake was not only to seek the source of the source but, in a certain sense, to block that source:

Will the source of Poetry be dried up? Or will the great black flood, in spite of everything, colour the sea into which it pours itself? It does not matter: every age has its own poetry; in every age the circumstances of history choose a nation, a race, a class to take up the torch by creating situations that can be expressed or transcended only through Poetry; sometimes the poetic impulse coincides with the revolutionary impulse, and sometimes they take different courses. Today let us hail the turn of history that will make it possible for the black men to utter 'the great Negro cry with a force that will shake the pillars of the world' (Césaire).[20]

And so it is not I who make a meaning for myself, but it is the meaning that was already there, pre-existing, waiting for me. It is not out of my bad nigger's misery, my bad nigger's teeth, my bad nigger's hunger that I will shape a torch with which to burn down the world, but it is the torch that was already there, waiting for that turn of history.

In terms of consciousness, the black consciousness is held out as an absolute density, as filled with itself, a stage preceding any invasion, any abolition of the ego by desire. Jean-Paul Sartre, in this work, has destroyed black zeal. In opposition to historical becoming, there had always been the unforeseeable. I needed to lose myself completely in negritude. One day, perhaps, in the depths of that unhappy romanticism....

In any case I *needed* not to know. This struggle, this new decline had to take on an aspect of completeness. Nothing is more unwelcome than the commonplace: 'You'll change, my boy; I was like that too when I was young ... you'll see, it will all pass.'

The dialectic that brings necessity into the foundation of my freedom drives me out of myself. It shatters my unreflected position. Still, in terms of consciousness, black consciousness is immanent in its own eyes. I am not a potentiality of something, I am wholly what I am. I do not have to look for the universal. No probability has any place inside me. My Negro consciousness does not hold itself out as a lack. It *is*. It is its own follower.

But, I will be told, your statements show a misreading of the processes of history. Listen then:

> Africa I have kept your memory Africa
> you are inside me
> Like the splinter in the wound
> like a guardian fetish in the centre of the village
> make me the stone in your sling
> make my mouth the lips of your wound

make my knees the broken pillars of your abasement
AND YET
I want to be of your race alone
workers peasants of all lands …
… white worker in Detroit black peon in Alabama
uncountable nation in capitalist slavery
destiny ranges us shoulder to shoulder
repudiating the ancient maledictions of blood taboos
we roll away the ruins of our solitudes
If the flood is a frontier
we will strip the gully of its endless
covering flow
If the Sierra is a frontier
we will smash the jaws of the volcanoes
upholding the Cordilleras
and the plain will be the parade ground of the dawn
where we regroup our forces sundered
by the deceits of our masters
As the contradiction among the features
creates the harmony of the face
we proclaim the oneness of the suffering
and the revolt
of all the peoples on all the face of the earth
    and we mix the mortar of the age of brotherhood
    out of the dust of idols.[21]

Exactly, we will reply, Negro experience is not a whole, for there is not merely *one* Negro, there are *Negroes*. What a difference, for instance, in this other poem:

The white man killed my father
Because my father was proud
The white man raped my mother
Because my mother was beautiful
The white man wore out my brother in the hot sun
    of the roads
Because my brother was strong
Then the white man came to me
His hands red with blood
Spat his contempt into my black face
Out of his tyrant's voice:
'Hey boy, a basin, a towel, water.'[22]

Or this other one:

> My brother with teeth that glisten at the compliments
> of hypocrites
> My brother with gold-rimmed spectacles
> Over eyes that turn blue at the sound of the Master's
> voice
> My poor brother in dinner jacket with its silk lapels
> Clucking and whispering and strutting through the
> drawing rooms of Condescension
> How pathetic you are
> The sun of your native country is nothing more now
> than a shadow
> On your composed civilized face
> And your grandmother's hut
> Brings blushes into cheeks made white by years of
> abasement and *Mea culpa*
> But when regurgitating the flood of lofty empty words
> Like the load that presses on your shoulders
> You walk again on the rough red earth of Africa
> These words of anguish will state the rhythm of your
> uneasy gait
> I feel so alone, so alone here![23]

From time to time one would like to stop. To state reality is a wearing task. But, when one has taken it into one's head to try to express existence, one runs the risk of finding only the non-existent. What is certain is that, at the very moment when I was trying to grasp my own being, Sartre, who remained The Other, gave me a name and thus shattered my last illusion. While I was saying to him:

> My negritude is neither a tower nor a cathedral,
> it thrusts into the red flesh of the sun,
> it thrusts into the burning flesh of the sky,
> it hollows through the dense dismay of its own pillar
> of patience ...

While I was shouting that, in the paroxysm of my being and my fury, he was reminding me that my blackness was only a minor term. In all truth, in all truth I tell you, my shoulders slipped out of the framework of the world, my feet could no longer feel the touch of the ground. Without a Negro past, without a Negro future, it was impossible for me to live my Negrohood. Not yet white, no longer wholly black, I was damned. Jean-Paul Sartre had forgotten that the Negro suffers in his body quite differently from the white man.[24] Between the white man and me the connection was irrevocably one of transcendence.[25]

But the constancy of my love had been forgotten. I defined myself as an absolute intensity of beginning. So I took up my negritude, and with tears in my eyes I put its machinery together again. What had been broken to pieces was rebuilt, reconstructed by the intuitive lianas of my hands.

My cry grew more violent: I am a Negro, I am a Negro, I am a Negro. ...

And there was my poor brother – living out his neurosis to the extreme and finding himself paralysed:

THE NEGRO: I can't, ma'am.
LIZZIE: Why not?
THE NEGRO: I can't shoot white folks.
LIZZIE: Really! That would bother them, wouldn't it?
THE NEGRO: They're white folks, ma'am.
LIZZIE: So what? Maybe they got a right to bleed you like a pig just because they're white?
THE NEGRO: But they're white folks.

A feeling of inferiority? No, a feeling of non-existence. Sin is Negro as virtue is white. All those white men in a group, guns in their hands, cannot be wrong. I am guilty. I do not know of what, but I know that I am no good.

THE NEGRO: That's how it goes, ma'am. That's how it always goes with white folks.
LIZZIE: You too? You feel guilty?
THE NEGRO: Yes, ma'am.[26]

It is Bigger Thomas – he is afraid, he is terribly afraid. He is afraid, but of what is he afraid? Of himself. No one knows yet who he is, but he knows that fear will fill the world when the world finds out. And when the world knows, the world always expects something of the Negro. He is afraid lest the world know, he is afraid of the fear that the world would feel if the world knew. Like that old woman on her knees who begged me to tie her to her bed:

'I just know, Doctor: Any minute that thing will take hold of me.'
'What thing?'
'The wanting to kill myself. Tie me down, I'm afraid.'

In the end, Bigger Thomas acts. To put an end to his tension, he acts, he responds to the world's anticipation.[27]

So it is with the character in *If He Hollers Let Him Go*[28] – who does precisely what he did not want to do. That big blonde who was always in his way, weak, sensual, offered, open, fearing (desiring) rape, became his mistress in the end.

The Negro is a toy in the white man's hands; so, in order to shatter the hellish cycle, he explodes. I cannot go to a film without seeing myself. I wait for me. In the interval, just before the film starts, I wait for me. The people in the theatre are watching me, examining me, waiting for me. A Negro groom is going to appear. My heart makes my head swim.

The crippled veteran of the Pacific war says to my brother, 'Resign yourself to your colour the way I got used to my stump; we're both victims.'[29]

Nevertheless with all my strength I refuse to accept that amputation. I feel in myself a soul as immense as the world, truly a soul as deep as the deepest of rivers, my chest has the power to expand without limit. I am a master and I am advised to adopt the humility of the cripple. Yesterday, awakening to the world, I saw the sky turn upon itself utterly and wholly. I wanted to rise, but the disembowelled silence fell back upon me, its wings paralysed. Without responsibility, straddling Nothingness and Infinity, I began to weep.

8
West Indians and Africans[1]

Two years ago I was finishing a work[2] on the problem of the coloured man in the white world. I knew that I must absolutely not amputate reality. I was not unaware of the fact that, within the very entity of the 'Negro people', movements could be discerned which, unfortunately, were utterly devoid of any attractive features. I mean, for example, that the enemy of the Negro is often not the white man but a man of his own colour. That is why I suggested the possibility of a study that could contribute to the dissolution of the affective complexes that could oppose West Indians and Africans.

Before taking up the discussion we should like to point out that this business of Negroes is a dirty business. A business to turn your stomach. A business which, when you are faced with it, leaves you wholly disarmed if you accept the premises of the Negro-baiters. And when I say that the expression 'Negro people' is an entity, I thereby indicate that, except for cultural influences, nothing is left. There is as great a difference between a West Indian and a Dakarian as between a Brazilian and a Spaniard. The object of lumping all Negroes together under the designation of 'Negro people' is to deprive them of any possibility of individual expression. What is thus attempted is to put them under the obligation of matching the idea one has of them.

Is it not obvious that there can only be a white race? What would the 'white people' correspond to? Do I have to explain the difference that exists between nation, people, fatherland, community? When one says 'Negro people', one systematically assumes that all Negroes agree on certain things, that they share a principle of communion. The truth is that there is nothing, *a priori*, to warrant the assumption that such a thing as a Negro people exists. That there is an African people, that there is a West Indian people, this I do believe.[3] But when someone talks to me about that 'Negro people', I try to understand what is meant. Then, unfortunately, I understand that there is in this a source of conflicts. Then I try to destroy this source.

I shall be found to use terms like 'metaphysical guilt' or 'obsession with purity'. I shall ask the reader not to be surprised: these will be accurate to the extent to which it is understood that, since what is important cannot really be attained, or, more precisely, since what is important is not really sought after, one falls back on what is contingent. This is one of the laws of recrimination and of bad faith. The urgent thing is to rediscover what is important beneath what is contingent.

What is at issue here? I say that in a period of fifteen years a revolution has occurred in West Indian–African relations. I want to show wherein this event consists.

In Martinique it is rare to find hardened racial positions. The racial problem is covered over by economic discrimination and, in a given social class, it is above all productive of anecdotes. Relations are not modified by epidermal accentuations. Despite the greater or lesser amount of melanin that the skin may contain, there is a tacit agreement enabling all and sundry to recognize one another as doctors, tradesmen, workers. A Negro worker will be on the side of the mulatto worker against the middle-class Negro. Here we have proof that questions of race are but a superstructure, a mantle, an obscure ideological emanation concealing an economic reality.

In Martinique, when it is remarked that this or that person is in fact very black, this is said without contempt, without hatred. One must be accustomed to what is called the spirit of Martinique in order to grasp the meaning of what is said. Jankelevitch has shown that irony is one of the forms that good conscience assumes. It is true that in the West Indies irony is a mechanism of defence against neurosis. A West Indian, in particular an intellectual who is no longer on the level of irony, discovers his Negritude. Thus, while in Europe irony protects against the existential anguish, in Martinique it protects against the awareness of Negritude.

It can be seen that a study of irony in the West Indies is crucial for the sociology of this region. Aggressiveness there is almost always cushioned by irony.[4]

It will be convenient for our purpose to distinguish two periods in the history of the West Indies: before and after the war of 1939–45.

BEFORE THE WAR

Before 1939, the West Indian claimed to be happy, or at least thought of himself as being so.[5] He voted, went to school, when he could, took part in the processions, liked rum and danced the beguine. Those who were privileged to go to France spoke of Paris, of Paris which meant France. And those who were not privileged to know Paris let themselves be beguiled.

There were also the civil servants working in Africa. Through them one saw a country of savages, of barbarians, of natives, or servants. Certain things need to be said if one is to avoid falsifying the problem. The metropolitan civil servant, returning from Africa, has accustomed us to stereotypes: sorcerers, makers of fetishes, tom-toms, guilelessness, faithfulness, respect for the white man, backwardness. The trouble is that the West Indian speaks of Africa in exactly the same way and, as the civil servant is not only the colonial administrator but the constable, the customs officer, the registrar, the soldier, at every level of West Indian society an inescapable feeling of superiority over the African develops, becomes systematic, hardens. In every West Indian, before the war of 1939, there was not only the certainty of a superiority over the African, but the certainty of a fundamental difference. The African was a Negro and the West Indian a European.

These are things everyone gives the impression of knowing, but which no one takes into account.

Before 1939 the West Indian who volunteered in the Colonial Army, whether he was illiterate or knew how to read and write, served in a European unit, whereas the African, with the exception of the natives of the five territories, served in a native unit. The result to which we wish to draw attention is that, whatever the field considered, the West Indian was superior to the African, of a different species, assimilated to the metropolitan. But inasmuch as externally the West Indian was just a little bit African, since, say what you will, he was black, he was obliged – as a normal reaction in psychological economy – to harden his frontiers in order to be protected against any misapprehension.

We may say that the West Indian, not satisfied to be superior to the African, despised him, and, while the white man could allow himself certain liberties with the native, the West Indian absolutely could not. This was because, between whites and Africans, there was no need of a reminder; the difference stared one in the face. But what a catastrophe if the West Indian should suddenly be taken for an African!

We may say also that this position of the West Indian was authenticated by Europe. The West Indian was not a Negro; he was a West Indian, that is to say a quasi-metropolitan. By this attitude the white man justified the West Indian in his contempt for the African. The Negro, in short, was a man who inhabited Africa.

In France, before 1940, when a West Indian was introduced in Bordeaux or Paris society, the introducer always added, 'from Martinique'. I say 'Martinique', because – as people may or may not know – Guadeloupe, for some reason or other, was considered to be a country of savages. Even today, in 1952, we hear Martiniquans insist that they (the natives of Guadeloupe) are more savage than we are.

The African, for his part, was in Africa the real representative of the Negro race. As a matter of fact, when a boss made too great demands on a Martiniquan in a work situation, he would sometimes be told: 'If it's a nigger you want, go and look for him in Africa', meaning thereby that slaves and forced labour had to be recruited elsewhere. Over there, where the Negroes were.

The African, on the other hand, apart from a few rare 'developed' individuals, was looked down upon, despised, confined within the labyrinth of his epiderm. As we see, the positions were clear-cut: on the one hand, the African; on the other, the European and the West Indian. The West Indian was a black man, but the Negro was in Africa.

In 1939 no West Indian in the West Indies proclaimed himself to be a Negro, claimed to be a Negro. When he did, it was always in his relations with a white man. It was the white man, the 'bad white man', who obliged him to assert his colour, more exactly to defend it. But it can be affirmed that in the West Indies in 1939 no spontaneous claim of Negritude rang forth.

It was then that three events occurred successively.

The first event was the arrival of Césaire.

For the first time a *lycée* teacher – a man, therefore, who was apparently worthy of respect – was seen to announce quite simply to West Indian society 'that it is fine and good to be a Negro'. To be sure, this created a scandal. It was said at the time that he was a little mad and his colleagues went out of their way to give details as to his supposed ailment.

What indeed could be more grotesque than an educated man, a man with a diploma, having in consequence understood a good many things, among others that 'it was unfortunate to be a Negro', proclaiming that his skin was beautiful and that the '*big black hole*' was a source of truth. Neither the mulattoes nor the Negroes understood this delirium. The mulattoes because they had escaped from the night, the Negroes because they aspired to get away from it. Two centuries of white truth proved this man to be wrong. He must be mad, for it was unthinkable that he could be right.

Once the excitement had died down, everything seemed to resume its normal course.... And Césaire was about to be proved wrong, when the second event occurred: I am referring to the French defeat.

The downfall of France, for the West Indian, was in a sense the murder of the father. This national defeat might have been endured as it was in the metropolis, but a good part of the French fleet remained blockaded in the West Indies during the four years of the German occupation. This needs to be emphasized. I believe it is essential to grasp the historic importance of those four years.

Before 1939 there were about 2,000 Europeans in Martinique. These Europeans had well-defined functions, were integrated into the social life, involved in the country's economy. Now, from one day to the next, the single town of Fort-de-France was submerged by nearly 10,000 Europeans having an unquestionable, but until then latent, racist mentality. I mean that the sailors of the *Béarn* or the *Emile-Bertin*, on previous occasions, in the course of a week in Fort-de-France, had not had time to manifest their racial prejudices. The four years during which they were obliged to live shut in on themselves, inactive, a prey to anguish when they thought of their families left in France, victims of despair as to the future, allowed them to drop a mask which, when all is said and done, was rather superficial, and to behave as 'authentic racists'.

It may be added that the West Indian economy suffered a severe blow, for it became necessary to find – again without any transition – at a time when nothing could be imported, the wherewithal to feed 10,000 men. Moreover, many of those sailors and soldiers were able to send for their wives and children, who had to be housed. The Martiniquan held those white racists responsible for all this. The West Indian, in the presence of those men who despised him, began to have misgivings as to his values. The West Indian underwent his first metaphysical experience.

Then came Free France. De Gaulle, in London, spoke of treason, of soldiers who surrendered their swords even before they had drawn them. All this contributed to convincing the West Indians that France, *their* France, had not lost the war but that traitors had sold it out. And where were these traitors, if not camouflaged in the West Indies? One then witnessed an extraordinary sight: West Indians refusing to take off their hats while the 'Marseillaise' was being played. What West Indian can forget those Thursday evenings when, on the Esplanade de la Savane, patrols of armed sailors demanded silence and attention while the national anthem was being played? What had happened?

By a process easy to understand, the West Indians had assimilated the France of the sailors into the bad France, and the 'Marseillaise' that those men respected was not their own. It must not be forgotten that those sailors were racists. Now 'Everybody knows that the true Frenchman is not a racist; in other words, he does not consider the West Indian a Negro.' Since these men did so consider him, this meant that they were not true Frenchmen. Who knows, perhaps they were Germans? And, as a matter of fact, the sailor was systematically considered as a German. But the consequence that concerns us is the following: before 10,000 racists, the West Indian felt obliged to defend himself. Without Césaire this would have been difficult for him. But Césaire was there, and people joined him in chanting the once-hated song to the effect that it is fine and good to be a Negro! ...

For two years the West Indian defended his 'virtuous colour' inch by inch and, without suspecting it, was dancing on the edge of a precipice. For after all, if the colour black is virtuous, I shall be all the more virtuous the blacker I am! Then there emerged from the shadows the very black, the 'blues', the pure. And Césaire, the faithful bard, would repeat that 'paint the tree trunk white as you will, the roots below remain black'. Then it became real that not only the colour black was invested with value, but fiction black, ideal black, black in the absolute, primitive black, the Negro. This amounted to nothing less than requiring the West Indian totally to recast his world, to undergo a metamorphosis of his body. It meant demanding of him an axiological activity in reverse, a valorization of what he had rejected.

But history continued. In 1943, weary of an ostracism to which they were not accustomed, irritated, famished, the West Indians, who had formerly been separated into closed sociological groups, broke all barriers, came to an agreement on certain things, among others that those Germans had gone too far and, supported by the local army, fought for and won the rallying of the colony to the Free French. Admiral Robert, 'that other German', yielded. And this leads us to the third event.

It can be said that the demonstrations on the occasion of the Liberation, which were held in the West Indies, in any case in Martinique, in the months of July and August 1943, were the consequence of the birth of the proletariat. Martinique for the first time systematized its political consciousness. It is logical that the elections that followed the Liberation should have delegated two communist deputies out of three. In Martinique, the first metaphysical, or, if one prefers, ontological experiment, coincided with the first political experiment. Auguste Comte regarded the proletarian as a systematic philosopher. The proletarian of Martinique is a systematized Negro.

AFTER THE WAR

Thus the West Indian, after 1945, changed his values. Whereas before 1939 he had his eyes riveted on white Europe, whereas what seemed good to him was escape from his colour, in 1945 he discovered himself to be not only black but a Negro, and it was in the direction of distant Africa that he was henceforth to put out his feelers. The West Indian in France was continually recalling that he was not a Negro: from 1945 on, the West Indian in France was continually to recall that he *was* a Negro.

During this time the African pursued his way. He was not torn; he did not have to situate himself simultaneously with reference to the West Indian and with reference to the European. These last belonged in the same bag, the bag of the starvers, of the exploiters, of the no-goods. To be sure, there had been Eboué, who, though a West Indian, had spoken to the Africans at the Brazzaville conference and had called them 'my dear brothers'. And this brotherhood was not evangelical; it was based on colour. The Africans had adopted Eboué. He was one of them. The other West Indians would come, but their pretensions to superiority were known. But to the Africans' great astonishment, the West Indians who came to Africa after 1945 appeared with their hands stretched out, their backs bowed, humbly suppliant. They came to Africa with their hearts full of hope, eager to rediscover the source, to suckle at the authentic breasts of the African earth. The West Indians, civil servants and military, lawyers and doctors, landing in Dakar, were distressed at not being sufficiently black. Fifteen years before, they said to the Europeans, 'Don't pay attention to my black skin, it's the sun that has burned me, my soul is as white as yours.' After 1945 they changed their tune. They said to the Africans, 'Don't pay attention to my white skin, my soul is as black as yours, and that is what matters.'

But the Africans were too resentful of them to allow them so easy a turnabout. Recognized in their blackness, in their obscurity, in what fifteen years before had been sin, they resented any encroachment on the West Indian's part in this realm. They discovered themselves at last to be the possessors of truth, centuries-old bearers of an incorruptible purity. They rejected the West Indian, reminding him that *they* had not deserted, that *they* had not betrayed, that *they* had toiled, suffered, struggled on the African earth. The West Indian had said no to the white man; the African was saying no to the West Indian.

The latter was undergoing his second metaphysical experience. He then suffered despair. Haunted by impurity, overwhelmed by sin, riddled with guilt, he was prey to the tragedy of being neither white nor Negro.

He wept, he composed poems, sang of Africa, of Africa the hard and the beautiful, Africa exploding with anger, tumultuous bustle, splash, Africa land of truth. At the Institute of Oriental Languages in Paris he learned Bambara. The African, in his majesty, rejected all approaches. The African was getting his revenge and the West Indian was paying....

If we now try to explain and summarize the situation, we may say that in Martinique, before 1939, there was not on one side the Negro and on the other side the white man, but a scale of colours the intervals of which could readily be passed over. One needed only to have children by someone less black than oneself. There was no racial barrier, no discrimination. There was that ironic spice, so characteristic of the Martinique mentality.

But in Africa the discrimination was real. There the Negro, the African, the native, the black, the dirty, was rejected, despised, cursed. There an amputation had occurred; there humanity was denied.

Until 1939 the West Indian lived, thought, dreamed (we have shown this in *Black Skin, White Masks*), composed poems, wrote novels exactly as a white man would have done. We understand now why it was not possible for him, as for the African poets, to sing the black night. 'The black woman with pink heels'. Before Césaire, West Indian literature was a literature of Europeans. The West Indian identified himself with the white man, adopted a white man's attitude, 'was a white man'.

After the West Indian was obliged, under the pressure of European racists, to abandon positions that were essentially fragile, because they were absurd, because they were incorrect, because they were alienating, a new generation came into being. The West Indian of 1945 is a Negro.

In *Cahier d'un retour au pays natal* (logbook of a return to the native land) there is an African period; we read:

By dint of thinking of the Congo
I have become a Congo humming with forests and rivers

Then, with his eyes on Africa, the West Indian was to hail it. He discovered himself to be a transplanted son of slaves; he felt the vibration of Africa in the very depth of his body and aspired only to one thing: to plunge into the great 'black hole'.

It thus seems that the West Indian, after the great white error, is now living in the great black mirage.

9
On National Culture

To take part in the African revolution it is not enough to write a revolutionary song; you must fashion the revolution with the people. And if you fashion it with the people, the songs will come by themselves, and of themselves.

In order to achieve real action, you must yourself be a living part of Africa and of her thought; you must be an element of that popular energy which is entirely called forth for the freeing, the progress and the happiness of Africa. There is no place outside that fight for the artist or for the intellectual who is not himself concerned with and completely at one with the people in the great battle of Africa and of suffering humanity.[1]

Each generation must, out of relative obscurity, discover its mission, fulfil it, or betray it. In underdeveloped countries the preceding generations have both resisted the work of erosion carried on by colonialism and also helped on the maturing of the struggles of today. We must rid ourselves of the habit, now that we are in the thick of the fight, of minimizing the action of our fathers or of feigning incomprehension when considering their silence and passivity. They fought as well as they could, with the arms that they possessed then; and if the echoes of their struggle have not resounded in the international arena, we must realize that the reason for this silence lies less in their lack of heroism than in the fundamentally different international situation of our time. It needed more than one native to say 'We've had enough', more than one peasant rising crushed, more than one demonstration put down before we could today hold our own, certain in our victory. As for those of us who have decided to break the back of colonialism, our historic mission is to sanction all revolts, all desperate actions, all those abortive attempts drowned in rivers of blood.

In this chapter we shall analyse the problem, which is felt to be fundamental, of the legitimacy of the claims of a nation. It must be recognized that the political party that mobilizes the people hardly touches on this problem of legitimacy. The political parties start from living reality and it is in the name of this reality, in the name of the stark facts that weigh down the present and the future of men and women, that they fix their line of action. The political party may well speak in moving terms of the nation, but what it is concerned with is that the people who are listening understand the need to take part in the fight if, quite simply, they wish to continue to exist.

Today we know that in the first phase of the national struggle colonialism tries to disarm national demands by putting forward economic doctrines. As soon as the first demands are set out, colonialism pretends to consider them, recognizing with ostentatious humility that the territory is suffering from serious underdevelopment which necessitates a great economic and social effort. And, in fact, it so happens that certain spectacular measures (centres of work for the unemployed which are opened here and there, for example) delay the crystallization of national consciousness for a few years. But, sooner or later, colonialism sees that it is not within its powers to put into practice a project of economic and social reforms that will satisfy aspirations of the colonized people. Even where food supplies are concerned, colonialism gives proof of its inherent incapability. The colonialist state quickly discovers that if it wishes to disarm the nationalist parties on strictly economic questions then it will have to do in the colonies exactly what it has refused to do in its own country. It is not mere chance that almost everywhere today there flourishes the doctrine of Cartierism.

The disillusioned bitterness we find in Cartier when up against the obstinate determination of France to link to herself peoples whom she must feed while so many French people live in want shows up the impossible situation in which colonialism finds itself when the colonial system is called upon to transform itself into an unselfish programme of aid and assistance. It is why, once again, there is no use in wasting time repeating that hunger with dignity is preferable to bread eaten in slavery. On the contrary, we must become convinced that colonialism is incapable of procuring for the colonized peoples the material conditions that might make them forget their concern for dignity. Once colonialism has realized where its tactics of social reform are leading, we see it falling back on its old reflexes, reinforcing police effectives, bringing up troops and setting up a reign of terror which is better adapted to its interests and its psychology.

Inside the political parties, and most often in offshoots from these parties, cultured individuals of the colonized race make their appearance. For these individuals, the demand for a national culture and the affirmation of the existence of such a culture represent a special battlefield. While the politicians situate their action in actual present-day events, men of culture take their stand in the field of history. Confronted with the native intellectual who decides to make an aggressive response to the colonialist theory of pre-colonial barbarism, colonialism will react only slightly, and still less because the ideas developed by the young colonized intelligentsia are widely professed by specialists in the mother country. It is in fact a commonplace to state that, for several decades, large numbers of research workers have, in the main, rehabilitated the African, Mexican and Peruvian civilizations. The passion with which native intellectuals defend the existence of their national culture may be a source of amazement; but those who condemn this exaggerated passion are strangely apt to forget that their own psyche and their own selves are conveniently sheltered behind a French or German culture that has given full proof of its existence and that is uncontested.

I am ready to concede that, on the plane of factual being, the past existence of an Aztec civilization does not change anything very much in the diet of the Mexican peasant of today. I admit that all the proofs of a wonderful Songhai civilization will not change the fact that today the Songhais are under-fed and illiterate, thrown between sky and water with empty heads and empty eyes. But it has been remarked several times that this passionate search for a national culture which existed before the colonial era finds its legitimate reason in the anxiety shared by native intellectuals to shrink away from that Western culture in which they all risk being swamped. Because they realize they are in danger of losing their lives and thus becoming lost to their people, these men, hot-headed and with anger in their hearts, relentlessly determine to renew contact once more with the oldest and most pre-colonial springs of life of their people.

Let us go farther. Perhaps this passionate research and this anger are kept up or at least directed by the secret hope of discovering beyond the misery of today, beyond self-contempt, resignation and abjuration, some very beautiful and splendid era whose existence rehabilitates us both in regard to ourselves and in regard to others. I have said that I have decided to go farther. Perhaps unconsciously, the native intellectuals, since they could not stand wonder-struck before the history of today's barbarity, decided to go back farther and to delve deeper down; and, let us make no mistake, it was with the greatest delight that they discovered that there was nothing to be ashamed of in the past, but rather dignity, glory and solemnity. The claim to a national culture in the past does not only rehabilitate that nation and serve as a justification for the hope of a future national culture. In the sphere of psycho-affective equilibrium it is responsible for an important change in the native. Perhaps we have not sufficiently demonstrated that colonialism is not simply content to impose its rule upon the present and the future of a dominated country. Colonialism is not satisfied merely with holding a people in its grip and emptying the native's brain of all form and content. By a kind of perverted logic, it turns to the past of the oppressed people, and distorts, disfigures and destroys it. This work of devaluing pre-colonial history takes on a dialectical significance today.

When we consider the efforts made to carry out the cultural estrangement so characteristic of the colonial epoch, we realize that nothing has been left to chance and that the total result looked for by colonial domination was indeed to convince the natives that colonialism came to lighten their darkness. The effect consciously sought by colonialism was to drive into the natives' heads the idea that if the settlers were to leave, they would at once fall back into barbarism, degradation and bestiality.

On the unconscious plane, colonialism therefore did not seek to be considered by the native as a gentle, loving mother who protects her child from a hostile environment, but rather as a mother who unceasingly restrains her fundamentally perverse offspring from managing to commit suicide and from giving free rein to its evil instincts. The colonial mother protects her child from itself, from its ego, and from its physiology, its biology and its own unhappiness, which is its very essence.

In such a situation the claims of the native intellectual are no luxury but a necessity in any coherent programme. The native intellectual who takes up arms to defend his nation's legitimacy and who wants to bring proofs to bear out that legitimacy, who is willing to strip himself naked to study the history of his body, is obliged to dissect the heart of his people.

Such an examination is not specifically national. The native intellectual who decides to give battle to colonial lies fights on the field of the whole continent. The past is given back its value. Culture, extracted from the past to be displayed in all its splendour, is not necessarily that of his own country. Colonialism, which has not bothered to put too fine a point on its efforts, has never ceased to maintain that the Negro is a savage; and for the colonist, the Negro was neither an Angolan nor a Nigerian, for he simply spoke of 'the Negro'. For colonialism, this vast continent was the haunt of savages, a country riddled with superstitions and fanaticism, destined for contempt, weighed down by the curse of God, a country of cannibals – in short, the Negro's country. Colonialism's condemnation is continental its scope. The contention by colonialism that the darkest night of humanity lay over pre-colonial history concerns the whole of the African continent. The efforts of the native to rehabilitate himself and to escape from the claws of colonialism are logically inscribed from the same point of view as that of colonialism. The native intellectual who has gone far beyond the domains of Western culture and who has got it into his head to proclaim the existence of another culture never does so in the name of Angola or of Dahomey. The culture which is affirmed is African culture. The Negro, never so much a Negro as since he has been dominated by the whites, when he decides to prove that he has a culture and to behave like a cultured person, comes to realize that history points out a well-defined path to him: he must demonstrate that a Negro culture exists.

And it is only too true that those who are most responsible for this racialization of thought, or at least for the first movement towards that thought, are and remain those Europeans who have never ceased to set up white culture to fill the gap left by the absence of other cultures. Colonialism did not dream of wasting its time in denying the existence of one national culture after another. Therefore the reply of the colonized peoples will be straight away continental in its breadth. In Africa, the native literature of the last twenty years is not a national literature but a Negro literature. The concept of Negro-ism, for example, was the emotional if not the logical antithesis of that insult which the white man flung at humanity. This rush of Negro-ism against the white man's contempt showed itself in certain spheres to be the one idea capable of lifting interdictions and anathemas. Because the New Guinean or Kenyan intellectuals found themselves above all up against a general ostracism and delivered to the combined contempt of their overlords, their reaction was to sing praises in admiration of each other. The unconditional affirmation of African culture has succeeded the unconditional affirmation of European culture. On the whole, the poets of Negro-ism oppose the idea of an old Europe to a young Africa, tiresome reasoning to lyricism, oppressive logic to high-stepping nature, and on one side stiffness, ceremony, etiquette and scepticism, while on the other frankness, liveliness, liberty and – why not? – luxuriance: but also irresponsibility.

The poets of Negro-ism will not stop at the limits of the continent. From America, black voices will take up the hymn with fuller unison. The 'black world' will see the light and Busia from Ghana, Birago Diop from Senegal, Hampaté Ba from the Sudan and Saint-Clair Drake from Chicago will not hesitate to assert the existence of common ties and a motive power that is identical.

The example of the Arab world might equally well be quoted here. We know that the majority of Arab territories have been under colonial domination. Colonialism has made the same effort in these regions to plant deep in the minds of the native population the idea that before the advent of colonialism their history was one that was dominated by barbarism. The struggle for national liberty has been accompanied by a cultural phenomenon known by the name of the awakening of Islam. The passion with which contemporary Arab writers remind their people of the great pages of their history is a reply to the lies told by the occupying power. The great names of Arabic literature and the great past of Arab civilization have been brandished about with the same ardour as those of the African civilizations. The Arab leaders have tried to return to the famous Dar El Islam which shone so brightly from the twelfth to the fourteenth century.

Today, in the political sphere, the Arab League is giving palpable form to this will to take up again the heritage of the past and to bring it to culmination. Today, Arab doctors and Arab poets speak to each other across the frontiers, and strive to create a new Arab culture and a new Arab civilization. It is in the name of Arabism that these men join together, and that they try to think together. Everywhere, however, in the Arab world, national feeling has preserved, even under colonial domination, a liveliness that we fail to find in Africa. At the same time, that spontaneous communion of each with all, present in the African movement, is not to be found in the Arab League. On the contrary, paradoxically, everyone tries to sing the praises of the achievements of his nation. The cultural process is freed from the lack of differentiation that characterized it in the African world, but the Arabs do not always manage to stand aside in order to achieve their aims. The living culture is not national but Arab. The problem is not as yet to secure a national culture, not as yet to lay hold of a movement differentiated by nations, but to assume an African or Arabic culture when confronted by the all-embracing condemnation pronounced by the dominating power. In the African world, as in the Arab, we see that the claims of the man of culture in a colonized country are all-embracing, continental and, in the case of the Arabs, world-wide.

This historical necessity, in which the men of African culture find themselves, to racialize their claims and to speak more of African culture than of national culture will tend to lead them up a blind alley. Let us take for example the case of the African Cultural Society. This society had been created by African intellectuals who wished to get to know each other and to compare their experiences and the results of their respective research work. The aim of this society was therefore to affirm the existence of an African culture, to evaluate this culture on the plane of distinct nations and to reveal the internal motive forces of each of their national cultures. But at the same time this society fulfilled another need: the need to exist side by side with the European Cultural Society, which threatened to transform itself into a Universal Cultural Society. There was therefore at the bottom of this decision the anxiety to be present at the universal trysting place fully armed, with a culture springing from the very heart of the African continent. Now, this Society will very quickly show its inability to shoulder these different tasks, and will limit itself to exhibitionist demonstrations, while the habitual behaviour of the members of this Society will be confined to showing Europeans that such a thing as African culture exists, and opposing their ideas to those of ostentatious and narcissistic Europeans. We have shown that such an attitude is normal and draws its legitimacy from the lies propagated by men of Western culture. But the degradation of the aims of this Society will become more marked with the elaboration of the concept of Negro-ism. The African Society will become the cultural society of the black world and will come to include the Negro dispersion, that is to say the tens of thousands of black people spread over the American continents.

The Negroes who live in the United States and in Central or Latin America in fact experience the need to attach themselves to a cultural matrix. Their problem is not fundamentally different from that of the Africans. The whites of America did not mete out to them any different treatment from that of the whites who ruled over the Africans. We have seen that the whites were used to putting all Negroes in the same bag. During the first congress of the African Cultural Society, which was held in Paris in 1956, the American Negroes of their own accord considered their problems from the same standpoint as those of their African brothers. Cultured Africans, speaking of African civilizations, decreed that there should be a reasonable status within the state for those who had formerly been slaves. But, little by little, the American Negroes realized that the essential problems confronting them were not the same as those that confronted the African Negroes. The Negroes of Chicago only resemble the Nigerians or the Tanganyikans in so far as they were all defined in relation to the whites. But once the first comparisons had been made and subjective feelings were assuaged, the American Negroes realized that the objective problems were fundamentally heterogeneous. The test cases of civil liberty whereby both whites and blacks in America try to drive back racial discrimination have very little in common in their principles and objectives with the heroic fight of the Angolan people against the detestable Portuguese colonialism. Thus, during the second congress of the African Cultural Society the American Negroes decided to create an American society for people of black cultures.

Negro-ism therefore finds its first limitation in the phenomena that take account of the formation of the historical character of men. Negro and African-Negro culture broke up into different entities because the men who wished to incarnate these cultures realized that every culture is first and foremost national, and that the problems that kept Richard Wright or Langston Hughes on the alert were fundamentally different from those that might confront Leopold Senghor or Jomo Kenyatta. In the same way, certain Arab states, though they had chanted the marvellous hymn of Arab renaissance, had nevertheless to realize that their geographical position and the economic ties of their region were stronger even than the past that they wished to revive. Thus we find today the Arab states organically linked once more with societies which are Mediterranean in their culture. The fact is that these states are submitted to modern pressure and to new channels of trade while the network of trade relations that was dominant during the great period of Arab history has disappeared. But, above all, there is the fact that the political regimes of certain Arab states are so different, and so far away from each other in their conceptions, that even a cultural meeting between these states is meaningless.

Thus we see that the cultural problem as it sometimes exists in colonized countries runs the risk of giving rise to serious ambiguities. The lack of culture of the Negroes, as proclaimed by colonialism, and the inherent barbarity of the Arabs, ought logically to lead to the exaltation of cultural manifestations which are not simply national but continental, and extremely racial. In Africa, the movement of men of culture is a movement towards the Negro-African culture or the Arab-Moslem culture. It is not specifically towards a national culture. Culture is becoming more and more cut off from the events of today. It finds its refuge beside a hearth that glows with passionate emotion, and from there makes its way by realistic paths, which are the only means by which it may be made fruitful, homogeneous and consistent.

If the action of the native intellectual is limited historically, there remains nevertheless the fact that it contributes greatly to upholding and justifying the action of politicians. It is true that the attitude of the native intellectual sometimes takes on the aspect of a cult or of a religion. But if we really wish to analyse this attitude correctly we will come to see that it is symptomatic of the intellectual's realization of the danger that he is running of cutting his last moorings and of breaking adrift from his people. This stated belief in a national culture is in fact an ardent, despairing turning towards anything that will afford him secure anchorage. In order to ensure his salvation and to escape from the supremacy of the white man's culture the native feels the need to turn backwards towards his unknown roots and to lose himself, at whatever cost, in his own barbarous people. Because he feels he is becoming estranged, that is to say, because he feels that he is the living haunt of contradictions which run the risk of becoming insurmountable, the native tears himself away from the swamp that may suck him down and accepts everything, decides to take all for granted and confirms everything, even though he may lose body and soul. The native finds that he is expected to answer for everything, and to all comers. He not only turns himself into the defender of his people's past; he is willing to be counted as one of them, and henceforward he is even capable of laughing at his past cowardice.

This tearing away, painful and difficult though it may be, is, however, necessary. If it is not accomplished there will be serious psycho-affective injuries and the result will be individuals without an anchor, without a horizon, colourless, stateless, rootless – a race of angels. It will be also quite normal to hear certain natives declare 'I speak as a Senegalese and as a Frenchman ...' 'I speak as an Algerian and as a Frenchman ...' The intellectual who is Arab and French, or Nigerian and English, when he comes up against the need to take on two nationalities, chooses, if he wants to remain true to himself, the negation of one of these determinations. But most often, since they cannot or will not make a choice, such intellectuals gather together all the historical determining factors which have conditioned them and take up a fundamentally 'universal standpoint'.

This is because the native intellectual has thrown himself greedily upon Western culture. Like adopted children who only stop investigating the new family framework at the moment when a minimum nucleus of security crystallizes in their psyche, the native intellectual will try to make European culture his own. He will not be content to get to know Rabelais and Diderot, Shakespeare and Edgar Allen Poe; he will bind them to his intelligence as closely as possible:

> La dame n'était pas seule
> Elle avait un mari
> Un mari très comme il faut
> Qui citait Racine et Corneille
> Et Voltaire et Rousseau
> Et le Père Hugo et le jeune Musset
> Et Gide et Valéry
> Et tant d'autres encore.[2]

But at the moment when the nationalist parties are mobilizing the people in the name of national independence, the native intellectual sometimes spurns these acquisitions which he suddenly feels make him a stranger in his own land. It is always easier to proclaim rejection than actually to reject. The intellectual who, through the medium of culture has filtered into Western civilization, who has managed to become part of the body of European culture – in other words who has exchanged his own culture for another – will come to realize that the cultural matrix, which now he wishes to assume since he is anxious to appear original, can hardly supply any figureheads that will bear comparison with those, so many in number and so great in prestige, of the occupying power's civilization. History, of course, though nevertheless written by the Westerners and to serve their purposes, will be able to evaluate from time to time certain periods of the African past. But, standing face to face with his country at the present time, and observing clearly and objectively the events of today throughout the continent that he wants to make his own, the intellectual is terrified by the void, the degradation and the savagery he sees there. Now he feels that he must get away from white culture. He must seek his culture elsewhere, anywhere at all; and if he fails to find the substance of culture of the same grandeur and scope as displayed by the ruling power, the native intellectual will very often fall back upon emotional attitudes and will develop a psychology that is dominated by exceptional sensitivity and susceptibility. This withdrawal, which is due in the first instance to a begging of the question in his internal behaviour mechanism and his own character, brings out, above all, a reflex and contradiction which is muscular.

This is sufficient explanation of the style of those native intellectuals who decide to give expression to this phase of consciousness that is in process of being liberated. It is a harsh style, full of images, for the image is the drawbridge that allows unconscious energies to be scattered on the surrounding meadows. It is a vigorous style, alive with rhythms, struck through and through with bursting life; it is full of colour, too, bronzed, sun-baked and violent. This style, which in its time astonished the peoples of the West, has nothing racial about it, in spite of frequent statements to the contrary; it expresses above all a hand-to-hand struggle and it reveals the need that man has to liberate himself from a part of his being that already contained the seeds of decay. Whether the fight is painful, quick or inevitable, muscular action must substitute itself for concepts.

If in the world of poetry this movement reaches unaccustomed heights, the fact remains that, in the real world, the intellectual often goes up a blind alley. When at the height of his intercourse with his people, whatever they were or whatever they are, the intellectual decides to come down into the common paths of real life, he only brings back from his adventuring formulas that are sterile in the extreme. He sets a high value on the customs, traditions and the appearances of his people; but his inevitable, painful experience only seems to be a banal search for exoticism. The sari becomes sacred and shoes that come from Paris or Italy are left off in favour of pampooties, while suddenly the language of the ruling power is felt to burn your lips. Finding your fellow countrymen sometimes means in this phase to will oneself to be a nigger, not a nigger like all other niggers but a real nigger, a Negro cur, just the sort of nigger that the white man wants you to be. Going back to your own people means to become a dirty wog, to go native as much as you can, to become unrecognizable and to cut off those wings that before you had allowed to grow.

The native intellectual decides to make an inventory of the bad habits drawn from the colonial world, and hastens to remind everyone of the good old customs of the people, that people which, he has decided, contains all truth and goodness. The scandalized attitude with which the settlers who live in the colonial territory greet this new departure only serves to strengthen the native's decision. When the colonialists, who had tasted the sweets of their victory over these assimilated people, realize that these men whom they considered as saved souls are beginning to fall back into the ways of niggers, the whole system totters. Every native won over, every native who had taken the pledge not only marks a failure for the colonial structure when he decides to lose himself and to go back to his own side, but also stands as a symbol for the uselessness and the shallowness of all the work that has been accomplished. Each native who goes back over the line is a radical condemnation of the methods and of the regime; and the native intellectual finds in the scandal he gives rise to a justification and an encouragement to persevere in the path he has chosen.

If we wanted to trace in the works of native writers the different phases that characterize this evolution, we would find spread out before us a panorama on three levels. In the first phase, the native intellectual gives proof that he has assimilated the culture of the occupying power. His writings correspond point by point with those of his opposite numbers in the mother country. His inspiration is European and we can easily link up these works with definite trends in the literature of the mother country. This is the period of unqualified assimilation. We find in this literature coming from the colonies the Parnassians, the Symbolists and the Surrealists.

In the second phase we find the native is disturbed; he decides to remember what he is. This period of creative work approximately corresponds to that immersion which we have just described. But since the native is not a part of his people, since he only has exterior relations with his people, he is content to recall their life only. Past happenings of the bygone days of his childhood will be brought up out of the depths of his memory; old legends will be reinterpreted in the light of a borrowed aestheticism and of a conception of the world that was discovered under other skies.

Sometimes this literature of just-before-the-battle is dominated by humour and by allegory; but often, too, it is symptomatic of a period of distress and difficulty, where death is experienced, and disgust too. We spew ourselves up; but already underneath laughter can be heard.

Finally, in the third phase, which is called the fighting phase, the native, after having tried to lose himself in the people and with the people, will on the contrary shake the people. Instead of according the people's lethargy an honoured place in his esteem, he turns himself into an awakener of the people; hence comes a fighting literature, a revolutionary literature and a national literature. During this phase a great many men and women who up till then would never have thought of producing a literary work, now that they find themselves in exceptional circumstances – in prison, with the Maquis or on the eve of their execution – feel the need to speak to their nation, to compose the sentence that expresses the heart of the people and to become the mouthpiece of a new reality in action.

The native intellectual nevertheless sooner or later will realize that you do not show proof of your nation from its culture but that you substantiate its existence in the fight that the people wage against the forces of occupation. No colonial system draws its justification from the fact that the territories it dominates are culturally non-existent. You will never make colonialism blush for shame by spreading out little-known cultural treasures under its eyes. At the very moment when the native intellectual is anxiously trying to create a cultural work he fails to realize that he is utilizing techniques and language that are borrowed from the stranger in his country. He contents himself with stamping these instruments with a hallmark that he wishes to be national, but which is strangely reminiscent of exoticism. The native intellectual who comes back to his people by way of cultural achievements behaves, in fact, like a foreigner. Sometimes he has no hesitation in using a dialect in order to show his will to be as near as possible to the people; but the ideas that he expresses and the preoccupations he is taken up with have no common yardstick to measure the real situation that the men and the women of his country know. The culture that the intellectual leans towards is often no more than a stock of particularisms. He wishes to attach himself to the people; but instead he only catches hold of their outer garments. And these outer garments are merely the reflection of a hidden life, teeming and perpetually in motion. That extremely obvious objectivity that seems to characterize a people is in fact only the inert, already forsaken result of frequent, and not always very coherent, adaptations of a much more fundamental substance which itself is continually being renewed. The man of culture, instead of setting out to find this substance, will let himself be hypnotized by these mummified fragments which, because they are static, are in fact symbols of negation and outworn contrivances. Culture never has the translucidity of custom; it abhors all simplification. In its essence it is opposed to custom, for custom is always the deterioration of culture. The desire to attach oneself to tradition or bring abandoned traditions to life again does not only mean going against the current of history but also opposing one's own people. When a people undertakes an armed struggle or even a political struggle against a relentless colonialism, the significance of tradition changes. All that has made up the technique of passive resistance in the past may, during this phase, be radically condemned. In an underdeveloped country during the period of struggle traditions are fundamentally unstable and are shot through by centrifugal tendencies. This is why the intellectual often runs the risk of being out of date. The peoples who have carried on the struggle are more impervious to demagogy; and those who wish to follow them reveal themselves as nothing more than common opportunists, in other words late-comers.

In the sphere of plastic arts, for example, the native artist who wishes at whatever cost to create a national work of art shuts himself up in a stereotyped reproduction of details. These artists, who have nevertheless thoroughly studied modern techniques and who have taken part in the main trends of contemporary painting and architecture, turn their back on foreign culture, deny it and set out to look for a true national culture, setting great store on what they consider to be the constant principles of national art. But these people forget that the forms of thought and what it feeds on, together with modern techniques of information, language and dress have dialectically reorganized the people's intelligences and that the constant principles which acted as safeguards during the colonial period are now undergoing extremely radical changes.

The artist who has decided to illustrate the truths of the nation turns paradoxically towards the past and away from actual events. What he ultimately intends to embrace are in fact the cast-offs of thought, its shells and corpses, a knowledge which has been stabilized once and for all. But the native intellectual who wishes to create an authentic work of art must realize that the truths of a nation are in the first place its realities. He must go on until he has found the seething pot out of which the learning of the future will emerge.

Before independence, the native painter was insensible to the national scene. He set a high value on non-figurative art, or more often was specialized in still-lifes. After independence his anxiety to rejoin his people will confine him to the most detailed representation of reality. This is representative art which has no internal rhythms, an art which is serene and immobile, evocative not of life but of death. Enlightened circles are in ecstasies when confronted with this 'inner truth' which is so well expressed; but we have the right to ask if this truth is in fact a reality, and if it is not already outworn and

denied, called in question by the epoch through which the people
are treading out their path towards history.

In the realm of poetry we may establish the same facts. After the
period of assimilation characterized by rhyming poetry, the poetic
tom-tom's rhythms break through. This is a poetry of revolt; but it
is also descriptive and analytical poetry. The poet ought, however, to
understand that nothing can replace the reasoned, irrevocable taking
up of arms on the people's side. Let us quote Depestre once more:

> The lady was not alone;
> She had a husband,
> A husband who knew everything,
> But to tell the truth knew nothing,
> For you can't have culture without making concessions.
> You concede your flesh and blood to it,
> You concede your own self to others;
> By conceding you gain
> Classicism and Romanticism,
> And all that our souls are steeped in.[3]

The native poet who is preoccupied with creating a national work of
art and who is determined to describe his people fails in his aim, for he
is not yet ready to make that fundamental concession that Depestre
speaks of. The French poet René Char shows his understanding
of the difficulty when he reminds us that 'the poem emerges out
of a subjective imposition and an objective choice. A poem is the
assembling and moving together of determining original values, in
contemporary relation with someone that these circumstances bring
to the fore.'[4]

Yes, the first duty of the native poet is to see clearly the people he
has chosen as the subject of his work of art. He cannot go forward
resolutely unless he first realizes the extent of his estrangement from
them. We have taken everything from the other side; and the other
side gives us nothing unless by a thousand detours we swing finally
round in their direction, unless by ten thousand wiles and a hundred
thousand tricks they manage to draw us towards them, to seduce us
and to imprison us. Taking means, in nearly every case, being taken:
thus it is not enough to try to free oneself by repeating proclamations
and denials. It is not enough to try to get back to the people in that
past out of which they have already emerged; rather we must join
them in that fluctuating movement to which they are just giving
a shape, and which, as soon as it has started, will be the signal for

everything to be called in question. Let there be no mistake about it; it is to this zone of occult instability where the people dwell that we must come; and it is there that our souls are crystallized and that our perceptions and our lives are transfused with light.

Keita Fodeba, today minister of internal affairs in the Republic of Guinea, when he was the director of the 'African Ballets' did not play any tricks with the reality that the people of Guinea offered him. He reinterpreted all the rhythmic images of his country from a revolutionary stand-point. But he did more. In his poetic works, which are not well known, we find a constant desire to define accurately the historic moments of the struggle and to mark off the field in which were to be unfolded the actions and ideas around which the popular will would crystallize. Here is a poem by Keita Fodeba which is a true invitation to thought, to de-mystification and to battle.

AFRICAN DAWN

(Guitar music)

Dawn was breaking. The little village, which had danced half the night to the sound of its tom-toms was awaking slowly. Ragged shepherds playing their flutes were leading their flocks down into the valley. The girls of the village with their canaries followed one by one along the winding path that leads to the fountain. In the marabout's courtyard a group of children were softly chanting in chorus some verses from the Koran.

(Guitar music)

Dawn was breaking – dawn, the fight between night and day. But the night was exhausted and could fight no more, and slowly died. A few rays of the sun, the forerunners of this victory of the day, still hovered on the horizon, pale and timid, while the last stars gently glided under the mass of clouds, crimson like the blooming flamboyant flowers.

(Guitar music)

Dawn was breaking. And down at the end of the vast plain with its purple contours, the silhouette of a bent man tilling the ground could be seen, the silhouette of Naman the labourer. Each time he lifted his hoe the frightened birds rose, and flew swiftly away to find the quiet banks of the Djoliba, the great Niger river. The man's grey cotton trousers, soaked by the dew, flapped against the grass on either side. Sweating, unresting, always bent over he worked with his hoe; for the seed had to be sown before the next rains came.

(Cora music)

Dawn was breaking, still breaking. The sparrows circled amongst the leaves announcing the day. On the damp track leading to the plain a child, carrying his little quiver of arrows round him like a bandolier, was running breathless towards Naman. He called out: 'Brother Naman, the head man of the village wants you to come to the council tree.'

(Cora music)

The labourer, surprised by such a message so early in the morning, laid down his hoe and walked towards the village, which now was shining in the beams of the rising sun. Already the old men of the village were sitting under the tree, looking more solemn than ever. Beside them a man in uniform, a district guard, sat impassively, quietly smoking his pipe.

(Cora music)

Naman took his place on the sheep-skin. The head man's spokesman stood up to announce to the assembly the will of the old men: 'The white men have sent a district guard to ask for a man from the village who will go to the war in their country. The chief men, after taking counsel together, have decided to send the young man who is the best representative of our race, so that he may go and give proof to the white men of that courage which has always been a feature of our *Manding*.'

(Guitar music)

Naman was thus officially marked out, for every evening the village girls praised his great stature and muscular appearance in musical couplets. Gentle Kadia, his young wife, overwhelmed by the news, suddenly ceased grinding corn, put the mortar away under the barn and, without saying a word, shut herself into her hut to weep over her misfortune with stifled sobs. For death had taken her first husband; and she could not believe that now the white people had taken Naman from her, Naman who was the centre of all her new-sprung hopes.

(Guitar music)

The next day, in spite of her tears and lamentations, the full-toned drumming of the war tom-toms accompanied Naman to the village's little harbour where he boarded a trawler that was going to the district capital. That night, instead of dancing in the market-place as they usually did, the village girls came to keep watch in Naman's outer room, and there told their tales until morning around a wood fire.

(Guitar music)

Several months went by without any news of Naman reaching the village. Kadia was so worried that she went to the cunning fetish-worker from the neighbouring village. The village elders themselves held a short secret council on the matter, but nothing came of it.

(Cora music)

At last one day a letter from Naman came to the village, to Kadia's address. She was worried as to what was happening to her husband, and so that same night she came, after hours of tiring walking, to the capital of the district, where a translator read the letter to her.

Naman was in North Africa; he was well, and he asked for news of the harvest, of the feastings, the river, the dances, the council tree … in fact, for news of all the village.

(Balafo music)

That night the old women of the village honoured Kadia by allowing her to come to the courtyard of the oldest woman and listen to the talk that went on nightly among them. The head man of the village, happy to have heard news of Naman, gave a great banquet to all the beggars of the neighbourhood.

(Bafalo music)

Again several months went by and everyone was once more anxious, for nothing more was heard of Naman. Kadia was thinking of going again to consult the fetish-worker when she received a second letter. Naman, after passing through Corsica and Italy, was now in Germany and was proud of having been decorated.

(Balafo music)

But the next time there was only a postcard to say that Naman had been made prisoner by the Germans. This news weighed heavily on the village. The old men held council and decided that henceforward Naman would be allowed to dance the Douga, that sacred dance of the vultures that no one who has not performed some outstanding feat is allowed to dance, that dance of the Mali emperors of which every step is a stage in the history of the Mali race. Kadia found consolation in the fact that her husband had been raised to the dignity of a hero of his country.

(Guitar music)

Time went by. A year followed another, and Naman was still in Germany. He did not write any more.

(Guitar music)

One fine day, the village head man received word from Dakar that Naman would soon be home. The mutter of the tom-toms was at once heard. There was dancing and singing till dawn. The village girls composed new songs for his homecoming, for the old men who were the devotees of the Douga spoke no more about that famous dance of the *Manding*.

(Tom-toms)

But a month later, Corporal Moussa, a great friend of Naman's, wrote a tragic letter to Kadia: 'Dawn was breaking. We were at Tiaroye-sur-Mer. In the course of a widespread dispute between us and our white officers from Dakar, a bullet struck Naman. He lies in the land of Senegal.'

(Guitar music)

Yes; dawn was breaking. The first rays of the sun hardly touched the surface of the sea, as they gilded its little foam-flecked waves. Stirred by the breeze, the palm-trees gently bent their trunks down towards the ocean, as if saddened by the morning's battle. The crows came in noisy flocks to warn the neighbourhood by their cawing of the tragedy that was staining the dawn at Tiaroye with blood. And in the flaming blue sky, just above Naman's body, a huge vulture was hovering heavily. It seemed to say to him 'Naman! You have not danced that dance that is named after me. Others will dance it.'

(Cora music)

If I have chosen to quote this long poem, it is on account of its unquestioned pedagogical value. Here, things are clear; it is a precise, forward-looking exposition. The understanding of the poem is not merely an intellectual advance, but a political advance. To understand this poem is to understand the part one has played, to recognize one's advance and to furbish up one's weapons. There is not a single colonized person who will not receive the message that this poem holds. Naman, the hero of the battlefields of Europe, Naman who eternally ensures the power and perenniality of the mother country, Naman is machine-gunned by the police force at the very moment that he comes back to the country of his birth: and this is Sétif in 1945, this is Fort-le-France, this is Saigon, Dakar and Lagos. All those niggers, all those wogs who fought to defend the liberty of France or for British civilization recognize themselves in this poem by Keita Fodeba.

But Keita Fodeba sees farther. In colonized counties, colonialism, after having made use of the natives on the battlefields, uses them as trained soldiers to put down the movements of independence. The ex-service associations are in the colonies one of the most anti-nationalist elements that exist. The poet Keita Fodeba was training the Minister for Internal Affairs of the Republic of Guinea to frustrate the plots organized by French colonialisms. The French secret service intend to use, among other means, the ex-service men to break up the young independent Guinean state.

The colonized man who writes for his people ought to use the past with the intention of opening the future, as an invitation to action and a basis for hope. But to ensure that hope and to give it form, he must take part in action and throw himself body and soul into the national struggle. You may speak about everything under the sun; but when you decide to speak of that unique thing in man's life that is represented by the fact of opening up new horizons, by bringing light to your own country and by raising yourself and your people to their feet, then you must collaborate on the physical plane.

The responsibility of the native man of culture is not a responsibility *vis-à-vis* his national culture but a global responsibility with regard to the totality of the nation, whose culture merely, after all, represents one aspect of that nation. The cultured native should not concern himself with choosing the level on which he wishes to fight or the sector where he decides to give battle for his nation. To fight for national culture means in the first place to fight for the liberation of the nation, that material keystone which makes the building of a culture possible. There is no other fight for culture that can develop apart from the popular struggle. To take an example: all those men and women who are fighting with their bare hands against French colonialism in Algeria are not by any means strangers to the national culture of Algeria. The national Algerian culture is taking on form and content as the battles are being fought out, in prisons, under the guillotine and in every French outpost that is captured or destroyed.

We must not therefore be content with delving into the past of a people in order to find coherent elements that will counteract colonialism's attempts to falsify and harm. We must work and fight with the same rhythm as the people to construct the future and to prepare the ground where vigorous shoots are already springing up. A national culture is not a folklore, nor an abstract populism that believes it can discover the people's true nature. It is not made up of the inert dregs of gratuitous actions, that is to say actions that are less and less attached to the ever-present reality of the people. A national culture is the whole body of efforts made by a people in the sphere of thought to describe, justify and praise the action through which that people has created itself and keeps itself in existence. A national culture in underdeveloped countries should therefore take its place at the very heart of the struggle for freedom that these countries are carrying on. Men of African cultures who are still fighting in the name of African-Negro culture and who have called many congresses in the name of the unity of that culture should today realize that all their efforts amount to is to make comparisons between coins and sarcophagi.

There is no common destiny to be shared between the national cultures of Senegal and Guinea; but there *is* a common destiny between the Senegalese and Guinean nations which are both dominated by the same French colonialism. If it is wished that the national culture of Senegal should come to resemble the national culture of Guinea, it is not enough for the rulers of the two peoples to decide to consider their problems – whether the problem of liberation is concerned, or the trade union questions, or economic difficulties – from similar view-points. And even here there does not seem to be complete identity, for the rhythm of the people and that of their rulers are not the same. There can be no two cultures that are completely identical. To believe that it is possible to create a black culture is to forget that niggers are disappearing, just as those people who brought them into being are seeing the break-up of their economic and cultural supremacy.[5] There will never be such a thing as black culture because there is not a single politician who feels he has a vocation to bring black republics into being. The problem is to get to know the place that these men mean to give their people, the kind of social relations that they decide to set up and the conception that they have of the future of humanity. It is this that counts; everything else is mystification, signifying nothing.

In 1959 the cultured Africans who met at Rome never stopped talking about unity. But one of the people who was loudest in the praise of this cultural unity, Jacques Rabemananjara, is today a minister in the Madagascan government and, as such, has decided, with his government, to oppose the Algerian people in the General Assembly of the United Nations. Rabemananjara, if he had been true to himself, should have resigned from the government and denounced those men who claim to incarnate the will of the Madagascan people. The 90,000 dead of Madagascar have not given Rabemananjara authority to oppose the aspirations of the Algerian people in the General Assembly of the United Nations.

It is around the peoples' struggles that African-Negro culture takes on substance, and not around songs, poems or folkore. Senghor, who is also a member of the Society of African Culture and who has worked with us on the question of African culture, is not afraid for his part either to give the order to his delegation to support French proposals on Algeria. Adherence to African-Negro culture and to the cultural unity of Africa is arrived at, in the first place, by upholding unconditionally the peoples' struggle for freedom. No one can truly wish for the spread of African culture if he does not give practical support to the creation of the conditions necessary to the existence of that culture; in other words, to the liberation of the whole continent.

I say again that no speech-making and no proclamation concerning culture will turn us from our fundamental tasks: the liberation of the national territory; a continual struggle against colonialism in its new forms; and an obstinate refusal to enter the charmed circle of mutual admiration at the summit.

RECIPROCAL BASES OF NATIONAL CULTURE
AND THE FIGHT FOR FREEDOM

Colonial domination, because it is total and tends to oversimplify, very soon manages to disrupt in spectacular fashion the cultural life of a conquered people. This cultural obliteration is made possible by the negation of national reality, by new legal relations introduced by the occupying power, by the banishment of the natives and their customs to outlying districts by colonial society, by expropriation, and by the systematic enslaving of men and women.

Three years ago at our first congress I showed that, in the colonial situation, dynamism is replaced fairly quickly by a substantification of the attitudes of the colonizing power. The area of culture is then marked off by fences and signposts. These are in fact so many defence mechanisms of the most elementary type, comparable for more than one good reason to the simple instinct for preservation. The interest of this period for us is that the oppressor does not manage to convince himself of the objective non-existence of the oppressed nation and its culture. Every effort is made to bring the colonized person to admit the inferiority of his culture, which has been transformed into instinctive patterns of behaviour, to recognize the unreality of his 'nation' and, in the last extreme, the confused and imperfect character of his own biological structure.

Vis-à-vis this state of affairs, the native's reactions are not unanimous. While the mass of the people maintain intact traditions which are completely different from those of the colonial situation, and the artisan style solidifies into a formalism which is more and more stereotyped, the intellectual throws himself in frenzied fashion into the frantic acquisition of the culture of the occupying power and takes every opportunity of unfavourably criticizing his own national culture, or else takes refuge in setting out and substantiating the claims of that culture in a way that is passionate but rapidly becomes unproductive.

The common nature of these two reactions lies in the fact that they both lead to impossible contradictions. Whether a turncoat or a substantialist, the native is ineffectual precisely because the analysis of the colonial situation is not carried out on strict lines. The colonial situation calls a halt to national culture in almost every field. Within the framework of colonial domination there is not and there will never be such phenomena as new cultural departures or changes in the national culture. Here and there valiant attempts are sometimes

made to reanimate the cultural dynamic and to give fresh impulses
to its themes, its forms and its tonalities. The immediate, palpable
and obvious interest of such leaps ahead is nil. But if we follow up the
consequences to the very end we see that preparations are being thus
made to brush the cobwebs off national consciousness, to question
oppression and to open up the struggle for freedom.

A national culture under colonial domination is a contested culture
whose destruction is sought in systematic fashion. It very quickly
becomes a culture condemned to secrecy. This idea of a clandestine
culture is immediately seen in the reactions of the occupying power,
which interprets attachment to traditions as faithfulness to the spirit
of the nation and as a refusal to submit. This persistence in following
forms of cultures that are already condemned to extinction is already
a demonstration of nationality; but it is a demonstration that is a
throwback to the laws of inertia. There is no taking of the offensive
and no redefining of relationships. There is simply a concentration
on a hard core of culture that is becoming more and more shrivelled
up, inert and empty.

By the time a century or two of exploitation has passed there
comes about a veritable emaciation of the stock of national culture.
It becomes a set of automatic habits, some traditions of dress and
a few broken-down institutions. Little movement can be discerned
in such remnants of culture; there is no real creativity and no
overflowing life. The poverty of the people, national oppression and
the inhibition of culture are one and the same thing. After a century
of colonial domination we find a culture that is rigid in the extreme,
or rather what we find are the dregs of culture, its mineral strata. The
withering away of the reality of the nation and the death-pangs of
the national culture are linked to each other in mutual dependence.
This is why it is of capital importance to follow the evolution of these
relations during the struggle for national freedom. The negation of
the native's culture, the contempt for any manifestation of culture,
whether active or emotional, and the placing outside the pale of all
specialized branches of organization contribute to breed aggressive
patterns of conduct in the native. But these patterns of conduct
are of the reflexive type; they are poorly differentiated, anarchic
and ineffective. Colonial exploitation, poverty and endemic famine
drive the native more and more to open, organized revolt. The
necessity for an open and decisive breach is formed progressively
and imperceptibly, and comes to be felt by the great majority of the
people. Those tensions that were hitherto non-existent come into

being. International events, the collapse of whole sections of colonial empires and the contradictions inherent in the colonial system strengthen and uphold the native's combativity while promoting and giving support to national consciousness.

These new-found tensions, which are present at all stages in the real nature of colonialism, have their repercussions on the cultural plane. In literature, for example, there is relative overproduction. From being a reply on a minor scale to the dominating power, the literature produced by natives becomes differentiated and makes itself into a will to particularism. The intelligentsia, which during the period of repression was essentially a consuming public, now themselves become producers. This literature at first chooses to confine itself to the tragic and poetic style; but later on novels, short stories and essays are attempted. It is as if a kind of internal organization or law of expression existed which wills that poetic expression become less frequent in proportion as the objectives and the methods of the struggle for liberation become more precise. Themes are completely altered; in fact, we find less and less of bitter, hopeless recrimination and less also of that violent, resounding, florid writing which, on the whole, serves to reassure the occupying power. The colonialists have in former times encouraged these modes of expression and made their existence possible. Stinging denunciations, the exposing of distressing conditions and passions that find their outlet in expression are in fact assimilated by the occupying power in a cathartic process. To aid such processes is, in a certain sense, to avoid their dramatization and to clear the atmosphere.

But such a situation can only be transitory. In fact, the progress of national consciousness among the people modifies and gives precision to the literary utterances of the native intellectual. The continued cohesion of the people constitutes for the intellectual an invitation to go farther than his cry of protest. The lament first makes the indictment; then it makes an appeal. In the period that follows, the words of command are heard. The crystallization of the national consciousness will both disrupt literary styles and themes, and also create a completely new public. While at the beginning the native intellectual used to produce his work to be read exclusively by the oppressor, whether with the intention of charming him or of denouncing him through ethnical or subjectivist means, now the native writer progressively takes on the habit of addressing his own people.

It is only from that moment that we can speak of a national literature. Here there is, at the level of literary creation, the taking up and clarification of themes that are typically nationalist. This may be properly called a literature of combat, in the sense that it calls on the whole people to fight for their existence as a nation. It is a literature of combat, because it moulds the national consciousness, giving it form and contours and flinging open before it new and boundless horizons; it is a literature of combat because it assumes responsibility and because it is the will to liberty expressed in terms of time and space.

On another level, the oral tradition – stories, epics and songs of the people – which formerly were filed away as set pieces are now beginning to change. The storytellers who used to relate inert episodes now bring them alive and introduce into them modifications that are increasingly fundamental. There is a tendency to bring conflicts up to date and to modernize the kinds of struggle that the stories evoke, together with the names of heroes and the types of weapons. The method of allusion is more and more widely used. The formula 'This all happened long ago' is substituted by that of 'What we are going to speak of happened somewhere else, but it might well have happened here today, and it might happen tomorrow.' The example of Algeria is significant in this context. From 1952–3 on, the storytellers, who were before that time stereotyped and tedious to listen to, completely overturned their traditional methods of storytelling and the contents of their tales. Their public, which was formerly scattered, became compact. The epic, with its typified categories, reappeared; it became an authentic form of entertainment that took on a cultural value once more. Colonialism made no mistake when, from 1955 on, it proceeded systematically to arrest these storytellers.

The contact of the people with the new movement gives rise to a new rhythm of life and to forgotten muscular tensions, and develops the imagination. Every time the storyteller relates a fresh episode to his public, he presides over a real invocation. The existence of a new type of man is revealed to the public. The present is no longer turned in upon itself but spread out for all to see. The storyteller once more gives free rein to his imagination; he makes innovations and he creates a work of art. It even happens that the characters, which are barely ready for such a transformation – highway robbers or more or less anti-social vagabonds – are taken up and remodelled. The emergence of the imagination and of the creative urge in the songs and epic stories of a colonized country is worth following. The storyteller replies to the expectant people by successive approximations, and makes his way, apparently alone but in fact helped on by his public, towards the seeking out of new patterns, that is to say national patterns. Comedy and farce disappear or lose their attraction. As for dramatization, it is no longer placed on the plane of the troubled intellectual and his tormented conscience. By losing its characteristics of despair and revolt, the drama becomes part of the common lot of the people and forms part of an action in preparation or already in progress.

Where handicrafts are concerned, the forms of expression that were formerly the dregs of art, surviving as if in a daze, now begin to reach out. Woodwork, for example, which formerly turned out certain faces and attitudes by the million, begins to be differentiated. The inexpressive or overwrought mask comes to life and the arms tend to be raised from the body as if to sketch an action. Compositions containing two, three or five figures appear. The traditional schools are led on to creative efforts by the rising avalanche of amateurs or of critics. This new vigour in this sector of cultural life very often passes unseen; and yet its contribution to the national effort is of capital importance. By carving figures and faces that are full of life, and by taking as his theme a group fixed on the same pedestal, the artist invites participation in an organized movement.

If we study the repercussions of the awakening of national consciousness in the domains of ceramics and pottery-making, the same observations may be drawn. Formalism is abandoned in the craftsman's work. Jugs, jars and trays are modified, at first imperceptibly, then almost savagely. The colours, of which formerly there were but few and which obeyed the traditional rules of harmony, increase in number and are influenced by the repercussions of the rising revolution. Certain ochres and blues, which seemed forbidden to all eternity in a given cultural area, now assert themselves without giving rise to scandal. In the same way the stylization of the human face, which according to sociologists is typical of very clearly defined regions, becomes suddenly completely relative. The specialist coming from the home country and the ethnologist are quick to note these changes. On the whole such changes are condemned in the name of a rigid code of artistic style and of a cultural life that grows up at the heart of the colonial system. The colonialist specialists do not recognize these new forms and rush to the help of the traditions of the indigenous society. It is the colonialists who become the defenders of the native style. We remember perfectly, and the example took on a certain measure of importance since the real nature of colonialism was not involved, the reactions of the white jazz specialists when, after the Second World War, new styles such as the be-bop took definite shape. The fact is that, in their eyes, jazz should only be the despairing, broken-down nostalgia of an old Negro who is trapped between five glasses of whisky, the curse of his race and the racial hatred of the white men. As soon as the Negro comes to an understanding of himself, and understands the rest of the world differently, when he gives birth to hope and forces back the racist universe, it is clear that his trumpet sounds more clearly and his voice less hoarsely. The new fashions in jazz are not simply born of economic competition. We must, without any doubt, see in them one of the consequences of the defeat, slow but sure, of the southern world of the United States. And it is not utopian to suppose that in fifty years' time the type of jazz howl hiccupped by a poor unfortunate Negro will be upheld only by the whites who believe in it as an expression of nigger-hood and who are faithful to this arrested image of a type of relationship.

We might in the same way seek and find, in dancing, singing, and traditional rites and ceremonies, the same upward-springing trend, and make out the same changes and the same impatience in this field. Well before the political or fighting phase of the national movement an attentive spectator can thus feel and see the manifestation of new vigour and feel the approaching conflict. He will note unusual forms of expression and themes that are fresh and imbued with a power which is no longer that of invocation but rather of the assembling of the people, a summoning together for a precise purpose. Everything works together to awaken the native's sensibility and to make unreal and unacceptable the contemplative attitude or the acceptance of defeat. The native rebuilds his perceptions because he renews the purpose and dynamism of the craftsmen, of dancing and music and of literature and the oral tradition. His world comes to lose its accursed character. The conditions necessary for the inevitable conflict are brought together.

We have noted the appearance of the movement in cultural forms and we have seen that this movement and these new forms are linked to the state of maturity of the national consciousness. Now, this movement tends more and more to express itself objectively, in institutions. From thence comes the need for a national existence, whatever the cost.

A frequent mistake, and one that is moreover hardly justifiable, is to try to find cultural expressions for and to give new values to native culture within the framework of colonial domination. This is why we arrive at a proposition which at first sight seems paradoxical: the fact that in a colonized country the most elementary, most savage and the most undifferentiated nationalism is the most fervent and efficient means of defending national culture. For culture is first the expression of a nation, the expression of its preferences, of its taboos and of its patterns. It is at every stage of the whole of society that other taboos, values and patterns are formed. A national culture is the sum total of all these appraisals; it is the result of internal and external extensions exerted over society as a whole and also at every level of that society. In the colonial situation, culture, which is doubly deprived of the support of the nation and of the state, falls away and dies. The condition for its existence is therefore national liberation and the renaissance of the state.

The nation is not only the condition of culture, its fruitfulness, its continuous renewal and its deepening. It is also a necessity. It is the fight for national existence that sets culture moving and opens to it the doors of creation. Later on it is the nation that will ensure the conditions and framework necessary to culture. The nation gathers together the various indispensable elements necessary for the creation of a culture, those elements which alone can give it credibility, validity, life and creative power. In the same way it is its national character that will make such a culture open to other cultures, and which will enable it to influence and permeate other cultures. A non-existent culture can hardly be expected to have bearing on reality or to influence reality. The first necessity is the re-establishment of the nation in order to give life to national culture in the strictly biological sense of the phrase.

Thus we have followed the break-up of the old strata of culture, a shattering that becomes increasingly fundamental; and we have noticed, on the eve of the decisive conflict for national freedom, the renewing of forms of expression and the rebirth of the imagination. There remains one essential question: what are the relations between the struggle – whether political or military – and culture? Is there a suspension of culture during the conflict? Is the national struggle an expression of a culture? Finally, ought one to say that the battle for freedom, however fertile *a posteriori* with regard to culture, is in itself a negation of culture? In short is the struggle for liberation a cultural phenomenon or not?

We believe that the conscious and organized undertaking by a colonized people to re-establish the sovereignty of that nation constitutes the most complete and obvious cultural manifestation that exists. It is not the success of the struggle alone that afterwards gives validity and vigour to culture; culture is not put into cold storage during the conflict. The struggle itself, in its development and in its internal progression, sends culture along different paths and traces out entirely new ones for it. The struggle for freedom does not give back to the national culture its former value and shapes; this struggle, which aims at a fundamentally different set of relations between men, cannot leave intact either the form or the content of the people's culture. After the conflict there is not only the disappearance of colonialism but also the disappearance of the colonized man.

This new humanity cannot do otherwise than define a new humanism both for itself and for others. It is prefigured in the objectives and methods of the conflict. A struggle which mobilizes all classes of the people and which expresses their aims and their impatience, which is not afraid to count almost exclusively on the people's support, will of necessity triumph. The value of this type of conflict is that it supplies the maximum of conditions necessary for the development and aims of culture. After national freedom has been obtained in these conditions, there is no such painful cultural indecision as is found in certain countries that are newly independent, because the nation, by its manner of coming into being and in the terms of its existence, exerts a fundamental influence over culture. A nation which is born of the people's concerted action and which embodies the real aspirations of the people while changing the state cannot exist save in the expression of exceptionally rich forms of culture.

The natives who are anxious for the culture of their country and who wish to give to it a universal dimension ought not, therefore, to place their confidence in the single principle of inevitable, undifferentiated independence written into the consciousness of the people in order to achieve their task. The liberation of the nation is one thing; the methods and popular content of the fight are another. It seems to us that the future of national culture and its riches are equally also part and parcel of the values that have ordained the struggle for freedom.

And now it is time to denounce certain pharisees. National claims, it is here and there stated, are a phase that humanity has left behind. It is the day of great concerted actions and retarded nationalists ought in consequence to set their mistakes aright. We, however, consider that the mistake, which may have very serious consequences, lies in wishing to skip the national period. If culture is the expression of national consciousness, I will not hesitate to affirm that, in the case with which we are dealing, it is the national consciousness that is the most elaborate form of culture.

The consciousness of self is not the closing of a door to communication. Philosophic thought teaches us, on the contrary, that it is its guarantee. National consciousness, which is not nationalism, is the only thing that will give us an international dimension. This problem of national consciousness and of national culture takes on in Africa a special dimension. The birth of national consciousness in Africa has a strictly contemporaneous connection with African consciousness. The responsibility of the African as regards national culture is also a responsibility with regard to African-Negro culture. This joint responsibility is not the fact of a metaphysical principle but the awareness of a simple rule which wills that every independent nation in an Africa where colonialism is still entrenched is an encircled nation, a nation which is fragile and in permanent danger.

If man is known by his acts, then we will say that the most urgent thing today for the intellectual is to build up his nation. If this building up is true, that is to say if it interprets the manifest will of the people and reveals the eager African peoples, then the building of a nation is of necessity accompanied by the discovery and encouragement of universalizing values. Far from keeping aloof from other nations, therefore, it is national liberation that leads the nation to play its part on the stage of history. It is at the heart of national consciousness that international consciousness lives and grows. And this two-fold emerging is ultimately the source of all culture.

(Statement made at the Second Congress of Black Artists and Writers, Rome, 1959)

Notes

FOREWORD: POSTCOLONIAL FANONISM

1. Albert Memmi, 'The Impossible Life of Frantz Fanon', *Massachusetts Review* (winter 1973), p. 10.
2. Ibid., p. 15.
3. Ibid., p. 16.
4. Ibid.
5. Ibid., p. 17.
6. Ibid., p. 18.
7. Frantz Fanon, *Black Skin, White Masks* (London, Pluto Press, 1986), p. 218.
8. Ibid., pp. 218–19.
9. Memmi, 'The Impossible Life of Frantz Fanon', p. 21.
10. Ibid., p. 20.
11. Ibid., p. 25.
12. Hussein Abdilahi Bulhan, *Frantz Fanon and the Psychology of Oppression* (New York and London, Plenum Press, 1985), p. 31.
13. Memmi, 'The Impossible Life of Frantz Fanon', p. 25.
14. Ibid., p. 28.
15. Ibid.
16. Ibid., p. 34.
17. Ibid.
18. Ibid.
19. Azzedine Haddour, 'Sartre and Fanon: On Negritude and Political Participation', in A. van den Hoven and A. Leak (eds) *Sartre Today*. (Oxford, Berghahn Books, 2005), pp. 285–301.
20. Fanon, *Black Skin, White Masks*, p. 203.
21. Ibid., p. 16.
22. Frantz Fanon, *Toward the African Revolution* (Harmondsworth, Penguin, 1970), p. 63.
23. Denis Hollier, 'Mosaic: Terminable and Interminable', *October 87* (winter 1999), p. 159.
24. Fanon, *The Wretched of the Earth* (Harmondsworth, Penguin, 1990), p. 199.
25. Ibid., p. 199.
26. Hollier, 'Mosaic: Terminable and Interminable', p. 159.
27. Homi K. Bhabha, 'Foreword: Framing Fanon', in Frantz Fanon, *The Wretched of the Earth*, trans. R. Philcox (New York, Grove Press, 2004), p. xvi.
28. Ibid., p. xvi.
29. Christiane Chaulet Achour, *Frantz Fanon: l'importun* (Montpellier, Éditions Chèvre-Feuille Étoilée, 2004), pp. 15–18.
30. Kebena Mercer, 'Busy in the Ruins of a Wretched Phantasia', in A.C. Alessandrini (ed.) *Frantz Fanon: Critical Perspectives* (London, Routledge, 1999), p. 197.

31. Stuart Hall, 'The After-life of Frantz Fanon: Why Fanon? Why Now? Why *Black Skin, White Masks?*', in Alan Read (ed.) *The Fact of Blackness: Frantz Fanon and Visual Representation* (London, ICA, 1996), p. 15.
32. Ibid., p. 16.
33. The Grove Press, 2004 edition.
34. Bhabha, 'Foreword: Framing Fanon', pp. ix–xi.
35. Fanon, *The Wretched of the Earth*, p. 28.
36. Ibid., pp. 27–28.
37. Ibid., p. 29.
38. Ibid., p. 48.
39. Ibid., p. 31.
40. Ibid., p. 28.
41. Bhabha, 'Foreword: Framing Fanon', pp. xxv–xxvi.
42. Ibid., pp. xix and xxi.
43. Ibid., p. xx.
44. Ibid., p. xx.
45. A. Haddour, *Colonial Myths, History and Narrative* (Manchester, Manchester University Press, 2000).
46. Bhabha, 'Foreword: Framing Fanon', p. xxii.
47. Hannah Arendt, *On Violence* (London, Allen Lane, The Penguin Press, 1970).
48. Jean-Paul Sartre, *Colonialism and Neocolonialism*, trans. A. Haddour, S. Brewer, T. McWilliams (London, Routledge, 2001), p. 147.
49. Ibid., p. 148.
50. Bhabha, 'Foreword: Framing Fanon', p. xxxvi.
51. Ibid., p. xl.
52. Henry Louis Gates Jr, 'Critical Fanonism', *Critical Inquiry* 17 (spring 1991), pp. 457–58.
53. Bhabha, 'Foreword: Framing Fanon', p. xii.
54. Ibid., p. xiv.
55. Ibid., p. xiv.
56. Ibid., p. xiv.
57. Ibid., p. xiv.
58. Fanon, *The Wretched of the Earth*, p. 59.
59. Ibid., p. 39.
60. Ibid., p. 76.
61. Ibid., p. 39.
62. Ibid., p. 64.
63. Ibid., p. 78.
64. Fanon, *Toward the African Revolution*, pp. 187–88.
65. Ibid., p. 197.
66. Bulhan, *Frantz Fanon and the Psychology of Oppression*, p. 254.
67. Bhabha, 'Foreword: Framing Fanon', p. xv.
68. Ibid., pp. xxvii–xxviii.

1   THE NEGRO AND LANGUAGE

1. *Charmes* (Paris, Gallimard, 1952).
2. *Le Langage et l'agressivité.*

3. By that I mean that Negroes who return to their original environments convey the impression that they have completed a cycle, that they have added to themselves something that was lacking. They return literally full of themselves.
4. Léon-G. Damas 'Hoquet', in *Pigments*, in Leopold S. Senghor, ed., *Anthologie de la nouvelle poésie nègre et malgache* (Paris, Presses Universitaires de France, 1948), pp. 15–17.
5. *Cahiers* (Paris, Présence Africaine, 1956), p. 30.
6. Literally, this dialect word means *European*; by extension it was applied to any officer. (Translator's note.)
7. 'Martinique-Guadeloupe-Haiti', *Les Temps Modernes*, February 1950, p. 1347.
8. Jean-Paul Sartre, *Orphée noir*, in *Anthologie de la nouvelle poésie nègre et malgache*, p. ix.
9. Quoted in Sir Alan Burns, *Colour Prejudice* (London, Allen and Unwin, 1948), p. 101.
10. Vulgar French for Arab. (Translator's note.)
11. 'I knew some Negroes in the School of Medicine ... in a word, they were a disappointment; the colour of their skin should have permitted them to give *us* the opportunity to be charitable, generous, or scientifically friendly. They were derelict in this duty, this claim on our good will. All our tearful tenderness, all our calculated solicitude were a drug on the market. We had no Negroes to condescend to, nor did we have anything to hate them for; they counted for virtually as much as we in the scale of the little jobs and petty chicaneries of daily life.' Michel Salomon, 'D'un juif à des nègres', *Présence Africaine*, No. 5, p. 776.
12. A generic term for *other people*, applied especially to Europeans.
13. Compare, for example, the almost incredible store of anecdotes to which the election of any candidate gives rise. A filthy newspaper called the *Canard Déchaîné* could not get its fill of overwhelming Monsieur B. with devastating Creolisms. This is indeed the bludgeon of the Antilles: *He can't express himself in French.*
14. '*Le français (l'élégance de la forme) était tellement chaud que la femme est tombée en transes*' [His French (the refinement of his style) was so exciting that the woman swooned away].
15. Introduction to *Cahier d'un retour au pays natal*, p. 14.
16. Michel Leiris, op. cit.

2   RACISM AND CULTURE

1. Text of Frantz Fanon's speech before the First Congress of Negro Writers and Artists in Paris, September 1956. Published in the Special Issue of *Présence Africaine*, June–November 1956.
2. A little-studied phenomenon sometimes appears at this stage. Intellectuals, students, belonging to the dominant group, make 'scientific' studies of the dominated society, its art, its ethical universe. In the universities the rare colonized intellectuals find their own cultural system being revealed to them. It even happens that scholars of the colonizing countries grow

enthusiastic over this or that specific feature. The concepts of purity, naïveté, innocence appear. The native intellectual's vigilance must here be doubly on the alert.

3 THE WOMAN OF COLOUR AND THE WHITE MAN

1. Mayotte Capécia, *Je suis Martiniquaise* (Paris, Corréa, 1948), p. 202.
2. Ibid., p. 150.
3. Gabriel Marcel, *Être et avoir* (Paris, Aubier, 1935).
4. Capécia, op. cit., p. 131.
5. Since he is the master and more simply the male, the white man can allow himself the luxury of sleeping with many women. This is true in every country and especially in colonies. But when a white woman accepts a black man there is automatically a romantic aspect. It is a giving, not a seizing. In the colonies, in fact, even though there is little marriage or actual sustained cohabitation between whites and blacks, the number of hybrids is amazing. This is because the white men often sleep with their black servants. None the less, that does not provide any foundation for this passage from Mannoni:

   > Thus one part of our drives would quite naturally impel us toward the most alien types. That is no mere literary illusion; there was no question of literature, and the illusion was probably very slight when Galliéni's soldiers chose young *ramatoa* as their more or less temporary wives. In fact these first contacts presented no difficulties at all. This was in part due to the healthy sex life of the Malagasies, which was unmarred by complexes. But this only goes to show that racial conflicts develop gradually and do not arise spontaneously. (*Prospero and Caliban*, p. 112)

   Let us not exaggerate. When a soldier of the conquering army went to bed with a young Malagasy girl, there was undoubtedly no tendency on his part to respect her entity as another person. The racial conflicts did not come later, they coexisted. The fact that Algerian colonists go to bed with their fourteen-year-old housemaids in no way demonstrates a lack of racial conflicts in Algeria. No, the problem is more complicated. And Mayotte Capécia is right: it is an honour to be the daughter of a white woman. That proves that one was not 'made in the bushes'. (This expression is applied exclusively to all the illegitimate children of the upper class in Martinique; they are known to be extremely numerous: Aubery, for example, is supposed to have fathered almost fifty.)
6. Capécia, op. cit., p. 59.
7. Here Fanon refers to *Black Skin, White Masks*. (Editor's note.)
8. The smile of the black man, the *grin* [in English in the original], seems to have captured the interest of a number of writers. Here is what Bernard Wolfe says about it: 'It pleases us to portray the Negro showing us all his teeth in a smile made for us. And his smile as we see it – as we make it – always means a *gift*. ...' ('L'oncle Rémus et son lapin', *Les Temps Modernes*, May, 1949, p. 888).

Gifts without end, in every advertisement, on every screen, on every food-product label.... The black man gives Madame the new 'dark Creole colours' for her pure nylons, courtesy of the House of Vigny; her 'imaginative, coil-like' bottles of Golliwog toilet water and perfume. Shoeshines, clothes white as snow, comfortable lower berths, quick baggage-handling; jazz, jitterbug, jive, jokes and the wonderful stories of Br'er Rabbit to amuse the little children. Service with a smile, every time.... 'The blacks', writes anthropologist Geoffrey Gorer in *The American Spirit: A Study in National Character* (New York, Norton, 1949), 'are kept in their obsequious attitude by the extreme penalties of fear and force, and this is common knowledge to both the whites and the blacks. Nevertheless, the whites demand that the blacks be always smiling, attentive and friendly in all their relationships with them....'.

 9. 'Sur le *Martinique* de M. Michel Cournot', *Les Temps Modernes*, February 1950.
10. Anna Freud, *The Ego and the Mechanism of Defence* (New York, International Universities Press, 1946), p. 111.
11. Capécia., op. cit., p. 65.
12. Ibid., p. 185.
13. After *Je suis Martiniquaise,* Mayotte Capécia wrote another book, *La Négresse blanche.* She must have recognized her earlier mistakes, for in this book one sees an attempt to re-evaluate the Negro. But Mayotte Capécia did not reckon with her own unconscious. As soon as the novelist allows her characters a little freedom, they use it to belittle the Negro. All the Negroes whom she describes are in one way or another either semi-criminals or 'sho' good' *niggers.*

 In addition – and from this one can foresee what is to come – it is legitimate to say that Mayotte Capécia has definitively turned her back on her country. In both her books only one course is left for her heroines: to go away. This country of niggers is decidedly accursed. In fact, there is an aura of malediction surrounding Mayotte Capécia. But she is centrifugal. Mayotte Capécia is barred from herself.

 May she add no more to the mass of her imbecilities.

 Depart in peace, mudslinging storyteller.... But remember that, beyond your 500 anaemic pages, it will always be possible to regain the honourable road that leads to the heart.

 In spite of you.
14. In *Présence Africaine*, 1–2–3.
15. A club frequented by the local young men. It stands across the street from the Civil Club, which is exclusively European.
16. Sadji, op. cit., in *Présence Africaine*, no. 2, p. 280.
17. Ibid., p. 286.
18. Ibid., p. 281–82.
19. Ibid., p. 281.
20. Ibid., p. 287. *Bougnoul* is one of those untranslatable coinages of the rabble like the American *jigaboo*. Originated by the North African colonists, *bougnoul* means, generically, any 'native' of a race *inferior* to that of the person using the word. (Translator's note.)
21. Ibid., p. 288.

22. Ibid., p. 289.
23. Ibid., p. 489.
24. Anna Freud, op. cit., p. 70.
25. Sadji, op. cit., p. 498.
26. Dublineau, *L'Intuition délirante*.
27. Jacques Lacan.
28. Alfred Adler, *Understanding Human Nature* (New York, Greenberg, 1927), p. 80.

4   THE MAN OF COLOUR AND THE WHITE WOMAN

1. René Maran, *Un homme pareil aux autres* (Paris, Éditions Arc-en-Ciel, 1947), p. 11.
2. Ibid., p. 87.
3. Ibid., pp. 18–19.
4. Ibid., pp. 45–46.
5. Ibid., p. 83.
6. Ibid.
7. Ibid., p. 36.
8. Ibid.
9. Ibid., pp. 152–54.
10. Ibid., p. 185.
11. Ibid., p. 162.
12. Ibid., p. 213.
13. 'Du jeu au Je, esquisse d'une géographie de l'action', *Les Temps Modernes*, April 1948, p. 1732.
14. *Rhythmes du monde*, 1949, p. 113.
15. G. Guex, *La Névrose d'abandon* (Paris, Presses Universitaires de France, 1950), p. 13.
16. E. Minkowski, *La Schizophrénie* (Paris, Payot, 1927).
17. Guex, op. cit., pp. 27–28.
18. My italics – F.F.
19. Maran, op. cit., p. 36.
20. Ibid., p. 227.
21. Ibid., p. 228.
22. Guex, op. cit., pp. 31–32.
23. Ibid., pp. 35–36.
24. Maran, op. cit., pp. 203–4.
25. Ibid., pp. 84–85.
26. Ibid., pp. 247–48.
27. Guex, op. cit., p. 39.
28. My italics – F.F.
29. Guex, op. cit., p. 44.
30. Maran, op. cit., p. 103.
31. Guex, op. cit., p. 54.
32. Claude Nordey, *L'Homme de couleur* (Paris, Collection 'Présences', Plon, 1939).

5   THE NEGRO AND PSYCHOPATHOLOGY

1. Jacques Lacan, 'Le Complèxe, facteur concret de la psychologie familiale', *Encyclopédie française*, 8–40, 5.

2. I should like to think that I am not going to be brought to trial for this sentence. Sceptics always have a fine time asking, 'What do you mean by *normal?*' For the moment, it is beyond the scope of this book to answer the question. In order to pacify the more insistent, let me refer them to the extremely instructive work by Georges Canguilhem, *Essai sur quelques problèmes concernant le normal et le pathologique* (Paris, Société d'Éditions, 1950), even though its sole orientation is biological. And let me add only that in the psychological sphere the abnormal man is he who demands, who appeals, who begs.

3. Although even this reservation is open to argument. See for example the question put by Mlle Juliette Boutonnier: 'Might not perversion be an extreme arrest in affect development, furthered, if not produced, by the conditions under which the child has lived, at least as much as by the congenital tendencies that are obviously factors in it but that probably are not alone responsible?' (*Revue Française de Psychanalyse*, No. 3, 1949, pp. 403–4).

4. Joachim Marcus, 'Structure familiale et comportements politiques', L'Autorité dans la famille et dans l'État, *Revue Française de Psychanalyse*, April–June 1949.

5. A quotation borrowed from Michel Leiris, 'Martinique, Guadeloupe, Haiti', *Les Temps Modernes*, February 1950, p. 1346.

6. In this connection, it is worth noting that the Caribs experienced the same fate at the hands of French and Spanish explorers.

7. In English in the original. (Translator's note.)

8. G. Legman, 'Psychopathologie des comics', French translation by H. Robillot, *Les Temps Modernes*, May 1949, pp. 919 ff.

9. One always sees a smile when one reports this aspect of education in Martinique. The smile comes because the comicality of the thing is obvious, but no one pursues it to its later consequences. Yet these are the important aspects, because three or four such phrases are the basis on which the young Antillean works out his view of the world.

10. In this connection it is worth remembering what Sartre said:

> Some children, at the age of five or six, have already had fights with schoolmates who call them 'Yids'. Others may remain in ignorance for a long time. A young Jewish girl in a family I am acquainted with did not even know the meaning of the word Jew until she was fifteen. During the Occupation there was a Jewish doctor who lived shut up in his home at Fontainebleau and raised his children without saying a word to them of their origin. But however it comes about, some day they must learn the truth: sometimes from the smiles of those around them, sometimes from rumour or insult. The later the discovery, the more violent the shock. Suddenly they perceive that others know something about them that they do not know, that people apply to

them an ugly and upsetting term that is not used in their own families. (*Anti-Semite and Jew*, p. 75.)

11. *Les Deux Sources consciente et inconsciente de la vie morale* (Neuchâtel, La Baconnière, 1943).

12. *Les Folies raisonnantes*, cited by A. Hesnard, *L'Univers morbide de la faute* (Paris, Presses Universitaires de France, 1949), p. 97.

13. I am thinking here particularly of the United States. See, for example, *Home of the Brave*.

14. On this point psychoanalysts will be reluctant to share my view. Dr Lacan, for instance, talks of the 'abundance' of the Oedipus complex. But even if the young boy has to kill his father, it is still necessary for the father to accept being killed. I am reminded of what Hegel said: 'The cradle of the child is the tomb of the parents'; and of Nicolas Calas' *Foyer d'incendie* and of Jean Lacroix' *Force et faiblesses de la famille*. The collapse of moral values in France after the war was perhaps the result of the defeat of that moral being which the nation represented. We know what such traumatisms on the family level may produce.

15. I recommend the following experiment to those who are unconvinced: attend showings of a Tarzan film in the Antilles and in Europe. In the Antilles, the young Negro identifies himself de facto with Tarzan against the Negroes. This is much more difficult for him in a European theatre, for the rest of the audience, which is white, automatically identifies him with the savages on the screen. It is a conclusive experience. The Negro learns that one is not black without problems. A documentary film on Africa produces similar reactions when it is shown in a French city and in Fort-de-France. I will go farther and say that Bushmen and Zulus arouse even more laughter among the young Antilleans. It would be interesting to show how in this instance the reactional exaggeration betrays a hint of recognition. In France a Negro who sees this documentary is virtually petrified. There he has no more hope of flight: he is at once Antillean, Bushman and Zulu.

16. More especially, they become aware that the line of self-esteem that they had chosen should be inverted. We have seen in fact that the Antillean who goes to France pictures this journey as the final stage of his personality. Quite literally I can say without any risk of error that the Antillean who goes to France in order to convince himself that he is white will find his real face there.

17. Hesnard, op. cit., p. 37.

18. *Anxiety and Magic Thinking* (New York, International Universities Press, 1956), p. 46. Originally, *L'Angoisse et la pensée magique* (Neuchâtel, Delachaux, 1947).

19. Ibid., p. 76.

20. Ibid., pp. 58 and 68.

21. Hesnard, op. cit., p. 38.

22. Ibid., p. 40.

23. In the work of Joachim Marcus we encounter the view according to which the social neurosis – or, if one prefers, abnormal behaviour in contact with the Other, whoever he may be – is closely related to the individual situation:

The study of our questionnaires showed that the most strongly anti-Semitic persons belonged to the most conflictual family structures. Their anti-Semitism was a reaction to frustrations suffered inside the family environment. What demonstrates that the Jew is a substitutive object in anti-Semitism is the fact that, depending on local conditions, the same family situations will produce hatred of Negroes, anti-Catholicism, or anti-Semitism. One can therefore state that, contrary to what is generally believed, it is the attitude that seeks the content rather than the content that creates the attitude. ('Structure familiale et comportements politiques', op. cit., p. 282)

24. To continue in Odier's terminology, it would be more accurate to say 'paralogical': 'The term "paralogical" might be suggested for the regression of the neurotic adult' (*Anxiety and Magic Thinking*, p. 118).

25. It would indeed be interesting, on the basis of Lacan's theory of the *mirror period*, to investigate the extent to which the *imago* of his fellow built up in the young white at the usual age would undergo an imaginary aggression with the appearance of the Negro. When one has grasped the mechanism described by Lacan, one can have no further doubt the real Other for the white man is and will continue to be the black man. And conversely. Only for the white man the Other is perceived on the level of the body image, absolutely as the not-self – that is, the unidentifiable, the unassimilable. For the black man, as we have shown, historical and economic realities come into the picture. 'The subject's recognition of his image in the mirror', Lacan says, 'is a phenomenon that is doubly significant for the analysis of this stage. The phenomenon appears after six months, and the study of it at that time shows in convincing fashion the tendencies that currently constitute reality for the subject; the mirror image, precisely because of these affinities, affords a good symbol of that reality: of its affective value, illusory like the image, and of its structure, as it reflects the human form' (*Encyclopédie française*, 8–40, 9 and 10).

We shall see that this discovery is basic: every time the subject sees his image and recognizes it, it is always in some way 'the mental oneness which is inherent in him' that he acclaims. In mental pathology, for instance, when one examines delirious hallucinations or interpretations, one always finds that this self-image is respected. In other words, there is a certain structural harmony, a sum of the individual and of the constructions through which he goes, at every stage of the psychotic behaviour. Aside from the fact that this fidelity might be attributed to affective content, there still remains evidence that it would be unscientific to misconstrue. Whenever there is a psychotic belief, there is a reproduction of self. It is especially in the period of anxiety and suspicion described by Dide and Guiraud that the Other takes a hand. At such times it is not surprising to find the Negro in the guise of satyr or murderer. But in the stage of systematization, when the conviction is being developed, there is no longer room for a stranger. In extreme cases, moreover, I should not hesitate to say that the theme of the Negro in certain deliriums (when it is not central) ranks with other phenomena such as zooscopy.[a] Lhermitte has described the liberation of the body image. This is what is clinically called heautophany or heautoscopy.[b]

The abruptness with which this phenomenon occurs, Lhermitte says, is inordinately strange. It occurs even among normal persons (Goethe, Taine, etc.). I contend that for the Antillean the mirror hallucination is always neutral. When Antilleans tell me that they have experienced it, I always ask the same question: 'What colour were you?' Invariably they reply: 'I had no colour.' What is more, in hypnagogic hallucinations and in what, by derivation from Duhamel, is called 'salavinization',ᶜ the same procedure is repeated. It is not I as a Negro who acts, thinks and is praised to the skies.

In addition, I suggest that those who are interested in such questions read some of the compositions written in French by Antillean children between the ages of ten and fourteen. Given as a theme 'My Feelings Before I Went on Vacation', they reacted like real little Parisians and produced such things as, 'I like vacation because then I can run through the fields, breathe fresh air and come home with *rosy* cheeks.' It is apparent that one would hardly be mistaken in saying that the Antillean does not altogether apprehend the fact of his being a Negro. I was perhaps thirteen when for the first time I saw Senegalese soldiers. All I knew about them was what I had heard from veterans of the First World War: 'They attack with the bayonet and, when that doesn't work, they just punch their way through the machine-gun fire with their fists.... They cut off heads and collect human ears.' These Senegalese were in transit in Martinique, on their way from Guiana. I scoured the streets eagerly for a sight of their uniforms, which had been described to me: red scarves and belts. My father went to the trouble of collecting two of them, whom he brought home and who had the family in raptures. It was the same thing in school. My mathematics teacher, a lieutenant in the reserve who had been in command of a unit of Senegalese troopers in 1914, used to make us shiver with his anecdotes: 'When they are praying they must never be disturbed, because then the officers just cease to exist. They're lions in a battle, but you have to respect their habits.' There is no reason now to be surprised that Mayotte Capécia dreamed of herself as pink and white; I should say that that was quite normal.

It may perhaps be objected that if the white man is subject to the elaboration of the *imago* of his peer, an analogous phenomenon should occur in the Antillean, visual perception being the sketch for such an elaboration. But to say this is to forget that in the Antilles perception always occurs on the level of the imaginary. It is in white terms that one perceives one's fellows. People will say of someone, for instance, that he is 'very black'; there is nothing surprising, within a family, in hearing a mother remark that 'X is the blackest of my children' – it means that X is the least white. I can only repeat the observation of a European acquaintance to whom I had explained this: in terms of people, it is nothing but a mystification. Let me point out once more that every Antillean expects all the others to perceive him in terms of the essence of the white man. In the Antilles, just as in France, one comes up against the same myth; a Parisian says, 'He is black but he is very intelligent'; a Martinican expresses himself no differently. During the Second World War, teachers went from Guadeloupe to Fort-de-France to correct the examinations of candidates for the baccalaureate and, driven by curiosity, I went to the hotel where they were staying, simply in order to see Monsieur B., a philosophy teacher who was supposed to be remarkably black; as the Martinicans say, not without a certain irony, he was 'blue'. One family in particular has an excellent reputation: 'They're very black, but they're all quite nice.' One of them, in fact, is a piano teacher and a former student at the Conservatoire in Paris, another is a teacher of natural science in the girls' academy, etc. The father was given to walking up and down his balcony every evening at sunset; after a certain time of night, it was always said, he became invisible. Of another family, who lived in the country, it was said that on nights when there was a power failure the children had to laugh so that their parents would know that they were there. On Mondays, very carefully got up in their white linen suits, certain Martinican officials, in the local figure of speech, 'looked like prunes in a bowl of milk'.

a. Hallucinations of animals. (Translator's note.)

b. The vivid psychological awareness and examination of one's own internal organs as if they were outside oneself – an extreme hypochondria. (Translator's note.)

c. See note 52.

26. [Dominique] O. Mannoni, *Prospero and Caliban: The Psychology of Colonization* (New York, Praeger, 1964), p. 111, note 1.

27. When we consider the responses given in waking-dream therapy we shall see that these mythological figures, or 'archetypes', do reside very deep in the human mind. Whenever the individual plunges down, one finds the Negro, whether concretely or symbolically.

28. Mannoni, op. cit., p. 111.

29. Let us remember, however, that the situation is ambiguous. Orin is also jealous of his sister's fiancé. On a psychoanalytic level, the film may be described thus: Orin, who suffers from the abandonment-neurosis, is fixated on his mother and is incapable of making a real object investment of his libido. Observe, for instance, his behaviour toward the girl to whom he is supposedly engaged. Vinnie, who for her part is fixated on their father, proves to Orin that their mother is unfaithful. But let us not make any mistakes. Her action is a bill of indictment (an introjective mechanism). Supplied with the evidence of the adultery, Orin kills his mother's lover. In reaction she commits suicide. Orin's libido, which requires investment in the same manner as before, turns toward Vinnie. In effect, through her behaviour and even through her physical appearance, Vinnie takes the place of their mother. Consequently – and this is beautifully handled in the film – Orin becomes an Oedipus in love with his sister. Hence it is understandable that Orin storms lamentation and reproach at his sister when she announces her marriage. But in his conflict with her fiancé it is emotion, affectivity, that he battles; with the Negro, the splendid natives, the conflict lies on a genital, biological level.

30. Karl Jaspers, *Psychopathologie générale* – French translation by Kastler and Mendousse, p. 49.

31. *Martinique* (Paris, Collection Metamorphoses, Gallimard, 1948), pp. 13–14.

32. Some writers have tried, thus accepting prejudices (in the etymological sense of the word), to show why the white man does not understand the sexual life of the Negro. Thus one can find in De Pédrals this passage, which, while it does nevertheless convey the truth, still leaves aside the deep causes of white 'opinion':

> The Negro child feels neither surprise nor shame at the facts of reproduction, because he is told whatever he wants to know. It is quite obvious, without having to fall back on the subtleties of psychoanalysis, that this difference cannot help having an effect on his way of thinking and hence on his way of acting. Since the sexual act is presented to him as the most natural, indeed the most commendable thing in view of the end that it pursues – impregnation – the African will retain this outlook as long as he lives; while the European, as long as he lives, will always unconsciously keep alive a guilt complex that neither reason nor experience will ever succeed in altogether dissipating. In this way the African is inclined to view his sexual life as only a part of his physiological life, just like eating, drinking and sleeping.... A conception of this kind, one would suppose, precludes the distortions into which the European is led in order to reconcile the conflicts of a tortured conscience, a vacillating intellect and a frustrated instinct. Hence the fundamental difference is not at all of natures, or of constitutions, but of conceptions; hence too the fact that the reproductive instinct, stripped of the halo with which the monuments of our literature have adorned it, is not at all the dominant element in the life of the African as it is in our own, in spite of the statements of *too many students inclined to explain what they have seen by the sole method of analysing themselves.* (Denis Pierre de Pédrals, *La Vie sexuelle en Afrique noire*, Paris, Payot, 1950, pp. 28–29) (My italies – F.F.)

33. 'Sur le *Martinique* de M. Michel Cournot', *Les Temps Modernes*, February 1950, p. 1505.
34. 'Une dangereuse mystification: la théorie de la négritude', *La Novelle Revue Critique*, June 1949.
35. The character of Uncle Remus was created by Harris. The figure of this gentle, melancholy old slave with his eternal *grin* is one of the most typical images of the American Negro.
36. See also the many Negro films of recent years. And yet all the producers were white.
37. Bernard Wolfe, 'L'oncle Rémus et son lapin', *Les Temps Modernes*, May 1949, pp. 898 ff.
38. It is usual to be told in the United States, when one calls for the real freedom of the Negro: 'That's all they're waiting for, to jump our women.' Since the white man behaves in an offensive manner toward the Negro, he recognizes that in the Negro's place he would have no mercy on his oppressors. Therefore it is not surprising to see that he identifies himself with the Negro: white 'hot-jazz' orchestras, white blues and spiritual singers, white authors writing novels in which the Negro proclaims his grievances, whites in blackface.
39. *The Psychology of Women* (New York, Grune and Stratton, 1944–1945).

40. *Female Sexuality* (New York, International Universities Press, 1953).
41. Marie Bonaparte, 'De la sexualité de la femme', *Revue Française de Psychanalyse*, April–June 1949.
42. Ibid., p. 180.
43. *Précis de psychiatrie* (Paris, Masson, 1950), p. 371.
44. Let me observe at once that I had no opportunity to establish the overt presence of homosexuality in Martinique. This must be viewed as the result of the absence of the Oedipus complex in the Antilles. The schema of homosexuality is well enough known. We should not overlook, however, the existence of what are called there 'men dressed like women' or 'godmothers'. Generally they wear shirts and skirts. But I am convinced that they lead normal sex lives. They can take a punch like any 'he-man' and they are not impervious to the allures of women – fish and vegetable merchants. In Europe, on the other hand, I have known several Martinicans who became homosexuals, always passive. But this was by no means a neurotic homosexuality: for them it was a means to a livelihood, as pimping is for others.
45. I am thinking particularly of this passage:

> Such then is this haunted man, condemned to make his choice of himself on the basis of false problems and in a false situation, deprived of the metaphysical sense by the hostility of the society that surrounds him, driven to a rationalism of despair. His life is nothing but a long flight from others and from himself. He has been alienated even from his own body; his emotional life has been cut in two; he has been reduced to pursuing the impossible dream of universal brotherhood in a world that rejects him.
>
> Whose is the fault? It is our eyes that reflect to him the unacceptable image that he wishes to dissimulate. It is our words and our gestures – *all* our words and *all* our gestures – our anti-Semitism, but equally our condescending liberalism – that have poisoned him. It is we who constrain him to choose to be a Jew *whether through flight from himself or through self-assertion*; it is we who force him into the dilemma of Jewish authenticity or inauthenticity.... This species that bears witness for essential humanity better than any other because it was born of secondary reactions within the body of humanity – this quintessence of man, disgraced, uprooted, destined from the start to either inauthenticity or martyrdom. In this situation there is not one of us who is not totally guilty and even criminal; the Jewish blood that the Nazis shed falls on all our heads. (pp. 135–36)

46. Baruk, *Précis de psychiatrie*, pp. 372–73.
47. This is what Marie Bonaparte wrote in *Myths de guerre*, No. 1, p. 145:

> The anti-Semite projects on to the Jew, ascribes to the Jew all his own more or less unconscious bad instincts.... Thus, in ridding himself of them by heaping them on the shoulders of the Jew, he has purged himself of them in his own eyes and sees himself in shining purity. The Jew thus lends himself magnificently to a projection of the Devil.... The Negro in the United States assumes the same function of fixation.

48. *Psychiatrie du médecin praticien* (Paris, Masson, 1922), p. 164.

49. Reverend Tempels, *La philosophie bantoue*.
50. I.R. Skine, 'Apartheid en Afrique du Sud', *Les Temps Modernes*, July 1950.
51. See, for example, *Cry, the Beloved Country*, by Alan Paton.
52. Salavin is a character created by Georges Duhamel, and is the prototype of the ineffectual man: a mediocrity, a creature of fleeting impulse and always the victim of his own chimeras. (Translator's note.)
53. *L'Air et les songes* (Paris, Corti, 1943).
54. Aimé Césaire, *Cahier d'un retour au pays natal* (Paris, Présence Africaine, 1956), pp. 94–96.
55. *Et les chiens se taisaient*, a tragedy, in *Les Armes miraculeuses* (Paris, Gallimard, 1946), pp. 144 and 122.
56. Ibid., p. 136.
57. Ibid., p. 65.
58. 'Premières réponses à l'enquête sur le "Mythe du nègre" ', *Présence Africaine*, No. 2.

6   ALGERIA UNVEILED

1. We do not here consider rural areas where the woman is often unveiled. Nor do we take into account the Kabyle woman who, except in the large cities, never uses a veil. For the tourist who rarely ventures into the mountains, the Arab woman is first of all one who wears a veil. This originality of the Kabyle woman constitutes, among others, one of the themes of colonialist propaganda bringing out the opposition between Arabs and Berbers. Such studies, devoted to the analysis of psychological modifications, neglect considerations that are properly historical. We shall presently take up this other aspect of Algerian reality in action. Here we shall content ourselves with pointing out that the Kabyle women, in the course of 130 years of domination, have developed other defence mechanisms with respect to the occupier. During the war of liberation their forms of action have likewise assumed absolutely original aspects.
2. *Djellaba* – a long, hooded cloak. (Translator's note.)
3. One phenomenon deserves to be recalled. In the course of the Moroccan people's struggle for liberation, and chiefly in the cities, the white veil was replaced by the black veil. This important modification is explained by the Moroccan women's desire to express their attachment to His Majesty Mohammed V. It will be remembered that it was immediately after the exiling of the King of Morocco that the black veil, a sign of mourning, made its appearance. It is worth noting that black, in Moroccan or Arab society, has never expressed mourning or affliction. As a combat measure, the adoption of black is a response to the desire to exert a symbolic pressure on the occupier, and hence to make a logical choice of one's own symbols.
4. The *haïk* – the Arab name for the big square veil worn by Arab women, covering the face and the whole body. (Translator's note.)
5. See Appendix at the end of this chapter.
6. The ground is prepared in the school establishments as well. The teachers to whom the parents have entrusted their children soon acquire the habit

of passing severe judgement on the fate of woman in Algerian society. 'We firmly hope that you at least will be strong enough to impose your point of view....' Schools for 'young Moslem girls' are multiplying. At their pupils' approach to puberty, the teachers or the nuns exercise a truly exceptional activity. The mothers are first felt out, besieged, and given the mission of shaking up and convincing the father. Much is made of the young student's prodigious intelligence, her maturity; a picture is painted of the brilliant future that awaits those eager young creatures and it is none too subtly hinted that it would be criminal if the child's schooling were interrupted. The shortcomings of colonized society are conceded and it is proposed that the young student be sent to boarding school in order to spare the parents the criticism of 'narrow-minded neighbours'. For the specialist in colonial affairs, veterans and the 'developed' natives are the commandos who are entrusted with destroying the cultural resistance of a colonized country. The regions are accordingly classified in terms of the number of developed 'active units', in other words, agents of erosion of the national culture that they contain.

7. *fellah* – a peasant. (Translator's note.)
8. Attention must be called to a frequent attitude, on the part of European women in particular, with regard to a special category of evolved natives. Certain unveiled Algerian women turn themselves into perfect Westerners with amazing rapidity and unsuspected ease. European women feel a certain uneasiness in the presence of these women. Frustrated in the presence of the veil, they experience a similar impression before the bared face, before that unabashed body which has lost all awkwardness, all timidity, and become downright offensive. Not only is the satisfaction of supervising the evolution and correcting the mistakes of the unveiled woman withdrawn from the European woman, but she feels herself challenged on the level of feminine charm, of elegance, and even sees a competitor in this novice metamorphosed into a professional, a neophyte transformed into a propagandist. The European woman has no choice but to make common cause with the Algerian man who had fiercely flung the unveiled woman into the camp of evil and of depravity. 'Really!' the European women will exclaim, 'These unveiled women are quite amoral and shameless.' Integration, in order to be successful, seems indeed to have to be simply a continued, accepted paternalism.
9. *djebel* – mountain. (Translator's note.)
10. We are mentioning here only realities known to the enemy. We therefore say nothing about the new forms of action adopted by women in the Revolution. Since 1958, in fact, the tortures inflicted on women militants have enabled the occupier to have an idea of the strategy used by women. Today new adaptations have developed. It will therefore be understood if we are silent as to these.
11. Front de Libération Nationale. (Editor's note.)
12. *fidaï* – a death volunteer, in the Islamic tradition. (Translator's note.)
13. *douar* – a village. (Translator's note.)
14. Froger, one of the colonialist leaders. Executed by a *fidaï* in late 1956.
15. The woman, who before the Revolution never left the house without being accompanied by her mother or her husband, is now entrusted with

special missions such as going from Oran to Constantine or Algiers. For several days, all by herself, carrying directives of capital importance for the Revolution, she takes the train, spends the night with an unknown family, among militants. Here too she must harmonize her movements, for the enemy is on the lookout for any false step. But the important thing here is that the husband makes no difficulty about letting his wife leave on an assignment. He will make it, in fact, a point of pride to say to the liaison agent when the latter returns, 'You see, everything has gone well in your absence.' The Algerian's age-old jealousy, his 'congenital' suspiciousness have melted on contact with the Revolution. It must be pointed out also that militants who are being sought by the police take refuge with other militants not yet identified by the occupier. In such cases the woman, left alone all day with the fugitive, is the one who gets him his food, the newspapers, the mail, showing no trace of suspicion or fear. Involved in the struggle, the husband or the father learns to look upon the relations between the sexes in a new light. The militant man discovers the militant woman and jointly they create new dimensions for Algerian society.

16. R.A.S. – *Rien à signaler* – a military abbreviation for 'Nothing to report'.
    We here go on to a description of attitudes. There is, however, an important piece of work to be done on the woman's role in the Revolution: the woman in the city, in the *djebel*, in the enemy administrations; the prostitute and the information she obtains; the woman in prison, under torture, facing death, before the courts. All these chapter headings, after the material has been sifted, will reveal an incalculable number of facts essential for the history of the national struggle.

17. See Chapter 5 ['Algeria's European Minority', in *Studies in a Dying Colonialism*].

18. This text which appeared in *Résistance Algérienne* in its issue of 16 May 1957 indicates the consciousness that the leaders of the National Liberation Front have always had of the important part played by the Algerian woman in the Revolution.

7   THE FACT OF BLACKNESS

1. Jean Lhermitte, *L'Image de notre corps* (Paris, Nouvelle Revue Critique, 1939), p. 17.
2. Sir Alan Burns, *Colour Prejudice* (London, Allen and Unwin, 1948), p. 16.
3. *Anti-Semite and Jew* (New York, Grove Press, 1960), pp. 112–13.
4. Ibid., p. 115.
5. Jon Alfred Mjoen, 'Harmonic and Disharmonic Race-crossings', The Second International Congress of Eugenics (1921), *Eugenics in Race and State*, vol. II, p. 60, quoted in Sir Alan Burns, op. cit., p. 120.
6. In English in the original. (Translator's note.)
7. 'Ce que l'homme noir apporte', in Claude Nordey, *L'Homme de couleur* (Paris, Plon, 1939), pp. 309–10.
8. Aimé Césaire, *Cahier d'un retour au pays natal* (Paris, Présence Africaine, 1956), pp. 77–78.

9. Ibid., p. 78.
10. Ibid., p. 79.
11. De Pédrals, *La Vie sexuelle en Afrique noire* (Paris, Payot), p. 83.
12. A.M. Vergiat, *Les Rites secrets des primitifs de l'Oubangui* (Paris, Payot, 1951), p. 113.
13. My italics – F.F.
14. My italics – F.F.
15. Léopold Senghor, 'Ce que l'homme noir apporte', in Nordey, op. cit., p. 205.
16. Léopold Senghor, *Chants d'ombre* (Paris, Éditions du Seuil, 1945).
17. Aimé Césaire, Introduction to Victor Schoelcher, *Esclavage et colonisation* (Paris, Presses Universitaires de France, 1948), p. 7.
18. Ibid., p. 8.
19. Jean-Paul Sartre, *Orphée noir*, preface to *Anthologie de la nouvelle poésie nègre et malgache* (Paris, Presses Universitaires de France, 1948), pp. xl ff.
20. Ibid., p. xliv.
21. Jacques Roumain, 'Bois-d'Ebène', Prelude, in *Anthologie de la nouvelle poésie nègre et malgache*, op. cit., p. 113.
22. David Diop, 'Le Temps du martyre', in ibid., p. 174.
23. David Diop, 'Le Renégat'.
24. Though Sartre's speculations on the existence of the Other may be correct (to the extent, we must remember, to which *Being and Nothingness* describes an alienated consciousness), their application to a black consciousness proves fallacious. That is because the white man is not only the Other but also the master, whether real or imaginary.
25. In the sense in which the word is used by Jean Wahl in *Existence humaine et transcendance* (Neuchâtel, La Baconnière, 1944).
26. Jean-Paul Sartre, *The Respectful Prostitute*, in *Three Plays* (New York, Knopf, 1949), pp. 189, 191. Originally, *La Putain respectueuse* (Paris, Gallimard, 1947). See also *Home of the Brave*, a film by Mark Robson.
27. Richard Wright, *Native Son* (New York, Harper, 1940).
28. By Chester Himes (Garden City, Doubleday, 1945).
29. *Home of the Brave.*

8   WEST INDIANS AND AFRICANS

1. First published in the review *Esprit*, February 1955.
2. *Peau noire, masques blancs* [*Black Skin, White Masks*] (Éditions du Seuil, Paris, 1952).
3. Let us say that the concessions we have made are fictitious. Philosophically and politically there is no such thing as an African people. There is an African world. And a West Indian world as well. On the other hand, it can be said that there is a Jewish people, but not a Jewish race.
4. See, for example, the Carnival and the songs composed on this occasion.
5. We might say: like the French lower middle class at this period, but that is not our point of approach. What we wish to do here is to study the change in attitude of the West Indian with respect to Negritude.

9   ON NATIONAL CULTURE

1. Sékou Touré, 'The political leader as the representative of a culture'. Address to the Second Congress of Black Artists and Writers, Rome, 1959.
2. The lady was not alone; she had a most respectable husband, who knew how to quote Racine and Corneille, Voltaire and Rousseau, Victor Hugo and Musset, Gide, Valéry and as many more again. (René Depestre, *Face à la nuit*.)
3. René Depestre, *Face à la nuit*.
4. Rene Char, *Partage formel*.
5. At the last school prize-giving in Dakar, the president of the Senegalese Republic, Leopold Senghor, decided to include the study of the idea of Negro-ism in the curriculum. If this decision was due to an anxiety to study historical causes, no one can criticize it. But if on the other hand it was taken in order to create black self-consciousness, it is simply a turning of his back upon history, which has already taken cognizance of the disappearance of the majority of Negroes.